PRAISE FOR STUART COSGROVE'S
DETROIT 67: THE YEAR THAT CHANGED SOUL

'Cosgrove weaves a compelling web of circumstance that maps
a city struggling with the loss of its youth to the Vietnam War, the
hard edge of the civil rights movement and ferocious inner-city
rioting. His prose is dense, not the kind that readers looking for a
quick tale about singers they know and love might take to, but a
proper music journalist's tome redolent of the field research that he
carried out in Detroit's public and academic libraries. It is rich in
titbits gathered from news reports. It is to be consumed rather than
to be dipped into, a whole-hearted evocation of people and places
filled with the confidence that it is telling a tale set at a fulcrum of
American social and cultural history.'

The Independent

'Broadcaster Stuart Cosgrove lifts the lid on the time when the fight
for civil rights and clash of cultures and generations came together
in an incendiary mix.'

Daily Record

'The set-up sparks like the finest pulp thriller. A harsh winter has
brought the city to its knees. The car factories are closed and Motown
major domo Berry Gordy is fighting to keep his empire afloat.
Stuart Cosgrove's immaculately researched account of a year in the
life of the Motor City manages a delicate balancing act. While his
love for the era – particularly the music, best exemplified by the
dominance of Motown, whose turbulent twelve months are
examined in depth – is clear, he maintains a dispassionate,
journalistic distance that gives his epic narrative authority and depth.
With the backdrop throughout of a seemingly never-ending
Vietnam War, *Detroit 67* plays out like a series of dispatches from
the frontline. History is quick to romanticise Hitsville USA but
Cosgrove is not quite so credulous, choosing to focus instead on the
dark shadows at the heart of his gripping story. *****'

The Skinny

Online reaction

'A thoroughly researched and fascinating insight into the music and the times of a city which came to epitomise the turmoil of a nation divided by race and class, while at the same time offering it an unforgettable, and increasingly poignant, soundtrack. With his follow-up, *Memphis 68*, on the way, Cosgrove is well set to add yet another string to his already well-strung bow, becoming a reliable chronicler of a neglected area of American culture, telling those stories which are still unknown to most. By using his love of the music as a starting point he has found the perfect way to explore further themes and ideas.'

Alistair Braidwood

'The story is unbelievably rich. Motown, the radical hippie underground, a trigger-happy police force, Vietnam, a disaffected young black community, inclement weather, The Supremes, the army, strikes, fiscal austerity, murders – all these elements coalesced, as Cosgrove noted, to create a remarkable year. In fact, as the book gathers pace, one can't help think how the hell did this city survive it all? In fact such is the depth and breadth of his research, and the skill of his pen, at times you actually feel like you are in Berry Gordy's office watching events unfurl like an unstoppable James Jamerson bass line. I was going to call this a great music book. Certainly, it contains some of the best ever writing and insight about Motown. Ever. But its huge canvas and backdrop, its rich social detail, negate against such a description. *Detroit 67* is a great and a unique book, full stop.'

Paolo Hewitt, *Caught by the River*

'The subhead for Stuart Cosgrove's *Detroit 67* is "the year that changed soul". But this thing contains multitudes, and digs in deep, well beyond just the city's music industry in that fateful year . . . All of this is written about with precision, empathy, and a great, deep love for the city of Detroit.'

Detroit Metro Times

'Big daddy of soul books . . . The riot that tore Detroit apart in 1967 was one of the worst in US history. Over twelve month-by-month chapters, the author – a TV executive and northern soul fanatic – weaves a thoroughly researched, epic tale of musical intrigues and escalating social violence.'

TeamRock

'As the title suggests, this is a story of twelve months in the life of a city. Subtitled "The Year That Changed Soul", it is much more than that. Leading black music label Motown is at the heart of the story, and 1967 is one of Motown's more turbulent years, but it's set against the backdrop of growing opposition to the war in Vietnam, police brutality, a disaffected black population, rioting, strikes in the Big Three car plants and what seemed like the imminent breakdown of society . . . *Detroit 67* is full of detailed information about music, politics and society that engages you from beginning to end. You finish the book with a real sense of a city in crisis and of how some artists reflected events. It is also the first in a trilogy by Cosgrove (*Memphis 68* and *Harlem 69*). By the time you finish this, you'll be eagerly awaiting the next book.'

Socialist Review

'A gritty portrait of the year Motown unravelled . . . *Detroit 67* is a wonderful book and a welcome contribution to both the history of soul music and the history of Detroit.'

Spiked

'A fine telling of a pivotal year in soul music'

Words and Guitars

MEMPHIS 68

The Tragedy of Southern Soul

STUART COSGROVE

First published in Great Britain in 2017 by Polygon,
an imprint of Birlinn Ltd.
Birlinn Ltd
West Newington House
10 Newington Road
Edinburgh
EH9 1QS

www.polygonbooks.co.uk

ISBN 978 1 84697 373 4
eBook ISBN 978 0 85790 938 1

British Library Cataloguing-in-Publication Data
A catalogue record for this book is available on request
from the British Library.

Typeset by 3btype.com
Printed by Clays Ltd, St Ives plc, Bungay, Suffolk

CONTENTS

FOREWORD

Memphis 68: The Tragedy of Southern Soul is the second part of a trilogy on the social history of soul music. The first part, *Detroit 67: The Year That Changed Soul* was published last year and the concluding book *Harlem 69: The Future of Soul* will be published later in 2018. It has been a mammoth task pulling together the unfolding stories of an era rich in music and social history, including the civil rights movement, the war in Vietnam, inner-city rebellion and riots, the rise of Black Power, and the FBI's secret war on social progress. I hope I have done these subjects justice and paid them due respect.

So many people have contributed to the research that it is not possible to thank everyone individually. But special thanks go to my friends and contemporaries on the UK northern soul scene, a remarkable source of knowledge, information and determination. I am also indebted to academic institutions across the USA and I'd like to thank the staff of the Harlan Hatcher Graduate Library at the University of Michigan, Ann Arbor, and the Ned R. McWherter Library at the University of Memphis, in particular the staff of the library's Special Collections Division who patiently located newspaper clippings, digital material and primary sources that have hopefully enriched this book. Thanks to the staff at the Hollis F.

Price Library on the LeMoyne-Owen campus in Memphis, the Stax Museum and Detroit Public Library, and for the co-operation of the FBI Academy Library in Quantico, Virginia.

Although I do not know them personally, two authors have paved the way in writing books about Stax Records that were invaluable – thanks to Rob Bowman and Robert Gordon.

Finally I'd like to thank the editorial team at Polygon in Edinburgh for requiring world-class standards from their independent base in Scotland, particularly my resilient editor Alison Rae and cover designer Chris Hannah.

Most of all, thanks and deepest love to my close friends and family.

Stuart Cosgrove
Glasgow
August 2017

Beale Street – the pumping artery of black Memphis life and self-styled Home of the Blues.

ROOSEVELT JAMISON'S BLOOD BANK

1 January

Generosity oozed from the pores of Roosevelt Jamison. He was a kind man, easy to like, and, surprisingly, for a man raised in the nefarious ways of Memphis soul music, he knew all there was to know about blood plasma. Jamison had a kind word for everyone, even the drifters who hung around his doorway, and he wished the world a good New Year as he navigated his way through the early-morning debris of Beale Street, bypassing the drunks, the panhandlers and the torn ticker-tape from the night before.

When he reached home he would sleep restlessly. He often complained that freight trains lumbering on the rail tracks along Old Southern Avenue kept him awake and he once told the singer James Carr that he thought the trains were trying to shake his old wooden-frame home to its foundations.

A small pack of dogs was scavenging from overturned garbage cans, and nothing about the first day of 1968 hinted at the dramas to come. It was a new year, but the old ways clung on in Memphis.

The city was reluctantly negotiating racial integration, a school bus programme was under way, and new legislation was set to challenge decades of segregation in the housing market. But, despite all the progress of the years of civil rights, the most basic commodity of human life – blood – was still stubbornly racist. Jamison knew it for a fact.

He ran the Interstate Blood Bank, which sat on the bustling corner of Beale Street and South 4th, at the intersection near the First Baptist Church of Memphis and the New Daisy Theater – between the Lord and late-night entertainment. Beale Street was the pumping artery of black Memphis life. Its legacy reached back to the itinerant blues singers of the Great Depression and it still had a reputation for attracting iridescent creatures of the night. It was the street where the first zoot suit was tailored, and among its many inhabitants were the Stax singer Rufus Thomas, who had worked as a teenage emcee at the Regal Theater on Beale, when a member of the boisterous Rabbit Foot Minstrels. Thomas once said, 'If you were black for one Saturday night on Beale, you'd never want to be white again.'

Beale Street was a place of sounds and smells. In his classic book *Hellhound on His Trail*, the historian Hampton Sides imagined 'a street of chitlin' joints, of hoodoos and fortune tellers, with jug bands playing on every corner. The street smelled of tamales and pulled pork, pot liquor and lard. Day and night, Beale throbbed with so much authentic and violent vitality that in the words of a song by the legendary originator of Memphis blues, W.C. Handy, "business never closes 'til somebody gets killed".'

Jamison felt at home on Beale. This was the stomping ground of Ma Rainey, Gene 'Bowlegs' Miller, Johnny Ace, Bobby Bland and B.B. King, and for a time they all played residencies on Beale. The Stax guitarist Lewie Steinberg, the original bassist of Booker T. and the M.G.'s, had been suckled on raw R&B; his father was the pianist at Pee Wee's Saloon and he remembers playing at his feet as the bar howled with drunken energy. Talent flocked there. At the back of his blood bank Jamison had opened a primitive recording studio and rehearsal room. A few streets away in a grubby office in the Mitchell Hotel, Stax housed unsolicited tapes and ran an offsite office for promising talent. Ernest Withers, society photographer, operated his studio on Beale, and it was there that Otis Redding, Carla Thomas, and Sam and Dave posed for promotional shots, and where a generation of Memphis lovers had their wedding photographs taken. Wilson Pickett, Bobby Womack and most of the local soul artists had been fitted with their stage suits at Lansky's, an old Jewish clothier at 126 Beale Street, where Elvis Presley had sung hillbilly elegies as he waited for his drapes to be fitted. When Bobby Bland was soundchecking at Club Handy, further along Beale, Jamison often watched silently from the rear of the empty club. He reckoned it was the best time to watch Bobby. Devoid of an audience, Bland would run the scales and stretch for notes that no ordinary soul could hope to reach, pleading amid the sticky carpets and faded lampshades for absolution.

By 1968 Jamison had invested much of his time and money in soul music but it had proved a fickle and cruel companion. He had lost the best of his singers to Goldwax Records and to other local independents, and all he had left in the whole wide world was blood: red, gushing and plentiful.

Just as the New Year bells finished chiming, Memphis swore in a new mayor, the obdurate Henry Loeb. Unconventionally, the rituals had not taken place in a civic building but in the sitting room of Loeb's home at 365 Colonial Road. Loeb was a local businessman, whose family owned a chain of laundries across the city, and he had won the election on the back of promises to turn back the hands of time and reverse integration. County Court Clerk Robert Gray administered the oath, standing self-consciously with a hefty bible between the settee and heavy draped curtains. The unusual circumstances had come about because of an acrimonious election and an ungracious handover by the previous lame duck mayor William B. Ingram. Seven contestants had put themselves forward for election; Rufus Thomas, the most recognisable black musician in the city, had canvassed exhaustively for the civil rights candidate, Walter A.W. Willis, but Willis fell far short of the vote required, and dogged by competing candidates from the African-American community the vote was split. Loeb's win was as much due to the fragmentation of the African-American community as his own policies. Being sworn in, in his own sitting room, cast a farcical start to Henry Loeb's tenure as mayor, but his unconventional and dogmatic reign was to worsen in the piercing heat of 1968 and eventually bring Memphis to the brink of civil war, pitting communities against each other and stretching the fabric of the city to its limits.

After the swearing-in ceremony, the new mayor arrived at his office long before his staff had gathered. Mayor Loeb was obsessively hard-working but his hyperactive demeanour masked a slowness to adapt to change in society. He was ultra-conservative, suspicious of the march of civil rights, and emotionally attached to the policies of racial segregation he had grown up with. On his office desk, the outgoing mayor had left only two objects: a tape recorder and a box of aspirins. The message was simple: the press would distort everything, so keep a record, and as for the aspirins they were there to ward off the headaches that he would inevitably encounter in the year ahead. It proved to be one of the greatest understatements in the city's unique history. Loeb's headaches in 1968 were to become an intense migraine that was to consume his life, blight his time in office, and scar his reputation for ever. Oblivious to what lay ahead, Loeb got to work. His first action as mayor was to dismiss eight senior municipal figures who had been appointed by the previous regime. He gave them twenty-four hours to proffer a letter of resignation or risk the humiliation of a public sacking. Loeb imagined it would show him as a decisive leader rejecting the cronyism of the Ingram era; in fact it revealed a belligerent and vengeful streak that was to worsen as the year unfolded. In his first press conference, Loeb told the assembled journalists that he was 'humbled by the magnitude of the problems we have at hand', saying prophetically that 'the next four years will not be easy ones'. It proved to be a serious miscalculation. The first four months of Mayor Loeb's tenure were among the most testing that any civic leader has ever faced, and, at least in part, he was the author of his own problems.

Loeb was the grandson of an entrepreneurial German-Jewish family who had established a chain of coin-operated launderettes across the city. He inherited his grandfather's suspicions of communism, and was among a group of conservative southern Democrats who supported McCarthyism and were naturally opposed to any form of radical social change. He had bequeathed from his family considerable wealth from one of the most luxurious whites-only Turkish baths, located on the corner of Main and Monroe. As late as 1968, he still clung to the belief that the races should be kept apart – 'separate but equal' – and, paradoxical as it may seem, heartily supported Roosevelt Jamison's Negro blood bank facilities as it provided a social service for a community on equal but segregated terms.

The Interstate Blood Bank was a business with an unconventional past. One day in the late forties, as Memphis sweltered in the heat, Jamison's life was changed irrevocably by a chance encounter with a professor at the University of Tennessee, one of America's leading haematologists, Dr Lemuel Whitley Diggs. At the time, blood was a massively controversial subject. Blood transfusion and contamination unlocked latent fears of racial integration, miscegenation and covert sexual intercourse. At the height of the Second World War, the American Red Cross had become embroiled in a deeply divisive dispute about transfusions. On the country's entry into the war, the Red Cross announced a nationwide drive to build up blood supplies for the military. Patriotic African-Americans responded to the call and lined up in most urban centres to donate blood, only to be turned away. Newspapers led with headlines like 'American Red Cross Bans Negro Blood!' and a furious backlash against the policy of exclusion engulfed the famous charity. It is now one of the forgotten struggles in the civil rights movements, but the Red Cross were forced into a hurried compromise, secretly meeting with the heads of the army and navy to thrash out a new policy that could defuse the situation. What they agreed was muddled and unhelpful. Under a new policy, Negro blood would be accepted, but, in line with the segregationist doctrines of the past, the blood of black donors was to be separated by race and ethnicity, presumed to be of lesser importance than blood donated by white donors. For many years this plasma apartheid public health policy dominated the southern states, opening up a wound in society that worsened after the war, as health centres and private hospitals sought new and separated sources of blood.

Memphis was already a city divided along racial lines, so it conceded to the prevailing orthodoxy and segregated its blood banks. Collection points targeting different communities sprang up across the city. But there was resistance, too. Many citizens boycotted the Red Cross and refused to donate to the charity, preferring to give blood to community blood banks. Gatemouth Moore, a gospel programmer with the Sound of Memphis, Radio Station WDIA, and the first blues singer to perform at Carnegie Hall, grew up accepting segregated healthcare as the norm. 'I remember when the black ambulances could not haul white people. They had a white company . . . called Thompsons,' he recounted. 'I was on my way to the station and when I came round the curve there was the ambulance from [the black healthcare company] S.W. Quails and there was a white lady lying in the ditch bleeding. And they were waiting for Thompsons to come and pick her up. I guess I waited thirty or forty minutes and still no ambulance. They tell me that the lady died.'

Roosevelt Jamison's Interstate Blood Bank was funded by the University of Tennessee and one of the most popular within the city's African-American community. Using the most basic equipment – rubber tubes and glass jars with metal bails – Jamison collected blood from Beale Street donors and frequently paid small sums of money to vagrants. He would do his rounds, first to John Gaston Hospital, and then on to the laboratories of the University of Tennessee, where Professor Diggs was the director of research. Remarkably, given the racial barriers of the time, they not only became colleagues but close friends who met on a weekly basis throughout the fifties. Diggs defied the laws of the day and began surreptitiously to teach Jamison about the basic science of haematology. It was against this backdrop of passionate research and separated blood that Diggs began the first experiment to understand the mutations of sickle cell anaemia. Eventually Jamison would come to share his knowledge with students at Druaghon's Business College where the apprentice blood scientist taught anatomy and physiology.

At the rear of Jamison's blood bank was a small cluttered warehouse, lined with jars, medical equipment and boxes of customer cards. A space had been cleared to accommodate a crude recording desk with a stand microphone, box speakers and a reel-to-reel tape, and makeshift soundproofing had been nailed to the walls. There was barely enough room for a band to rehearse but the blood bank tapped into the talent on Beale Street and quickly became one of the city's many busy and underfunded studios. Not as famous as Stax, nor as historic as the old Royal Theater – a primitive rockabilly studio transformed by the legendary Willie Mitchell into the House of Instrumentals (Hi Records) – the blood bank played a vital community role in the southern soul scene. Like Detroit in the north, Memphis had become a creative Klondike for aspiring musicians, who flooded to the city in search of a break. This was where the tense trinity of blues, gospel and country music met and merged. Southern soul was raw and unpolished compared to the more metropolitan music of the north; its blood was thick and heavy.

Every day, Jamison drove around Memphis collecting blood, hauling musical instruments from place to place, and delivering flyers to promote his shows. It was a journey that took him around a city coursing with soul music, each new artery leading to a studio, a record store or some makeshift venue at the rear of a sidewalk bar. Jamison had a regular 'arm' – a very good customer – who lived in a two-storey low-income block on Azalia Street. The man was B negative, one of only a tiny percentage of people in America with that blood type, and so his blood was highly sought after. The man had long since retired, and Jamison knew that one day soon he would die, so he treated him like a rare bird's egg, being soft and tender with his arm, and stroking his skin like feathers. He always gave the agreed price of $10 in a crisp new note, nothing crumpled or grubby. The man's wife looked on proudly as the blood flowed into Jamison's jar, standing by with sweet tea and an Oreo cookie. It was the only money the couple earned beyond welfare. When enough blood had been extracted from her husband's arm, his wife kissed him sweetly, as if he was special, which according to the Red Cross almanac he most certainly was.

On his weekly visit to Stax, Jamison hugged the rail tracks along Southern where freight trains lumbered slower than life itself and remembered the days when it was nothing but a dirt-track road. He drove on past parched blue signs implausibly selling catfish and diesel oil from the same paint-blistered shack. Jamison felt an affinity with the owner; the needs of business bringing two unlikely products together in the same company – in his case, blood and soul. Then, after bumping over the McLemore and Dunavant rail crossing, his car dipped bumpily into a new kind of poverty in the hidden side streets above the darting tunnels of the Mississippi Boulevard, on through a sad desperation, and on again to Stax where the old movie sign came into view – 'Soulsville U.S.A.'.

Since 1964, Jamison had helped to develop the careers of two of the city's greatest vocalists – James Carr and Overton Vertis (O.V.) Wright. Neither was an easy option. Both were brilliant singers who drew effortlessly on blues and gospel, but they were also difficult and, in many respects, troubled individuals. Carr suffered throughout his life with debilitating bouts of depression, and was unable to read or write. His illiteracy and dark moods made him incoherent and at times painfully withdrawn. O.V. Wright was a heroin user who, despite numerous attempts to overcome his addiction, suffered several heart attacks before dying in the back of an ambulance on his way to emergency care in Birmingham, Alabama, at the relatively young age of forty-two. In an obituary in the *Wall Street Journal*, Jesse Drucker hinted at Wright's pained self-destruction: 'There is a tortured, sometimes even menacing feel to many of his recordings. Many soul singers of that period could sing sad lyrics, but the grief was often feigned. Not Wright. His hurt was real.' The titles of some of the songs he recorded provide a clue: 'Drowning On Dry Land' (1972), 'I'd Rather Be Blind, Crippled And Crazy' (1973), 'You're Gonna Make Me Cry' (1965), and Wright's masterpiece, an emotional tribute to the instruments of his addiction, 'A Nickel And A Nail' (1971).

It was as if the three men – the blood bank clerk, the depressive and the addict – were destined to find each other. The renowned music critic Peter Guralnick saw in Jamison an unrestrained generosity: 'He seemed to possess an empathy gene, a need to be of service that carried over into every aspect of his life. He was the kind of person who couldn't see a stray dog without needing to feed him.' In the early sixties, Jamison began to manage local groups, often rehearsing them in the blood bank's back-office. Among them were two of Memphis's great gospel groups, the Jubilee Hummingbirds and the Harmony Echoes. James Carr and O.V. Wright emerged from their ranks. Wright rehearsed by night in the blood bank and by day worked as a garbage man for the Department of Public Works, a place of desperate conditions, and one soon to become the source of the city's notoriety in 1968. Excited by the raw talent he had discovered, Jamison, a wiry extrovert man with a distinctive goatee beard, dragged Carr and Wright to Stax Records. The timing was unfortunate; the studios on McLemore were bursting at the seams and Stax boss Jim Stewart turned them away, recommending that they talk to Quinton Claunch. They were given similar advice by a local saxophonist, Richard Sanders, and so, with two separate recommendations, the unlikely trio went on a late-night journey to Claunch's suburban home on the outskirts of East Memphis.

Claunch was a one-time country guitarist who in his early years had played for the Blue Seal Pals, a hillbilly group who took their name from a southern brand of refined flour. He moved north from Tishomingo, Mississippi, a dirt-track town near Highway 25, and settled in Memphis, where he was a featured musician on early releases by Carl Perkins, on the city's most famous rockabilly label, Sun Records. By day Claunch had a job selling hardware supplies and repairing air-conditioning units but in the evenings he operated in the city's start-up studios. One night in early 1964, he was woken by the sound of knocking on his front door. 'Here's what happened,' Claunch relates. 'I was layin' in bed, twelve o'clock, big knock on this door . . . it was Roosevelt Jamison, James Carr, O.V. Wright.' They had a crude tape of demo songs in their possession and a portable tape recorder. Jamison charmed the sleepy Claunch into sitting on his front-room floor to listen to the songs. They were by all accounts primitive but outstanding. Among the tracks was a song Jamison had written for his girlfriend, 'That's How Strong My Love Is', sung by O.V. Wright. Within days of hearing the raw tapes, Claunch took Wright to American Sound Studio, on the corner of Thomas and Chelsea, where master-producer Chips Moman cut a recording that became Goldwax's stepping stone to deep soul immortality – O.V. Wright with the Keys' 'There Goes My Used

To Be'/'That's How Strong My Love Is' (1964). It was destined to become an international best-seller and was subsequently recorded by Otis Redding, the Rolling Stones, Taj Mahal and a host of others. Jamison never received the full remuneration he should have. Over a lifetime royalties trickled in, always underestimated, from a system that was heavily skewed to the famous major labels and to those most connected to the powerful collection agencies. It was blood not deep soul that funded his family.

On 15 January 1968, Jamison called in at the Satellite record store next door to the Stax studios to buy tickets for a concert by James Brown and the Famous Flames, who were scheduled to perform at the Mid-South Coliseum. His was a regular face at all the major concerts in Tennessee, where he promoted Carr and O.V. Wright, and often took the opportunity to distribute blood-donor information leaflets to what was guaranteed to be an all-black crowd, yet success had neither been instant nor straightforward. There were the obligatory legal disputes, first with Peacock Records, a company owned by the mercurial Houston-based hustler Don Robey. According to Jerry Leiber of the renowned songwriting team of Leiber and Stoller, Robey was a gangster who managed his various entertainment enterprises 'using violence, the threat of violence, and murder'. Unbeknown to the gentler and more generous-spirited Jamison, Wright had previously signed a gospel contract with Robey that had to be untangled. Then there were disputed contract agreements with Goldwax, and various failed attempts to cure Wright's addictions, and the endless efforts to drag Carr from the pits of clinical depression. None worked entirely successfully, but he kept on trying. He felt an obligation to Carr that went far beyond simple kindness. He had first met the vocalist in the early sixties when they were both featured singers on the gospel caravan circuit. Jamison had been a member of the Memphis gospel group the Redemption Harmonizers, who travelled the Delta towns crammed into a Cadillac. He sang with some of the unheralded giants of deep soul and shared a stage with Wee Willie Walker, and remembered meeting Carr backstage as far back as 1962.

Carr was a mystifying genius. He was born in Coahoma County near Clarksdale, Mississippi, in 1942. During his infant years, his parents moved to Memphis, where his father, a street-corner preacher, formed a gospel group called the Southern Wonders. Carr was only nine years of age when he first took to the stage. Rarely in school, he never learned how to read or write, and although Jamison tried to tutor him with simple stories and basic word recognition, Carr lived his life functionally illiterate. As an adult, he gained most of his experience on the road as a member of in-demand gospel circuit groups, the Sunset Travellers and the Harmony Echoes, while working part-time as a labourer, breaking up with partners, and trying, not always successfully, to support a young family. He followed Wright to the doors of the emergent Goldwax label, with Jamison acting as his manager and confidant, and between 1966 and 1969 he released ten singles, breaking into the R&B charts with his third single, 'You've Got My Mind Messed Up', in 1966. By January 1968, with his mentor hawking discs from the back of his car, Carr came to record songs that were poised to join the great legacy of southern soul music. His definitive version of the illicit-love song 'The Dark End Of The Street' (1967) was a stone-cold classic and his rousing 'Freedom Train' (1969) became one of the great anthems of the civil rights era. 'The Dark End Of The Street' was a visceral and challenging number about secret love and betrayal in the dark streets of downtown Memphis. It had been hurriedly written by Dan Penn and Chips Moman in a hotel during a break in a marathon poker session. Moman had earned the nickname 'Chips' from his lust for gambling, and, according to music historian Robert Gordon, the two friends were 'pilled up at a music convention in Nashville [when] they took a break from a poker break, went to a piano, and hammered out the song in less than an hour, returning to play another hand'. The ballad's lasting complexity eclipsed its humdrum origins and it was recorded first by Percy Sledge, then by Aretha Franklin, as well as Ry Cooder and Linda Ronstadt. *The New York Times* was to describe his voice as 'a robust baritone that embraced amber-toned purity and desperate growls'. He could turn an already unhappy love song into three minutes of tortured heartsick drama. But mental illness hampered his career, and none of his releases seriously bothered the pop charts. 'He had a hard life,' Quinton Claunch said. 'He lived the blues and was not always good at taking medication.' Author Hank Cherry saw in Carr's depression a route to a profound depth: 'When you listen to him sing his songs, a freeway opens up and drives right to the soul of raw emotion. While Otis Redding certainly sang with supreme emotion, that emotion was predicated on confidence. James Carr dove into his own embattled soul, and pulled from the painful reaches of his psyche.'

When the Goldwax label eventually folded in 1969 they left James Carr, O.V. Wright and Wee Willie Walker with no royalties to show for their careers. Walker continued to work in a corrugated cardboard plant and Wright could not even afford his own apartment, and so shared a low-income home with his mother on the notorious Le Moyne Gardens, relying largely on welfare. There were many honourable attempts to resurrect Carr's professional career, but his apparent lack of energy and an inclination to drift into lengthy depressive silences undermined them. He suffered from what Peter Guralnick described as 'a crippling paralysis of spirit, a graver and graver malaise'. His fear and anxiety about the outside world led him to move into his sister's home in Memphis, after which he rarely emerged from his depression and eventually died of lung cancer in 2001.

Throughout the early months of 1968, as his career as a community haematologist and blood-bank manager grew, Roosevelt Jamison's role in trying to develop the career of the lost spirit of Carr inevitably took second place. He promoted Wee Willie Walker's full-throttle cover version of the Beatles' 'Ticket To Ride', but always alerted friends to the B-side, the peerless 'There Goes My Used To Be', an agonising tale of lost love. He remained a concerned friend to Carr even as his final two Goldwax releases, 'A Man Needs A Woman'/ 'Stronger Than Love' (Goldwax 332, 1968) and 'Life Turned Her That Way'/'A Message To Young Lovers' (Goldwax 335, 1968) stalled and failed. The slower Carr's life became, the more it seemed to propel Jamison forward. He kept up a relentless pace, racing around the small towns of the South handing out promotional copies to radio DJs, then back to the corner of Beale Street and Fourth, where the blood bank rehearsal room was attracting the next generation of hopeful singers. By 1968 he had befriended yet another Memphis act, the Ovations, and directed them to Goldwax. He would juggle the demands of soul and blood, the values of gospel and haemoglobins, as he accelerated east along E Trigg Avenue and turned onto Lauderdale where he would park at Royal Studios, the old nickelodeon that was now a factory of instrumental soul under the guidance of local bandleader Willie Mitchell. The owner, Joe Cuoghi, was well known in the music industry for his pioneering store Poplar Records, which had been a local institution since 1946. It was where Elvis hung out and where the different strands of Memphis music, from hillbilly to R&B, found common company. Cuoghi was usually good for a pint of blood, but since a serious illness he had all but disappeared. Willie Mitchell had always promised him an 'armful' but that never seemed to happen; the time was never right, his arm was always elsewhere, and so Jamison hung out with the Hodges brothers: Charlie, Leroy or Teenie. They were the rhythm section at Hi Studios and a reliable source of music gossip, but curiously reluctant to allow their blood to flow.

The evenings would bring Jamison full circle back to Beale Street. This was the busiest time of his working day, when the singers and musicians arrived from their day job and rehearsals would begin. It was also the time that regular donors, many from Baptist churches across the city, finished their work for the day and could take time to donate, and when alcoholics turned up, needing a few cents for a drink. Jamison had been told by the university not to take blood from drunks for fear of contamination, and he tried to stick scrupulously to the rules, but witnessing the broken lives and gaunt faces around him tested his deeply held Christian views, so he kept a small jar of quarters under the desk to give out to the most needy. Generosity oozed from the pores of Roosevelt Jamison, but charity alone could not solve the problems of Memphis. Powerful forces were gathering outside the Interstate Blood Bank, and they came with a mandate to challenge the deep discrimination that still lingered in the city. Within a matter of months, the decaying corners of Beale Street would be visited by righteous fury, pathological racism and unprecedented grief.

A soul requiem. Otis Redding's death hurt Stax to the core,
and the role of talking to the press fell on the young shoulders
of crash survivor Ben Cauley of the Bar-Kays.

CARL CUNNINGHAM'S CARDBOARD REQUIEM

8 January

It was a routine delivery. A parcel truck parked illegally outside a dilapidated cinema on East McLemore Avenue in South Memphis. No one even looked at the driver as he stacked a tower of cardboard boxes and delivered them to the foyer, to the ramshackle offices of one of the most prodigious independent recording studios in the world. This was Stax Records, the flagship home of Memphis soul and a beacon of hope for hundreds of young musicians and teenagers who hung around its doors as if it were a fairground. The boxes were addressed only to the company and they lay by the entrance, unacknowledged, for several days. It was only when a curious staff member opened them that their sad significance came to light. They contained the remains of the drum kit of Carl Lee Cunningham, the deceased drummer of the Bar-Kays, the backing band of Stax's most famous star, Otis Redding. The cardboard lay scattered over the lavender carpeting, a banal requiem to the tragic events of the previous month, when seven young people plunged to their death in a plane crash. The drum cases were in a bad state, battered by the waves and rusted by cold waters, with their skins partly torn from the rims. The red strips of tape that had once secured the cases top to bottom had peeled off in the deep, and now hung pathetically.

Carl Cunningham's death hurt Stax to the core. He was a familiar face around the studios, a boy obsessed with music and bewitched by the beat, who came from a famous family of drummers well known at Stax and on the streets of Orange Mound. Like many of his generation, he lived a hand-to-mouth existence, holding down a low-paid job as a shoeshine boy at King's Barbershop on the corner of College Street and East McLemore. Cunningham's drums were the last items to be salvaged from the crash site. His horn-rimmed glasses had disappeared, and the drumsticks he had cradled in his hand as the plane plummeted were never recovered. They were presumed lost in the frozen waters of Lake Monona, Dane County, Wisconsin.

Talking to the press was a tough thing to ask anyone to do and that role fell heavily on the shoulders of Cunningham's friend, the trumpeter Ben Cauley, who was still only twenty. He had been hospitalised in the immediate aftermath of the crash and had spent a difficult Christmas recuperating. Now that 1968 had arrived, he was facing up to the loss of his best friends. He stood in the reception area at Stax, head bowed down in grief and holding back the tears, barely managing to answer the questions in a stammering, fading voice. He was dressed in a double-breasted military raincoat with epaulettes and an Ushanka hat that perched perilously on his head and looked as if he had bought it second-hand from the Russian army. It was in fact a hat that he had bought in Wisconsin as the winter winds grew stronger. On his left arm he wore a new wristwatch, to replace the one he lost in the deep waters of the lake. Ben held his hands in front of him as if he were at a wake and his eyes gazed wearily at the floor. He started to explain his ordeal. He had all but passed out in the freezing lake but miraculously survived by clinging on to a soaking wet seat cushion. Hallucinating with hypothermia, he had watched each of his friends try to escape from the wreckage, but fail to keep their heads above the surface. All drowned before the rescue party arrived. Cauley spent twenty-five minutes in the water. When he could no longer hold the sodden cushion in his numb and frozen hands any longer, he drifted into unconsciousness. 'Just as soon as I let it go, somebody yanked me up,' Cauley remembered, still bewildered by the randomness that had saved his life and killed his friends. He admitted to the journalists that his near-drowning provoked recurring nightmares in which 'the rush of the lake's icy water, the chill of fear, and the helplessness' lapped through his mind.

The Stax songwriter David Porter watched the press conference in disbelief. From that day on, he described Cauley's survival as divine: 'Ben is a miracle. It's really that simple.' Yet Cauley was not alone in his luck; bass guitarist James Alexander had travelled by a different route and survived, and the Stax singer Mary Frierson, who had been given the stage name Wendy Rene by Otis Redding and was pencilled to appear as a warm-up act and a backing singer, stayed in Memphis, having just given birth to a baby boy. Frierson eventually drifted away from music as a consequence of the crash, leaving only a few obscure songs as her legacy. Cauley then told the press that he was rushed to the Methodist Hospital in Wisconsin, suffering from exposure and shock, where he remained for several days. His first visitor was James Alexander, another member of the Bar-Kays, who had missed the doomed flight. The group had drawn lots. Alexander lost out and, with no seat available on the private plane, flew safely by commercial airline via Milwaukee. On his arrival at Mitchell airport, Alexander had been met by police who drove him to visit his friend in hospital. Then he was taken on the grimmest visit of his life – to the mortuary, where he was asked to identify the naked bodies of his friends, name tags hanging limply from their big toes.

When he was asked what had caused the crash, Cauley hesitated, then looked around to Stax's staff members for guidance. He explained nervously that he had been visited by aviation investigators and had told them that the aircraft had been cold when they first boarded. The Bar-Kays had asked the young pilot if he could crank up the heat, but ominously he told them that the battery reading was too low for extra heat and almost certainly too low to guide the plane to safety.

The crash that killed Otis Redding and six others was a mess of misinformation. Even eye witnesses were unsure of what had happened. It seems that around 3.30 p.m. on 10 December 1967, just three miles from the safety of Dane County's regional airport Truax Field, a twin-engine Beechcraft-18 plane plunged through low-lying clouds and fog. The gusting rain and squally conditions seemed to tip the plane into a tailspin and it crashed down into Lake Monona. Only a few witnesses saw the crash, but many more claimed to have heard the engine fighting with itself as the pilot tried desperately to descend into an instrument-led landing pattern. What no one knew at the time was that the plane was a private jet owned by soul singer Otis Redding, one he had bought several months earlier from James Brown. The distinctive green-and-white livery, recently painted and emblazoned with Redding's name, was barely visible in the low-lying clouds, and, according to one of the few eye witnesses, the plane seemed to break apart as soon as it hit the surface of the lake. If it had continued for another mile it would have crash-landed into Madison's heavily populated East Side. By some small mercy a major catastrophe was averted. That was cold comfort to Stax, whose heart had been ripped out by the crash.

Police divers and volunteers, including a small contingent of local doctors, quickly gathered at the scene. Defying the freezing cold, they plunged into the water to look for survivors, but when it became clear that there was little likelihood of saving lives, a crane was hired from a local contractor, and police began what was to become a painstaking rescue operation. A razor-thin film of ice formed on the bitterly cold waters of the lake, the temperature plunged, and after a day of searching, the search was called off. Later, they managed to winch the wreckage up from the lake. The body of Otis Redding, one of the greatest soul singers in the world, was slowly dragged up from the water. A police photographer captured the moment. Redding's head was inelegantly trapped between the winch and the police barge, his mouth battered and blood clotted around his lips – those lips that had sung the saddest of songs with such elegance and pleading – 'Fa-fa-fa-fa-fa-fa-fa-fa, I keep singing them sad, sad songs y'all, Sad songs is all I know.'

The police barge headed at a glacial pace to the shore, obscured by the dense fog that hung over the lake's surface. The remnants of the Bar-Kays' stage suits, bought at Lansky's on Beale Street back home, floated pathetically to the surface. Only these freezing waters knew the full story of what had actually happened. On board was the plane's log, which had been found near the aircraft. It was eventually turned over to Federal Aviation Agency officials, but by the time it was in their safe hands, the impact of one of soul music's greatest tragedies was reverberating around the world.

Redding had been scheduled to play a concert at the Factory, a club in a converted garage in the city's West Gorham Street. Local art student William Barr had designed a surreal psychedelic poster advertising Otis, the Bar-Kays and a warm-up group from Illinois, prophetically known as the Grim Reapers, who later morphed into the rock band Cheap Trick. By the time Redding's body arrived at the laboratory of Dane County, much was still to be unexplained. Coroner Clyde Chamberlain trundled the gurney down a corridor past the county sheriff's department, with no idea whose the body was or its significance. Chamberlain had never heard of Otis Redding, Stax was a name he was entirely unfamiliar with, and Memphis was a remote southern city he had never visited. Nor was he expecting the attention that would descend on his office. Usually, dead bodies arrived at his autopsy room on gurneys or carried on police stretchers, and with a brown paper carrier bag containing the personal effects of the deceased, typically small sums of cash, a wristwatch, a cigarette lighter, a wallet and a photograph of wife and family.

Otis Redding had always been conscious of his appearance. His colleague and collaborator at Stax, Isaac Hayes, called him 'a statue of a man', Jerry Wexler, the emperor of Atlantic Records, described him as 'a natural prince', and others talked about him as being of 'chiselled marble' and 'god-like'. A keen amateur pilot, Redding had been sitting upfront, and had been propelled forward into the control panel at the time of the crash. His leg was broken, and a small attaché in which the soul singer kept his cash earnings from two previous concerts was missing, but unlike Cunningham's drum kit the missing attaché was never found. It has always been the subject of unresolved intrigue – and long-term family resentment. Redding had just completed a lucrative three-night concert trip to Cleveland and the attaché was presumed to have contained $10,000 in cash. Redding's widow Zelma always presumed that it was stolen by rescue workers or expropriated by a rogue police officer. However, it is more likely to have remained in the silty grey unforgiving waters of Lake Monona.

Redding had died at the pinnacle of his career. His now classic album *Otis Blue*, released in the autumn of 1965, had gone to number one in the R&B charts and stayed in the pop charts for thirty-four weeks. Rock critic Dave Marsh was convinced it was vocal range that set Redding apart, describing him as 'one of the great live showmen . . . a masterful ballad singer and a true rocker in the spirit of his boyhood hero, Little Richard'. Three months prior to his death, *Melody Maker* selected him as the world's top male vocalist, dethroning Memphis's most famous son, Elvis Presley, who had held the top spot since 1956. Redding's fame had brought him to the attention of the White House and he had recently accepted an invitation from Vice President Hubert Humphrey to head a troupe of Stax/Volt artists to entertain US troops in Vietnam in the spring of 1968. He had destroyed all before him when he appeared the previous summer at the celebrated Monterey Pop Festival. In the few weeks prior to his death, Redding had undergone a period of intense creativity, scribbling lyrics down on notepaper as he travelled, improvising ideas on stage, and soaking up influences from urban soul to the new festival rock. Excitedly, Otis was in daily contact with his collaborator and sometime producer Steve Cropper, who as a teenager had bought his first guitar by mail order and was now a mainstay of the Stax studio system. Redding rarely completed songs. He threw ideas out there like confetti, often asking for help to complete the best of them. Cropper was his sounding board and often brought shape to the initial idea, moulding it until it was ready to record. Unlike the more controlled Motown system, or, more famously, the Hollywood studio system, Stax was informal, haphazard and collegiate, and in contrast to the urban sounds from the north, Stax was heavy with southern heat. Cropper was drawn to a ballad that Otis had sketched out while relaxing on a houseboat on Waldo Point, California, after a residency at the Fillmore. He sensed that '(Sittin' On) The Dock Of The Bay' had a wider appeal, way beyond the narrow register of Redding's trademark deep soul ballads, like 'I've Been Loving You Too Long' or 'Try A Little Tenderness'. The song's narrative was one of departure, loneliness and yearning for home, universal themes that could appeal far beyond the ghetto bar-rooms. It was one of a catalogue of songs Redding recorded in a period of intense activity at Stax studios in December 1967, and his death brought the songs prophetically to life. In a fast turnaround, motivated by a mixture of remembrance and market greed, Stax – with the help of their distrusted colleagues at Atlantic Records in New York – rush-released the song. It hit the streets on 8 January 1968 and became an instant success – number one in the USA, the UK and much of Europe – selling over four million copies and dominating awards throughout the year. Out there on radio stations, and in the stores, it took on a watery mournfulness, as if Otis had written the song as his final farewell. Suddenly, a song about love took on much greater significance, and the metaphor of the dock of the bay came to mean a lover's requiem, suicidal self-reflection, or the chronicle of a death foretold. The song ends with Otis whistling the final refrain, as if he is lost for words, fading into a distant forever. Many have claimed that in the recording session Redding had simply run out of words and ideas, but keyboardist Booker T. Jones was adamant that it was all planned, observing that the song was 'beautifully simplistic – all major chords. Otis's lyrics touched me – about leaving home and watching the bay, trying to figure things out as everyone's pulling at you. My notes on the piano fed into that. I wanted to capture a maritime feel – the sound of a boat on the Mississippi River, and the sounds of gospel and New Orleans. I put those flourishes around Otis's voice.' Cropper filled out the under-produced parts of the song by borrowing sound effects from a rival studio on Union Avenue. 'I went over to a local jingle company [called] Pepper-Tanner, and got into their sound library and came up with some seagulls and some waves, and I made the tape loop of that, brought them in and out of the holes, you know. Whenever the song took a little breather, I just kind of filled it with a seagull or a wave.' The finished recording remains one of the greatest posthumous pop songs of all time: enriched by death and given profundity by the circumstances. Writer Jack Hamilton describes the song as 'another thing entirely, a song about homesickness that Redding turns into something elemental, existential . . . It is personal, bold, warm and warming, completely magnificent. And written and performed by a man who was only twenty-six years old.'

The coroner's office in Madison had become a place of chaotic activity. One by one, the bodies of young black men were brought in, and all were pronounced dead due to drowning: Jimmy King (18), guitarist with the Bar-Kays; the drummer, Carl Lee Cunningham (18); organist Ronnie Caldwell (19); Matthew Kelly (17), a personal valet to Otis Redding; and pilot Richard 'Dick' Fraser (26). Fraser had been raised in Warner Robins, Georgia, near Otis Redding's hometown of Macon. Although there was talk of low battery power and ice on the carburettor, the consensus within the light-aviation industry was pilot error.

The Bar-Kays had been students together at Booker T. Washington High School, deep in South Memphis. It was the informal academy of southern soul, and many of its most precocious pupils had gravitated to Stax Records as odd-job staff, session musicians and eventually soul superstars. In the improvisational world of the East McLemore studios, the Bar-Kays hustled a Top Ten hit with the infectious 'Soul Finger', a storming party track that opened with the riff from the nursery rhyme 'Mary Had A Little Lamb'. Propelled by Cunningham's relentless drums, it became a street funk anthem. The song captured the spirit of the place and the times. Young neighbourhood kids from the Memphis ghettos had packed into the studio to add authenticity as they chanted effusively to the music. A few days after high-school graduation, the Bar-Kays joined Otis Redding on the road, and once performed at the famous Apollo Theater in Harlem, where, unrehearsed, James Brown had jumped onto the stage and performed an unscripted duet with Redding. Resplendent in their canary-yellow suits, the Bar-Kays tore up the theatres on the old Chitlin' Circuit and were blasting a reputation nationwide until the day that the last remnants of their yellow suits floated to the surface of Lake Monona.

It was to be death, rather than street funk, that bound the lost Stax boys together. Between registering the deaths of the teenage band members and liaising with the Madison police, Clyde Chamberlain eventually managed to make phone contact with Redding's widow, Zelma. She insisted on travelling to the Wisconsin morgue together with her father-in-law, Otis Redding Sr, in order to accompany her husband's body back to his native Georgia. Redding's father, a southern preacher, had resented his son's career as a soul singer and chastised him for appearing in godless nightclubs, but fame, critical respect and money had tempered his criticism. With the unspoken blessing of the dead star, they agreed that the final resting place would not be Memphis, but Redding's 300-acre Big O Ranch, which was situated about twenty-five miles north of his hometown. Redding had bought the ranch in 1965 for $125,000 on the back of two years of hits and a relentless itinerary of live shows. 'He always wanted a ranch,' Zelma told the US news broadcaster CNN, recalling the 'freedom I could see him have when he came home off the road'. Redding's ranch was a world apart from where Carl Cunningham and the teenage Bar-Kays grew up. They were from the blistering segregated streets of Memphis's Orange Mound, the biggest African-American community outside Harlem. It was this contrast and contradiction that gave Stax uniqueness – urban and country were thrown fortuitously together. Redding was most at home in rural environments, raising cattle, riding horses and working away in his barn while Cunningham grew up thrashing skins on a makeshift drum kit in his family's overcrowded shotgun-style house near Kimball Avenue.

Unintentionally, Redding's death has always overshadowed those who died with him and the funerals reflected that hierarchy. The young members of the Bar-Kays were remembered together as a band of brothers; Redding was given a dedicated service, a lying-in-state, and a memoriam that reflected his remarkable status. Although he had become synonymous in music circles with Memphis, it was not a city Redding knew particularly well. Unlike Cunningham, who had lived and breathed the city's tense discriminations, Redding had a more rural upbringing. He was born in Dawson, in southwest Georgia, and raised in the central state city of Macon; a place with its own claim to fame, it was where both Little Richard and James Brown were raised. Always a creative magpie and not yet fully settled in a distinctive style of his own, Redding borrowed heavily from both of them. At times, his grunting 'gotta, gotta, gotta' refrain in live shows made him sound too much like James Brown – and dangerously short of subtlety – but his derivativeness was also a strength.

At seventeen, he was winning weekly talent shows at Macon's Douglass Theater, wiping away decent opposition. He hung out with Little Richard's old band, the Upsetters, and then became the featured singer with a local band called Pat T. Cake and the Mighty Panthers, before migrating to yet another Macon band, Johnny Jenkins and his Pinetoppers. With Redding acting as his driver, Jenkins travelled north for a studio session at Stax, and when the house band Booker T. and the M.G.'s wrapped up early to fulfil a local engagement, Redding hustled the gap in the timetable and recorded his first significant release, 'These Arms Of Mine' (1962), a ballad as much influenced by country as by soul. His rocking cover version of the Rolling Stones' '(I Can't Get No) Satisfaction' (1965) had the imported energy of the UK R&B beat scene, and his cover version of the ubiquitous 'Louie Louie' (1963) was unfettered garage R&B. Redding had never heard of the Rolling Stones, nor had he heard their music, but in his almost naïve enthusiasm he spontaneously burst into their song, mispronouncing words but giving it a unique energy all of his own. He was a steam train who careered into music, recording whole songs live in the studio without a break, looking out to imagined audiences, signing autographs in his mind before the song was finished, and even rewriting songs as he sang them. His manager, Phil Walden, said, 'He was successful and he liked that lifestyle, being a star and having people like him. He was into being Otis Redding.'

In the Stax studios Redding personified the company's unwritten philosophy of unrestrained work and live takes. It was not a place prone to much pre-planning or technological aftercare. Wayne Jackson, who sat in on one of the numerous Stax sessions as one of the famed Memphis Horns, described Redding as a hurricane of effort: 'The man was physical. Emotional and physical . . . He'd just get right in front of you with that big fist up in the air and strut and sing that stuff at you until you were just foaming at the mouth. He'd have you so excited. We had to calm him down sometimes.' Redding had grown up understanding that hard work was always a bridge to success and he was by some distance the pace-setter in Stax's fierce cauldron. 'Otis gave ten thousand per cent,' said the then-Stax publicist Al Bell. 'He lost pounds in the studio. He'd come into the studio and strip down to his waist . . . and just sing until the water was coming off him, like someone was pouring out of a bucket.'

Redding was in many ways bewitched by the whole process of being a star. He frequently recounted one of the great myths of African-American music, the story of the legendary bluesman Robert Johnson who 'sold his soul to the devil' at a rural crossroads near Dockery Plantation in Mississippi. Redding often embroidered the story, relocating it closer to his own home in Georgia and describing it happening in land that he only knew fleetingly through childhood memories of the dirt-poor sharecropper shacks dotted along the Old River Road near the Jarrell cotton plantation. When Redding faced his own crossroads in the sixties, it was not the devil who stood in his path but his own Christian father and the fragmenting music of the South. The Reddings had by then moved into Tindall Heights, Macon's first public housing development for black families, and Otis had taken on menial work as a well digger and as a gas station attendant. Much of his money went towards funding his father's healthcare, yet as his father's tuberculosis worsened, his loathing of Redding's musical career deepened, and the singer was forced to conceal his whereabouts at night.

For all his rousing performances, it was as a balladeer that Otis Redding found his true persona. On a tour of New York State in the mid sixties, he was rooming with Jerry Butler, who had been raised in Chicago's notorious Cabrini-Green housing projects and had recently left the Impressions to pursue a solo career. It was fortunate happenstance, after one show, that the two sat up together and composed the blistering ballad 'I've Been Loving You Too

Long', which not only became a success in its own right, but was the stand-out song in Redding's critically acclaimed 1965 album *Otis Blue*, recorded live over a hectic twenty-four-hour period.

Memphis had grown and thrived on the back of slavery, and then segregation, but history was forcing it to reappraise its ways. The city's wealth had been founded on the cotton empire that meandered across the Mississippi Delta, a raging river that connected Memphis to the slave port of New Orleans and which Stax guitarist Steve Cropper described as a great thoroughfare. 'Memphis is in a very lucky position on the map,' he once said. 'Everything just gravitated to Memphis for years.'

Schools were acclimatising to the difficult early days of desegregation and downtown restaurants were now required to serve black customers, but the law proved easier to change than attitudes, and inequality and subtle forms of segregation have remained a constant in Memphis society to the current day. In 1968 Memphis had a population of 500,000. Around forty per cent of the population was African-American and fifty-eight per cent of black families lived in poverty. The vast majority of men worked as labourers while most black women with paid jobs worked in the homes of white families or in the service economy. Behind the picket fences and white shutters was a world of orders, hierarchies and thinly disguised racism.

Yet, when Otis Redding first walked into Stax on McLemore as an unknown driver, the studio had already shattered segregationist rules. Drivers were not expected to stay hidden away in their cars or at a parking lot nearby; they were allowed into the studio to watch, listen or drink coffee. Black and white musicians would work and play together, but they were separate in their lifestyle, with the majority living in different neighbourhoods, attending different schools and barely acknowledging each other as they passed in the street. Songwriter William Bell described the situation: 'Those were heavy times and the best of times . . . When we walked out of the studio, the reality hit us in the face, with all the segregation and everything. But inside the studio it was like utopia.'

Stax historian Rob Bowman, who wrote his doctoral thesis on

the company, claimed in an interview: 'It's impossible to conceive what Stax did in terms of integration unless you've spent time in the South. Stax was in the heart of the Mid South. When Stax began, Memphis was as racially segregated and polarized as a city could get. The city was fifty per cent white and fifty per cent black. But nothing was integrated except Stax. I call Stax an oasis of racial sanity in an otherwise insane world. A lot of the people who worked at Stax commented on how going to work was like going to church. You stepped into the Stax building and the world was somehow different. Black and white people were working together and becoming friends at Stax in a way that was totally organic. Stax was the organic manifestation of Dr Martin Luther King's dream, where black and white people came together through a common purpose. Working together toward a common goal – making music – black and white people realized that their differences were a matter of culture and not a matter of species.'

The original owners of Stax, Jim Stewart and his sister Estelle Axton, whose abbreviated surnames bequeathed the company its name, acted as quiet trailblazers in a society where integration was still a troublesome concept. Jim Stewart was a white farm boy from Tennessee and a part-time fiddle player who had been raised on hoedown and hillbilly music in an Ulster-Scots farming community, where the preferred music was Highland and barn-dance reels. He had been immersed in country music from childhood, listening to the Grand Ole Opry on Radio Station WSM on his father's vintage Emerson radio, and so was an unlikely figure on the southern soul scene. He was thin and bookish, and favoured heavy black-rimmed glasses, patterned rayon shirts, pressed flannels and polished shoes. He was, in the parlance of the time, a 'square'. Having moved from the farmlands of Mississippi to urban Memphis, he worked at the Union Planters Bank, holding down a secure salaried job. Trumpeter Wayne Jackson described him as 'an accountant and an introvert' who routinely took pills to combat nerves and anxiety. Deeply insecure about the vulnerable fortunes of the recording industry, he remained at his bank job many years after Stax was formed. Stewart was always more comfortable with country music than with soul, and according to music critic Barney

Hoskyns in his pioneering book *Say It One More Time for the Brokenhearted*, 'Stax had grown on a country foundation' and Stewart considered Otis Redding's 'These Arms Of Mine' to be a classic example of 'black country'.

Understandably, given his upbringing and conservative views, Stewart was concerned that the music could not be trusted to provide an income for himself and his family, and, although they were very different characters, he shared his sister's strong streak of moral responsibility. Estelle Axton had moved from the family farm to work as a teacher in the Memphis education system, a role that influenced her attitudes to music. She eventually became the likeable matriarch of Satellite Records, the vinyl store next door to the Stax studios which became a gathering place for the neighbourhood's young and aspiring African-American talent. For a few unsuccessful years, Jim Stewart released country and western records on the Satellite label (named after the record store), but the location of the shop in what was a blighted ghetto area brought black music teeming to its doors. William Bell, then an emergent songwriter, described Satellite as 'a teenage hangout' and many of Stax's greatest acts found their first words of encouragement from the lips of Axton, as they shopped for the latest releases or came to her with their ideas. The songwriter Homer Banks was an assistant at the record store and was patiently guided through the craft of writing lyrics by Axton. Although she was no longer a teacher, it was a profession she never truly abandoned, taking her skills into the community as a mentor of raw and often rough young teenagers. She had pioneered a crude but effective data system within the shop in which she recorded on file cards and a Rolodex all the records that ever sold well in the shop. The data was frequently consulted to try to fathom the appeal of the most successful. Axton claims it was 'the workshop of Stax Records' and told the writer Rob Bowman in his book *Soulsville U.S.A.* that 'when a record would [become a] hit on another label, we would discuss what makes the record sell. We analysed it. That's why we had so many good writers. They knew what would sell.' Next door, within the flaking walls of the old Capitol Movie Theater, the company that became Stax set up home, and for years the shop and the studio worked in mutually reinforcing tandem: improvising, producing and selling records.

Stax could not have flourished without the local Memphis school system, and two pioneering schools stood out, separated not just by the sprawling geography of the city, but by the deep cultural apartheid of Tennessee; they were the exclusively black Booker T. Washington High School and the predominantly white Messick High School. Although black students made up forty-five per cent of the Memphis educational roll, discrimination was ingrained and institutionalised; not a single black parent, politician or elder served on a school board. Divisions ran deep in Memphis life but somehow music found a cross-over. It was at Messick High in February 1955 that the teenage Elvis Presley performed a pioneering show that triggered the moment of rock 'n' roll, a musical eruption that Greil Marcus described as the 'Big Bang' – the event that changed the universe of teenage music. 'If ever there was music that bleeds,' Marcus wrote, 'this was it.' Messick bled music. It was an urban high school but it had once drawn its students from the farmlands on the periphery of the city. It sat in a tree-lined block on Spottswood Avenue and was exclusively white. Although the legal system was slowly recognising civil rights, segregation was still powerfully in force: the Memphis district had fifty-five all-black schools, eighteen that were all white, twenty-five that were predominately black and sixty-eight that were predominately white. Stax drew on them all, regardless of colour. One Messick High student stood out from the crowd. Charles 'Packy' Axton, the wayward son of Stax co-owner Estelle, was a tenor saxophonist, a provocative outsider and one of the school's teenage delinquents. His father Everett was an alcoholic, and, although he was married to the Stax clan, Packy was kept at arm's length from the studios and, for a spell, banned from the studios. Packy's wayward life led his cautious uncle to believe that alcoholism surged through the family and unresolved resentments flared into open warfare. It was a battle of generational attitudes. Packy enjoyed shaming his conservative uncle; he flagrantly hung out with black kids in the wrong parts of town, flaunted the sexual divisions of the day by dating black girls, and drank copiously in feared local nightclubs, such as the notorious Plantation Inn across the Mississippi Bridge in West Memphis. Packy had hooked up with an emergent high-school band called the Royal Spades, who rehearsed in the school auditorium, on the stage that Elvis Presley had once graced. The Spades became the nucleus of Stax road band the Mar-Keys, and among their number were lead guitarist Steve Cropper, Donald 'Duck' Dunn, a promising bass guitarist who had grown up in semi-rural Tennessee, saxophonist Don Nix, Terry Johnson, a precociously talented drummer who played in his father's country and western group, trumpeter Wayne Jackson, a latter-day member of the Memphis Horns, and vocalist Ronnie 'Stoots' Angel, a talented graphic designer who designed Stax's original label – an untidy pile of vinyl discs. Most were from Messick High and all from high schools in the exclusively white neighbourhoods of East Memphis. Cropper had arrived in the city as a ten-year-old from his home on a tiny farmstead in Dora, Missouri, on Route 181 – territory steeped in racial suspicion and hillbilly values. According to the Memphis historian and music critic Robert Gordon, 'Memphis music is an approach to life, defined by geography, dignified by the bluesmen.' In his obsessively researched local history *It Came from Memphis*, Gordon describes the uniqueness of the place and its people. 'This is the big city surrounded by farmland, where snug businessmen gamble on the labor of field hands, widening the gap between them, testing the uneasy alliance. Memphis has always been a place where cultures came together to have a wreck: black and white, rural and urban, poor and rich. The music of Memphis is more than a soundtrack to these confrontations. It is the document of it.'

Civil rights legislation was chipping away at discrimination. In 1964 1.2 per cent of African-American students in the South were attending school with whites, and by the first days of 1968 the figure had risen to over thirty per cent. But Memphis had not yet reflected the scale of that change. Booker T. Washington High School was almost entirely black. It was an urban oasis named after the great educationalist, and was staffed by teachers who encouraged black ambition. Booker was hemmed in between the Danny Thomas Boulevard and East Railroad Avenue, in an area that echoed to the percussion of railroad wagons lumbering along an old rail network that connected the Tennessee River to Charleston, South Carolina, the capital of the slave trade. Many of the teenagers who would go on to shape southern soul walked those tracks: Stax organist Booker T. Jones was named after the educationalist, and his father was a science teacher at the school; another teacher Nat D. Williams became the first DJ to broadcast to black audiences via Radio Station WDIA; Rufus Thomas, the clown prince of Stax, had studied there; Isaac Hayes, David Porter and William Bell were all students there before graduating to the writing rooms and the main studio at Stax as writer-producers. Even the old bluesmen of a different generation had walked those railroads. John Lee Hooker once said: 'I hitchhiked, took trucks 'n' trains – anything that would pick me up. I stopped in Memphis for about six months and they found me and come got me. Staid [sic] about a month and then split.'

In its earliest days, Stax was colour blind. Estelle Axton commented that 'we never saw colour, we saw talent'. Musicians from all the various strands of music and society found expression in the glorious 1962 hit 'Green Onions' by Booker T. and the M.G.'s, which broke through the fragile harmonies of Memphis society to trailblaze southern soul to the summit of the *Billboard* charts and launch an act with near perfect racial symmetry. The song was improvised at the tail-end of a studio session and hawked around local radio stations, from where it grew steadily into a worldwide club classic. The group consisted of Booker T. Jones and a drumming prodigy called Al Jackson Jr, both of whom were black. Steve Cropper and Lewie Steinberg were white. In time Steinberg was replaced by another white bassist, Donald Dunn. Booker T. and the M.G.'s were the band that openly defied segregation. The celebrated Memphis guitarist Jim Dickinson claims that 'Booker T. and the M.G.'s was a perfect example of racial collision – four men who under normal circumstances would not have known each other, much less work with each other in ensemble like that.' It is a theme that runs like oil through the history of Memphis music. According to Al Bell, Stax's dynamic publicist, producer and, ultimately, its most aggressive executive, Stax was a 'haven, because it allowed us to escape all of the segregation and racism outside.

When we left Stax and went back to our communities, the blacks went back to the black community and the whites to the white community . . . When we left and went out that door, *then* we went into a different world, but inside of Stax it didn't exist.' The label's greatest achievement was that it challenged orthodoxy and attracted musicians from across the ethnic divide: they came from the hillbilly homes of the Appalachian mountains, from the country bars of Nashville, from the rural roadside shacks of gut-bucket blues and from the glorious gospel churches of the southern states.

News of the plane crash that killed Otis Redding spread like wildfire through the R&B community. Aretha Franklin and her sister Carolyn were at home in Detroit when the news reached them. Although she was now a Detroit citizen, Aretha had been born in a crowded clapboard house at 406 Lucy Avenue on the Southside of Memphis and remained emotionally attached to her birthplace. She spent the remainder of the day on the phone with Redding's wife and executives at Stax Records in Memphis, trying to make sense of the patchy information that was leaking out from news services. Soul music had just been denied one of its greatest collaborations. According to Redding's manager Phil Walden, he had negotiated a deal that would bring Otis and Aretha into the Stax studios to record a series of as yet unidentified duets. Both had recorded the anthemic 'Respect', a song likely to have been on the notional roster. Aretha called Atlantic Records in New York, and although Atlantic and Stax, one-time close partners, were now lurching towards a bitter dispute, Franklin sensed that her mentor Jerry Wexler would want to hear the news directly. She couldn't reach him. Wexler, a boss at Atlantic Records and a long-time distributor of Redding's hits, had been at a record executives' convention and was subsequently paged at Kennedy airport when he touched down. Although he had already fallen out with the Stax management, and had no great love of the city of Memphis, he had maintained a good, if proprietorial, relationship with Redding, who he described in his memoirs *Rhythm and the Blues* as a man with 'a strong inner life. He was emotionally centered, his manners were impeccable. His humour was sly and roguish.'

Stax singer Eddie Floyd was on tour in Europe and a delayed flight prevented him reaching the funeral service in time. Motown boss Berry Gordy was at the corporation's Los Angeles offices when he heard, and he promptly called his old friend and label mate Mable John. She was now signed to Stax and living locally, and was closer to the Memphis scene. John had toured extensively with Redding and knew him well, but such was the paucity of hard information she knew only the sketchiest details of the crash. James Brown was on stage in St Louis, Missouri, when the news reached him. Drummer Clyde Stubblefield, then a member of Brown's Famous Flames, describes the audience falling silent and how the effervescent and usually unflappable James Brown looking genuinely shell-shocked.

Zelma Redding has since admitted that she barely coped with the pain of managing the 'frightened emotions' of her three young children. She was advised to delay the funeral arrangements until the family was able to function and to allow Redding's body to lie in state at the Macon City Auditorium in Georgia. More than 4,500 people snaked through the building to pay their respects to Redding. Many white mourners admitted that they had never heard of him but felt so touched by the way his death had troubled their neighbours or friends that they felt compelled to pay their respects.

The bodies of the Bar-Kays were eventually flown back to Memphis and the body of Otis Redding to home. On Monday, 18 December 1967, Redding was buried at his home in Round Oak, Georgia. Jerry Wexler delivered the eulogy to a congregation of southern soul's aristocracy. There was a tension in the air. Wexler's relationship with the mourners from Stax was changing. Having once been a sage from the north and the company's route to national distribution, he was now less well liked and viewed suspiciously by some. The year 1968 would bring the relationship crashing to an end. The pallbearers were mostly southern-based singers – Joe Tex, Jo Simon, Johnnie Taylor, Arthur Conley and Solomon Burke – and among the ranks of the mourners were James Brown, Rufus Thomas and Aretha Franklin, one of the few to make the journey south from Detroit. The supremely gifted Johnnie Taylor, who in six short months would be Stax's most successful artist, in part filling the void left by Redding, sang the rousing gospel standard 'I'll Be Standing By' with Booker T. Jones accompanying him on organ.

Two uniformed nurses accompanied Zelma Redding throughout the ceremony, watching out for her wellbeing and prepared to help out if she became overcome with emotion. She came perilously close at times, shouting, 'Oh God, what am I going to do?' and hugging her children as if they might be snatched from her, too. Redding's burial had the heightened atmosphere of a state funeral, but, significantly in a music scene still largely regionalised, Motown's northern-based superstars stayed away. It was not a snub as such; a North–South divide still shaped the rhythm and blues scene, and the mourners were mostly drawn from Redding's world – the still segregated country towns of the Deep South. Crowds besieged James Brown, nearly tearing his coat from his back, and singer Joe Tex was forced to seek sanctuary in a nearby parking lot, hidden from the crowd by publicist Lee Ivory. Police with nightsticks were called to restore order, and only when the requiem reached its most solemn moment was there enough calm for Joe Simon to sing the hymn 'Jesus Keep Me Near The Cross' and Johnnie Taylor to deliver his version of 'I'll Be Standing By'. Both songs were rooted in Redding's era – rural Christianity ignited by the passions of civil rights. His father, who had always opposed his son's chosen career, could finally relax in his untimely death; the old songs were sung in the proper way and the sexual temptations of secular soul music were beyond him now.

Jim Stewart spoke fulsomely of Redding's importance to the recording industry and his adopted city of Memphis, saying in his funeral address, 'To us Otis exemplified the Memphis Sound, he represented everything the Memphis Sound should be: verve, vitality and excitement.' But the address tipped into brand posturing as he declared that Redding would always remain on his throne as the King of the Memphis Sound. Stax had simultaneously released statements to the national press and the image of the King of the Memphis Sound recurred throughout. It stopped short of cashing in on death – but only just. Redding's death had reached out across the nation. Vice President Hubert Humphrey delivered his own personal tribute, thanking Redding for supporting the government's ghetto outreach projects; his simple and emotionally enduring tribute paraphrased a single prophetic line from Redding's current single, '(Sittin' On) The Dock Of The Bay': 'I roamed two thousand miles from Georgia, never to go back home again'. It was an oft repeated line that captured the tragic futility of the plane crash and added a fateful sense of loss to the disintegrating world of sixties soul. 'Dock Of The Bay' became the most popular song among Vietnam veterans in the months, years and decades to come, capturing an as yet unspoken realisation of a war already lost.

Myth has it that Redding was laid to rest within hearing distance of the bells of Vineville Baptist Church, where he had sung in the choir. This was a sentimental exaggeration. His church was miles away from the ranch that would carry on his memory. While Redding's funeral attracted international attention, comment from the White House and fanatical grief among the fans he had charmed in Europe and on American campuses, the funeral of the dead members of the Bar-Kays was a more down-home affair. The families agreed to pool their resources and hire Clayborn Temple A.M.E. Church near Fourth Street and Linden Avenue, an African Episcopal church which across the angry summer of 1968 would become a gathering place for the discriminated and the dispossessed of Memphis. The interior of the church was a breathtaking vision of southern devotion; arched ceilings reached upwards to heaven and stained-glass windows depicting Christ's Ascension gazed down on the congregation. An old ceremonial pipe organ played sonorously throughout the service, its haunting sounds echoing with tears and cries to the Lord. The Cunningham family occupied an entire pew to the front; ten children, one delivered in almost every year, and almost all of them talented drummers. Dressed elegantly in his funeral suit, Carl's brother Blair was barely ten years old. He would grow up to become a drummer in the UK with Haircut 100, the Pretenders and Paul McCartney.

Because four young men were being buried at the same service, a cluster of pallbearers had to meet hurriedly in advance. Brothers, school friends and local musicians were coordinated by the funeral directors to carry the coffins into the church, where a congregation of distraught teenagers, familiar ghetto faces and attentive teachers mingled with the grieving families and the gospel choir. Afterwards, a lengthy cortege of cars drove to New Park Cemetery, due south of Elvis Presley's Graceland mansion. It was there on the quiet hillside that the Bar-Kays, together with valet and school friend Matthew Kelly, were finally laid to rest. Even as the families mourned, Stax swiftly recruited a new generation of Bar-Kays to fulfil outstanding engagements. In the weeks and months to come, a new group emerged featuring saxophonist Harvey Henderson, recruited from teen band the Wildcats, local guitarist Michael Toles, and vocalist Larry Dodson from Memphis harmony group the Temprees. One young hopeful, who in time replaced Carl Cunningham as drummer of the Bar-Kays, was still in high school. Willie Hall was playing midnight sessions with the house band at the Tiki Club near Bellevue Parkway. On the day of the plane crash, Memphis was besieged with a horrendous rain storm, and Hall was bedridden with double pneumonia. He had an omen that he would become the band's new drummer, and within a few months the surreal daydream came true.

By the time Hall came to the attention of Stax, his predecessor Carl Cunningham had been dead for at least two months. The cardboard boxes that had been delivered to 926 East McLemore had been opened and the remains of his drum kit were transported south to his parents' home. Don Nix, a saxophonist with the Mar-Keys, remembers the delivery as if it were a dagger to the heart of the Stax community. 'They were all warped,' he told Stax historian Robert Gordon. 'They had been at the bottom of the lake all that time. And everybody just sighed. We were getting over it, and I remember how that made me feel, 'cause everyone was friends – a neighbourhood. It was guys that cared about each other.'

I AM A MAN. Striking sanitation workers walk the gauntlet of military occupation in the weeks after the deaths of Echol Cole and Robert Walker.

ECHOL COLE'S LONG HARD DAY

1 February

Echol Cole worked long hard days. His job was brutal and demeaning, and the cuts and blemishes of hard labour encircled his wrists. The putrid smell of rotting garbage followed him around all day, clinging to his clothes, hanging on his skin, and even coming home with him at the end of the day, where the smell hung heavy in his crowded wooden-frame home in South Memphis. On the first morning of February 1968, Cole had been working since 5 a.m. for the local Department of Public Works, lugging huge garbage cans into the back of an old Weiner Barrel truck. The antisocial hours, the back-breaking physical demands and the most unhygienic working conditions in the city made it a job that was dangerous and poorly paid, and so only ever undertaken by poor black men. In his peerless history of the Memphis sanitation workers, *Going Down Jericho Road*, historian Michael K. Honey described workers like Echol Cole existing in a life just beyond slavery, 'in a netherworld between the plantation and the modern economy'.

Irrespective of the weather, which was often humid and unpredictable, the city's 1,100 sanitation workers collected over 2,000 tons of household garbage daily. They were all male, all black and usually with limited formal education. They worked six days a week, with a miserly fifteen-minute break for a hand-held lunch, which they took either in their truck or huddled by the roadside. They had no access to washing facilities and were forced to take toilet breaks hidden behind cinder walls or crouched behind privet hedges away from householders and passing traffic. Pay rates were controversial – based on the routes they worked, not the hours – as sanitation workers would be expected to clear an area irrespective of how long it took, and with no hope of overtime pay. There was no uniform and no safety suits; workers were expected to supply their own clothing and gloves, and maintain them to a reasonable standard. Back at the depot, there was no place to shower, clean up or change into fresh clothes before returning home. Most of the men lived in low-income housing projects in the city's Southside and tried to make ends meet with government-sponsored food stamps and small items of value they could scavenge from garbage cans or backyards. The city paid most of its sanitation workers a minimum wage of one dollar and sixty cents per hour, and despite working in a full-time job, over forty per cent were poor enough to draw welfare. It was a miserable existence at the very bottom of the social ladder of Memphis life where fifty-eight per cent of the black population lived in poverty. Coby Smith, a Memphis community organiser, and sometime member of the city's Black Power group, the Memphis Invaders, described the role of the sanitation worker as 'a job a white man could not have, it was beneath the level of a white man, it was a social caste, this is a job reserved for blacks, it was not a clean job. They had to wear filthy clothes, they had to work in filth, they had to drag garbage cans, I mean tubs of garbage.' Taylor Rogers, who worked on the trucks, told a newsreel reporter that 'those tubs had holes in them, garbage leaking all over ya when you got home in the evening, you had to stop at the door to pull off your shoes, pull off those real dirty clothes because maggots had fallen all on ya'. Such was their lot in life, the sanitation workers had earned the unflattering name 'walking buzzards'.

Echol Cole's route snaked eastward out through the suburban homes that fringed the Botanic Gardens, east on Park Avenue, until his truck rumbled to the corner of Verne and Colonial Road, near the end of its daily route. The air was claustrophobic and unforgiving. Humidity seemed to be leaking up from the Mississippi Delta, exaggerating a tense feeling of entrapment, and then the clouds burst. Cole was wearing only a torn sweat-stained shirt when suddenly and spectacularly the heavens opened. He ran to the garbage truck through the fierce thunderstorm to grab his overcoat. As the rain increased in its intensity, the men jostled for shelter. Willie Crain, the driver and chief of the four-man crew, allocated space for the journey back to the municipal garbage dump. Two of the men, Elester Gregory and Eddie Ross Jr, squeezed alongside Crain in the driver's cab. The two younger members of the crew, Robert Walker (29) and Echol Cole (35), were directed to the rear to find shelter. They had two choices: to hang on to the exterior perches and platforms and find partial shelter as the truck lurched back to base through torrential rains; or climb inside the barrel and wedge themselves between the wall and the machinery that compressed the refuse against the rear of the cab. Cole and Walker opted to stay dry and scrambled aboard the back of the truck.

A white housewife living at 4762 Verne had been sitting at her kitchen table when the storm broke and got up to look out of her window across the cropped lawns and neat hedges that separated her home from the exposed corner. Mrs C. E. Hinson then heard the grinding and screeching of the garbage truck's hydraulic ram. The rusting and decaying motor had short-circuited and cruelly pulled both men into the barrel. 'It was horrible,' she told the *Memphis Press-Scimitar* newspaper. 'His body went in first and his legs were hanging out. Suddenly it looked like that big thing just swallowed him whole.' Then, the man's legs vanished. Mrs Hinson called for an ambulance but it was already too late. The gruesome job of rescuing the crushed workers from the back of the truck took several agonising hours before they were eventually pronounced dead at John Gaston Hospital.

Death was not the final humiliation. Although the city offered a voluntary, self-financed life insurance policy covering death benefits up to the cost of $2,000, neither of the dead men could afford the payments, and because the city listed them on their employment rotas as 'unclassified, hourly employees' they were not covered by compensation. The one month's salary due to the deceased was a meagre $500, which fell far short of their burial expenses. Neither had personal life insurance. Both left behind wives and children, and Walker's wife Earline was pregnant when he died.

The deaths deepened resentment among the African-American workforce at the Department of Public Works and provoked a face-off between the workers and the new mayor of Memphis, Henry Loeb, a convinced segregationist, who in successive elections had described court-ordered integration policies as 'anarchy'. Loeb had taken office just a month ago 'over the determined opposition of practically the entire black community', as a local press source claimed, and was proving to be an uncompromising man whose views were stated with such dogmatism that negotiation was impossible. On his appointment, the unbending Loeb returned to a Public Works regime that had been rife in the fifties, using equipment that was decrepit and dangerous, and had a history of causing industrial accidents including deaths.

On the positive side he embarked on an ambitious project to clean the city streets – fixing potholes and exterminating snakes from the drainage system – but those noble aims were achieved on the back of punishing work schedules that discriminated against black workers. They could be sent home in torrential rain and not paid for a full day's work or struck off the work register if hand, shoulder or arm injuries prevented them working effectively. Loeb's truculence was to become a weeping sore in the months ahead and his refusal to give ground to workers' demands made a city-wide strike inevitable. Two days before Cole and Walker were crushed to death, twenty-one members of the sewer and drainage division had been sent home with only two hours of 'show-up pay' because of bad weather. In a climate where rain fell frequently, Loeb's initiatives had taken away black workers' ability to predict their income. It was dependent on the weather. After years of setbacks and minor defeats, the sanitation workers' union, Local 1733, of the American Federation of State, County and Municipal

Employees (AFSCME), began to regroup. From a pitiful base of only forty fully subscribed members from nearly 1,300 sanitation workers, interest in collective action was reignited. One of the barriers to union action was membership; the City of Memphis refused to compromise with AFSCME and collect union dues at source, raising an anxiety that anyone who joined the union would be sacked. Fear of the sack reduced workers to what was called 'fist collections', small sums of money surreptitiously exchanged at workplaces, as if they were drug deals. The collector was inevitably a tubby and avuncular public services worker called Thomas Oliver 'T.O.' Jones, whose comic-book appearance belied a dogged determination. Jones was from Douglass in North Memphis, a ghetto neighbourhood hemmed in by rail tracks to the north, south and west. Even as a teenager, he bore an uncanny resemblance to the R&B pianist Fats Domino, and his chubby vaudeville appearance meant that he was frequently underestimated by the managers he came up against. Jones was neither a fool nor an easy touch. He went on to become a critical figure in the Memphis of 1968, leading the sanitation workers in what was to become one of the most historic strikes of the civil rights era. In a stand-up row with city officials, Jones used the evangelical language of the local churches, calling the deaths of Cole and Walker 'a disgrace and a sin'. It proved to be a prophetic statement as a generation of ministers and local preachers rallied behind him and carried their campaign far and wide.

On the Sunday after the deaths, 800 black workers packed into the Memphis Labor Temple on South Second Street. Righteous fury gripped the hall. With neither a vote nor a plan of action, the emotional energy tipped towards strike action, at a time when striking against public services was illegal. The next morning, a clear majority of the city's sanitation workers failed to show up for work, and Mayor Loeb began the hurried and contentious job of recruiting agency labour and scab workers. A protest march was called, one of the many that would divide Memphis in the months ahead. Eight hundred workers gathered at the Firestone plant – a vast smoke-stacked industrial sprawl that scarred the North Memphis skyline while pumping out 20,000 car tyres a day – and then marched downtown to the new city hall on Main Street. It was a march about pay and conditions, civil rights and, in a more subtle sense, a march against anonymity. Maxine Smith, the executive secretary of the Memphis branch of the National Association for the Advancement of Colored Peoples (NAACP), said starkly, 'I've lived in this city all my life and I've never seen a white garbage worker.'

The strike received an early boost when Radio Station WDIA, the voice of black Memphis, held a minute's silence on air for the dead workers. On the surface it was an act of respect for the dead, but it was interpreted as tacit support for the strike, silently sending a message out to a community who saw the radio station as an informal leader. WDIA had dominated the airwaves in black homes since the early fifties. It had stumbled on air in 1947 but grew in self-confidence with the emergence of Memphis blues. B.B. King and Dwight 'Gatemouth' Moore were among its most popular entertainers, and then Rufus Thomas, the minstrel turned soul singer, connected the station to Stewart and Axton and the early days of Stax Records. WDIA attracted listeners and talent from across the Mid South, and it became the place-on-the-dial that people tuned to in order to hear the new faces of black music: Jimmy Reed, Little Walter, Big Joe Williams, the Platters, Muddy Waters and Bobby 'Blue' Bland. In 1956, at the height of his first wave of fame, Elvis Presley showed up at WDIA's annual revue, the most influential talent competition in the city. He clowned about backstage with Rufus Thomas and posed for the 'Two Kings' snapshot with B.B. King – a now iconic image taken by local photographer Ernest Withers. Presley is dressed in a dapper striped jacket, his arm casually wrapped around the shoulders of B.B. King, who is dressed in a plaid band suit. That lingering and friendly arm screamed of significance in a city that Martin Luther King described as a place 'still sadly crippled by the manacles of segregation'. Elvis was the most famous white singer on the planet, and to see an image of him acknowledging a debt to black Memphis underlined the awesome power of rhythm and blues. WDIA was building up to a triumphant year. Lou Rawls, the Fifth Dimension, Jackie Wilson, and Peaches and Herb were all due to appear on Dwight 'Gatemouth' Moore specials in the weeks to come and the station's flagship talent show, *Starlite Revue 1968*, was to be held in

June at the Mid-South Coliseum. It would feature Joe Tex, Percy Sledge, the Intruders and local acts. The Bar-Kays, Rufus Thomas and, most current of all, the Box Tops – whose hit song 'The Letter', produced by Dan Penn, was a stand-out hit in an era crowded with soulful white garage bands – were also scheduled to appear.

The sounds of Memphis jammed the airwaves across America, but apart from a minute of commemorative silence on a local radio station, Echol Cole and Robert Walker were anonymous and dead. Nor was their anonymity all to do with their lowly station in life. By one of the many curious twists of fate that were to visit Memphis in the years ahead, the death of the two sanitation workers had directly coincided with the birth of Elvis Presley's daughter Lisa Marie. The pack of press photographers and local journalists who might have given greater coverage to the deaths largely ignored the events unfolding at John Gaston Hospital and were instead crowded by the doorways of the ten-storey Baptist Memorial Hospital waiting for news of Memphis's most famous musical family, the Presleys. The coverage of the birth dominated front pages and entertainment columns across the USA and came with the breathless reportage of the celebrity press. The baby weighed six pounds fifteen ounces and, as the mother was pushed in a wheelchair to the parking lot, her beauty was unconfined. 'Mrs. Presley, dressed in a pink dress and with long, flowing hairdo, was pretty pleased with her daughter.' 'She's perfect, she couldn't be any better,' Priscilla Presley told a reporter.

The Sanitation Workers Strike had to create its own visibility. The bold and dramatic I AM A MAN posters that the strikers adopted while picketing made even the most thinly attended demonstration seem bold and assertive. Rather than huddling together, the strikers walked in single file, a half-block apart: planned, dignified and unbowed. Many of the bigger strike meetings attracted performers from the gospel and soul fraternities, either singing songs from the civil rights catalogue or warming up the audience for speeches that were often inspired rhetoric rather than a mundane restatement of the workers' key demands. On 5 March, Memphis City Council's weekly meeting broke conclusively with the norm. Rather than speaking to a half empty room of barely engaged councillors, the hall was packed with strike supporters. Like many civil rights protests in the years gone by, charismatic ministers were at the forefront of the protest movement. The Reverend Ezekiel Bell, pastor of Parkway Gardens Presbyterian Church – 'a man of small stature but a giant among us' according to fellow civil rights leader Dwight Montgomery – had already challenged the council with an impassioned address at a previous meeting. 'This is a racist country,' he declaimed. 'You call our sons off to be killed to protect your way of life. It takes about $350,000 to kill a Vietnam soldier. They came back here and don't have a place to live.' Bell then went on to argue that the city should accept a 'dues check-off', the right of the union to recruit members and collect their dues at source.

Irritated council members began to drift away when a protestor, NAACP leader Maxine Smith, who in her teenage years had been refused entry to the then all-white Memphis State University, shouted, 'Don't leave me here by myself!' and launched into a powerful gospel rendition of 'We Shall Not Be Moved'. Smith's voice rang with authority. She had been a leading force in the battle to desegregate the school system in Memphis and had acted as the 'surrogate mother' when she led the first thirteen black children into a whites-only school. As Smith sang, raising her voice as if on stage, others joined in. They continued to belt out songs from the civil rights songbook, and what had begun as a protest meeting gradually became a sit-in. Police were called to clear the council chamber, but their efforts fell on stony ground and they were faced down by a determined audience who had no intention of moving. They awaited arrest one by one. One hundred and seventeen people, some tied to the chamber banisters with belts and shoelaces, were eventually hauled from the chamber and taken to jail. They appeared the following morning at the Chancery Court in what was the biggest day of arrests in the history of the Memphis police. Thirteen ministers were among the convicted. Maxine Smith was jailed for supposedly having led the revolt and her colleague the Reverend Rosalyn Nichols later said of her: 'Maxine took hell into her heart, went to jail, paid the price, took the stand, gave her all, so you and I could sit and stand, go and play and dream. She took which was impure and gave us back hope, faith and love.'

As the fury of the sanitation workers grew, the strike attracted the attention of the nation's most famous civil rights activist, Dr Martin Luther King Jr, whose commitment to support the strike set the context for momentous events ahead. The historian Taylor Branch wrote: 'Echol Cole and Robert Walker soon became the anonymous cause that diverted Martin Luther King to Memphis for his last march. City flags flew at half-mast for them, but they never were public figures . . . Cole and Walker would not be listed among civil rights martyrs, nor studied like Rosa Parks as the catalyst for a new movement.' They died anonymously, known not for their dignity and toil but for the horrendous filth they worked in and the gruesome circumstances of their death. This was not a joyous moment in the resistance of civil rights movement but poverty and exploitation at its very worst. Slavery was long gone but its legacy lived on.

WILSON PICKETT

ATLANTIC RECORDS

Wilson Pickett: wicked to the core.

WILSON PICKETT'S FEROCIOUS TEMPER

23 February

'Who would ever have thought that a butcher boy from Youngstown, Ohio, would end up with twenty-four million smackers in his pocket?' With these self-aggrandising words, the movie mogul Jack L. Warner, one-time owner of Warner Brothers, turned his back on Hollywood. What no one knew at the time was that his characteristically mouthy departure would trigger a series of events that would reverberate around the music scene and, by 1968, strike a body blow to the very survival of Stax Records.

Back in September 1965, Jack Warner had sold 1.6 million shares in the world-famous studio to an ambitious equity investment company called Seven Arts Inc., who at the time were stalking the entertainment industry, looking to diversify away from movie production. They had a fanciful management plan to dominate the so-called seven arts: architecture, sculpture, painting, music, poetry, dance, theatre/cinema, along with the modern additions of photography and comics. It smacked of corporate narcissism based on a surprisingly thin portfolio of proven success. The company's greatest success to date was a part-share in the Hammer horror movie *The Plague of the Zombies*, and a back-share in the 1961 film *The Misfits*, starring Marilyn Monroe. At the time of the acquisition, Warner Brothers had built a small soul music subsidiary called Loma Records, aimed principally at the singles market in urban areas. The roster of artists included Ben Aiken, Carl Hall, Linda Jones and the Apollas – talented artists but hardly household names. Never likely to break big, let alone reach the fantastical levels of profitability promised in the Seven Arts management strategy, the hunt was now on for a bigger scalp, a company with proven success in music. Within a matter of months, the conglomerate made an audacious bid for Atlantic Records in New York, the self-proclaimed West Point of rhythm and blues. Suddenly, through acquisition, the Warner Bros.–Seven Arts group could claim leverage over the careers of many of soul music's most inspirational voices – Aretha Franklin, Wilson Pickett, Percy Sledge, Don Covay, Solomon King, Ben E. King, Carla Thomas, Sam and Dave – and the highly exploitable back catalogue of the late Otis Redding. Only the effervescent stars of Detroit's Motown Corporation were out of their avaricious reach.

Ominously for Stax Records, and for Memphis, the game that they thought they knew had changed for ever. A spate of mergers and acquisitions had gripped every sector of the US corporate landscape, threatening the wellbeing of small independent record labels and making scale all but essential. Everything that had once seemed settled was suddenly up for grabs. The very idea of regionality – making music in a small southern city – came under strain and a Stax–Atlantic national distribution deal that had been signed in 1965, and had existed before that as a gentleman's agreement, finally and dramatically unravelled.

In the spring of 1968 Stax stared mortality in the face. Relationships with their one-time big brother Atlantic came under strain and then finally broke down, never to be repaired. Stax tried to negotiate a solution but came up against a new generation of faceless management who knew nothing of Memphis music and everything about contract law. Jim Stewart, his sister Estelle and their passionate publicity manager Al Bell flew to New York to try to argue their case but were coldly rebuffed. Buried within the small print of old contracts was a requirement that all of Stax's master tapes were the property of Atlantic Records, and so they now came under the ownership of the decidedly less chummy conglomerate. Nor was their ownership in any way settled, either. Having splashed out on Atlantic, Warner Bros.-Seven Arts faced serious cash flow problems, which in turn weakened their market position and made *them* vulnerable to takeover. Even higher up the corporate food chain, the giant Kinney National, a parking-lot company that faced accusations of price fixing across America, had become aware of Warner's weakness and pounced. It was an unholy mess of confused ownership, anti-trust suits and complicated legal disputes that only full-blown American corporate capitalism could have scripted.

Suddenly, Stax's existence, its status, and most of all its creative history, was torn from its control. The best records and the cream of Memphis music – Booker T. and the M.G.'s, Rufus Thomas, Otis Redding, the Mad Lads, Eddie Floyd, Arthur Conley, Johnnie Taylor and William Bell – were gone, drowned in the small print and sucked into a legal minefield.

For over two months, until they rediscovered the will to fight back, Stax were thrown into disarray. Cursing their friendship with Jerry Wexler, the one-time sage who had brought them into the Atlantic fold, they had come to realise that they had been the victims of emollient duping and had simply become a service company providing studio production duties for Atlantic in return for distribution. The initial friendship was forged back in 1960, when Stax were touting a local R&B record by father-and-daughter act Rufus and Carla Thomas around southern radio stations. A distributor mentioned the local buzz on a raucous record called 'Cause I Love You' to Wexler, who, as a writer with the industry magazine *Billboard*, had coined the phrase 'rhythm and blues'. Although he left fulltime writing, Wexler never lost his loquaciousness, and throughout his formidable career he remained an articulate and witty man. On leaving journalism, he set up Atlantic Records with the sons of the Turkish ambassador to the USA, Ahmet and Nesuhi Ertegun, and, after a stuttering start, Atlantic became home to a generation of

African-American stars including Ray Charles, Lavern Baker, Clyde McPhatter & the Drifters, Sam and Dave, and Wilson Pickett.

Jerry Wexler described himself in his autobiography as a 'Bronx window-cleaner-turned-R&B-maestro'. He grew up in Washington Heights, an area of New York nicknamed 'Frankfurt-on-the-Hudson' where an influx of Jews from Germany and Austria had settled after their escape from fascism in Europe. Prone to clever turns of phrase and always putting himself in the centre of the action, Wexler once christened the emotionally troubled Aretha Franklin as 'Our Lady of Mysterious Sorrows'. His wordplay was the equal of his exquisite taste in music, and as the Atlantic roster of artists grew in size and reputation, Wexler became enthralled by the funk-soul sounds coming like a midnight train from the southern recording studios, first working with Stax until their fall-out, and then American Sound Studio in Memphis and finally moving on again to Fame Studios in Muscle Shoals, Alabama.

When Wexler first met Jim Stewart it was in every respect a meeting of opposites: Wexler was a self-confident and at times showy extrovert; Jim Stewart took pills for high blood pressure and was painfully introverted. Wexler was a fan of sophisticated jazz; Stewart a child of rural hillbilly. Although the Civil War was ancient history, Wexler was a product of the urbane north while Stewart was steeped in the ways of Dixie and the Deep South. For a time – rich in output – their differences worked and their culture clash produced some of the greatest soul music ever. Over a period of three years, Wexler sent Atlantic's best singers south to Memphis. It proved to be a creative period rich in quality but high in emotional anxiety. Wexler had not only dispatched his best singers, he had dumped a flammable cargo of personalities on Memphis, singers with deeply complex and volatile personalities, who constantly teetered on the edge of eruption.

By February 1968, relations between north and south had soured. The long history of co-operation had turned into resentment, and a myth had settled in the minds of the studio staff on East McLemore. They had come to believe that Wexler – once seen as a visionary – was deliberately dumping soul music's most cantankerous talent on the studio. It was a misreading of Wexler's motives, but for several stressful years in the mid sixties, Atlantic sent Stax the 'Wicked' Wilson Pickett, a gun-toting vocalist whom Wexler himself found troublesome. He described Pickett with two unflattering words – 'the pistol' – that hinted at his lawless, violent and sexual temperament. Atlantic also sent Stax Don 'Pretty Boy' Covay, a former chauffeur for Little Richard and a turbulent singer-songwriter, who had an inferiority complex that nearly wrecked his career. Covay had trawled the studios of New York with patchy success and bore a grudge that his talent was not sufficiently recognised. Then, to add gasoline to the flames, Wexler talked Stax into recording the most combustible duo ever to record soul music, the warring and dysfunctional Sam and Dave. Isaac Hayes, a man who was familiar with demanding Memphis musicians and had witnessed bad behaviour close-up in his years working in bar-room soul groups across Memphis, described the visiting Atlantic talent as 'a fucking war zone'. Inflammatory disagreements, appalling personal behaviour and violent fistfights were common, but out of the highly charged studio environment greatness was born.

Don Covay and Wilson Pickett had both enjoyed some success in the era of dance-craze soul. Among their various hits were Covay's 1962 release 'The Popeye Waddle' for Cameo Parkway, a novelty song that promoted a dance based on the exaggerated movements of the cartoon character Popeye. R&B music had always had a comic sensibility, which Stax took to new heights of vaudeville, exploiting the stage persona of Rufus Thomas. His recordings – 'Walking The Dog', 'Can Your Monkey Do The Dog' and 'Do The Funky Chicken' – were low-rent animal impersonation routines taken wholesale from the minstrel shows of Beale Street. Mining a similar vein, Covay subsequently wrote the song 'Pony Time' for his stablemate Chubby Checker, the Philadelphian abattoir worker tuned superstar, whose worldwide hit 'The Twist' (1960) became the high point of novelty dance records. Pickett also recorded a prolific seam of dance-craze songs – 'Land Of 1000 Dances' (1966) – a frenetic homage that paid tribute to the Pony, the Mashed Potato and the Alligator. Frustratingly difficult to work with, Covay and Pickett also had radically different personalities. Covay was more suited to songwriting than performance; he was unconfident on stage and, even in front of the studio microphone, looked nervous and intimidated. When backing singers joined the fray his insecurities would grow; he would fret that behind him were more naturally gifted singers – and often there were. Covay's anxieties dated back to childhood. His father was a Baptist preacher, who first encouraged him to sing as a member of the family's travelling gospel group the Cherry-Keys, and who died when Don was only eight. Covay then lived an itinerant life throughout his early teens, moving first to Washington, DC, where he briefly sang with Marvin Gaye in a local doo-wop group called the Rainbows, and then north to join the Little Richard caravan. Covay tried his luck as a performer with half a dozen small independent R&B labels, being signed and then dumped in short order. Each new rejection or failure ate away at his soul before he found a modicum of success with the song 'Mercy Mercy' (1964) on the tiny Rosemart label. It was a song that brought him cult attention on the musical grapevine (the song featured Jimi Hendrix on guitar) when he was still a session musician in New York and became part of Hendrix's repertoire. After the Jimi Hendrix Experience was formed in London the song was picked up and recorded by the Rolling Stones, and it became the blueprint for Mick Jagger's vocal stylisation. At risk of being lost in the discount bins, Atlantic picked up the distribution rights of the Rosemart single and tried to give 'Mercy Mercy' greater national visibility in the USA, eventually taking it to number one in the R&B Top Fifty, by which time it had become an underground classic in Europe.

Now signed to Atlantic but riven with uncertainty, Covay was sent south to Stax, mainly to give him an identity and more substantial backing tracks. But from the outset his relationship with the Memphis studio musicians was at best tense. More tellingly, a gulf of misunderstanding opened up between him and Jim Stewart, who was unimpressed by the singer's idiosyncrasies and thought he was strange, unpredictable and only playing at genius. Covay seemed to avoid the microphone, fearing its challenges, and only really settled when he was in the more creative act of writing, or in the reassuring company of Stax's master-guitarist Steve Cropper, who told author Rob Bowman: 'I loved Don to death. We get along great but I don't think Jim and them understood Don. He thinks in different areas and he was kind of driving people bananas.'

At least in part, Covay's truculence grew from insecurity, not from arrogance. He was not only an anxious performer; as a writer he was uncertain about lyrics. He would often interrupt sessions to write on small scraps of paper and pages torn from school notebooks, worrying away at lyrics on songs he was supposed to be recording to tape. He would then misplace his pencil, or forget the nuance of a line, and so his reputation for chronic indecision grew. Yet he had some success with his 1965 hit 'See-Saw' – a charmingly naïve song that tapped into childhood memories but was kept credible by the relentless southern beat and blaring Memphis horns which drove away any sentimentality.

In marked contrast to Covay, Wilson Pickett was never a prisoner to doubt. Arrogant, demanding and projecting an unbridled superiority complex, Pickett imagined himself as a gifted and flawless singer, better than those around him, and, tragically, those who tried to help him. Pickett had been born in Alabama, where he stayed with his violent mother, then as a child moved north to Detroit to live with his estranged father. He grew up in the Motor City when it was thronged with gifted African-American soul singers. Over 400 small independent labels sprouted up in a city on the cusp of being dominated by the Motown corporation. Still a teenager, Pickett joined a local group, the Falcons, which also featured vocalists Eddie Floyd and 'Sir' Mack Rice, who subsequently joined Pickett in Memphis. It was there that they gave shape to two of Atlantic-Stax's greatest ever releases, 'Knock On Wood' by Eddie Floyd (1966) and Pickett's irrepressible sex and soul song 'Mustang Sally' (1965).

In Detroit, Pickett replaced Joe Stubbs, the older brother of Levi Stubbs, as lead singer of the Falcons, but it was clear from the outset that he was not temperamentally suited to being in a group. Stubbs once said that Pickett could start a fight in an empty dressing room, and others who travelled with him spoke of his vaulting ambition. The Falcons were a vocal sensation locally and gave Pickett an early taste for celebrity, one he craved to the point of addiction later in life. In the Detroit of the late fifties, the Falcons had recorded an early hit, 'Let Me Be Your Boy', which was eventually issued on the local Correc-tone label; the song became famous as much for its backing vocals as Pickett's own performance. The backing singers were Florence Ballard and the Primettes, another group of local hopefuls poised to become Detroit's most famous group, the Supremes.

Pickett's reputation as a vocalist came to the attention of Jerry Wexler in New York when he sent a demo tape of songs for consideration, and which Atlantic ostensibly set aside for Solomon King. Recognising his potential, Wexler sent Pickett to Memphis, unintentionally creating the impression that he kept his most stable singers in New York and offloaded his most unruly south to Memphis. Having tasted local success in Detroit, Pickett already had an overblown sense of his own importance, and, given the growing reputation of the city where he grew up, his reputation came tinged with a swaggering arrogance. Wexler fed his ego, once describing him as having 'matinee idol looks, flaming eyes, lustrous ebony skin [and] a sleek muscular torso'. His voice was 'a cyclone of conviction' and he was 'a black panther' before the phrase was political. Many who worked with Pickett, including the very best session musicians at Stax, knew he had talent in abundance but felt that he was condescending about Memphis and could barely disguise his contempt for those around him. Paradoxically, it was Memphis and not Detroit that provided the streak of success that was to become the bedrock of Wilson Pickett's career. In one unprecedented year in 1966, Pickett fronted a stream of songs that were only ever matched by Otis Redding, among them '634-5789' (Soulsville U.S.A.), 'Ninety-Nine And A Half (Won't Do)', 'Land Of 1000 Dances' and 'Mustang Sally'. Pickett had much to thank Memphis for but rarely got round to doing it.

Pickett was driven by risk and was an unrestrained gambler, playing craps and dice between sets. His biographer, Tony Fletcher, claims: 'In his dressing room at the Apollo it wasn't uncommon for him and his entourage to engage in a $20,000 freeze-out, which meant that if you bet such a sum and lost it, you were done, no going back . . .' At American Sound Studio, where Pickett's lifetime associate the guitarist and vocalist Bobby Womack had joined the rhythm section, he recorded the self-aggrandising classic 'Stagger Lee', a song so saturated in the myths of reckless gambling and violent nightlife it could have been Pickett's biography. By March 1968, Pickett returned to American Sound Studio, where the local session musicians were on a high, having taken local band the Box Tops to an unexpected number one with the song 'The Letter'. By now Womack was a fixture, and he embarked on a reckless and drug-fuelled friendship with Pickett based on overconfidence and limitless lines of cocaine. The talented and unpredictable pairing wrote numerous songs together, not least another story of unrestrained nightlife and garrulous sexuality, 'I'm A Midnight Mover'.

When Pickett first arrived in Memphis, the relationship between Stax and Atlantic was a thriving two-way street, mutually beneficial to both parties. Atlantic provided a distribution system that had tentacles in communities Stax could never reach, including suburban homes in the north and west, and richer white neighbourhoods across the USA. But, in turn, Stax was a production nerve centre, offering a raw, robust and unique studio sound that regularly enriched Atlantic's reservoir of talent. A contractual deal eventually emerged out of informal arrangements, giving Atlantic the sole rights to distribute Stax Records and providing a stream of studio work for Stax. Buried deep in the contract was a clause, of which Wexler has always claimed he was unaware, that in effect gave Atlantic or its owners rights in the master tapes. The Warner Bros.-Seven Arts takeover upset the informality that had once defined the relationship and suddenly Stax faced an unimagined threat: the lion's share of their back catalogue was being swept away to New York and into the grasp of a soulless conglomerate.

As a teenager growing up in Detroit, Pickett had become perilously obsessed with guns and was less than discreet about carrying weapons. Covay described him as 'young and wild', but others were less kind. Several Stax musicians had witnessed close up his volcanic moods, which could be triggered by even the smallest setback, and had come to avoid him even within the corridors of the studio. Jim Stewart refused to have him back again and banned Pickett from the Stax studios. Rather than take Pickett back north, Atlantic bosses then traded him like a belligerent NBA star to another team; this time he was moved to American Sound

Studio on Thomas Street in Memphis where he recorded with Bobby Womack and, finally, when tolerance ran out there, to Rick Hall's Fame Studios in Muscle Shoals, Alabama, a southern rival to Stax that had also come within Wexler's radar as relationships with Stax soured. For a year in Memphis, Pickett's friendship with Womack was a crazed round of drugs, guns and debauchery: soul out of control.

Throughout his life Pickett failed to control his temper and his obsession with hand guns never receded for long. In 1987 he faced prison for carrying a loaded shotgun in his car but he struck a deal and paid a heavy fine. He was then arrested for recklessly driving his car across the mayor of Englewood's lawn, in an aggressive act of misplaced revenge for a civic misdemeanour that no one was ever able to ascertain. He was fined on several other occasions for drunken driving, drug offences and spousal abuse, and then, most tragically of all, he played a role in the death of an eighty-six-year-old pedestrian. Pickett was at the wheel of the car that ran down retired animator Pepe Ruiz in New Jersey. Ruiz had once been vice president of the Animators' Union in New York City, and his funeral brought a grieving congregation of friends and colleagues. Yet, despite the catalogue of criminal offences, broken promises and misadventures that marred his life, the 'Wicked' Wilson Pickett was frequently lauded by the music fraternity, his great Memphis releases still somehow overshadowing his dark and threatening personality.

By February 1968, having been rebuffed by Atlantic's new lawyers, Stax were waking up to the ice-cold realisation that their entire business was at risk and that the good old days were now firmly in the past. Atlantic was changing, and so, too, was the entire recording industry. The consolidated sales figures for 1967 landed on the desks of Atlantic's new owners in the early weeks of February. There were three obvious factors. The first was that Atlantic was a successful business that, with the help of Stax, had taken eighteen different singles into the *Billboard* charts that summer. Second, despite the previously cordial relations, Atlantic viewed Stax as only one in a myriad of independent companies in a wealthy chain of distribution. It announced that another slate of southern-based soul labels were joining the family, including Henry Stone's Dade Records in Miami, which included the much admired vocalist Benny Latimore, and South Camp from Alabama, which included vocalists Don Varner and Bill Brandon. Third, and perhaps most significant of all, it was clear that Atlantic and its new parent company Warner Bros.-Seven Arts had identified a new and growing market opportunity: album sales. In January 1968, at a sales convention in Nassau, Atlantic launched a new push into the LP market, in part buoyed by the rise of stereo sound and the sales spike in home entertainment furniture systems. That momentum was about to be boosted by two posthumous Otis Redding albums, *The Dock Of The Bay* and *The Immortal Otis Redding*. The direction of travel was clear: death sells, and the dominance of the teenage singles market was in retreat. Diversification into new adult markets was the next big thing.

Sam and Dave were unquestionably the greatest male duo to emerge out of the classic era of sixties soul but their energetic partnership was founded on an underlying tension: they hated the sight of each other. When Sam Moore and Dave Prater first met, they were rivals on the Miami amateur-night scene, trying to hack out a professional contract in one of soul music's outlying cities. Reputedly, they had shared the same bill on gospel tours but first spoke to each other on stage in 1960 at a crime-riddled nightclub called the King of Hearts on 7th Avenue and then performed as a duo at Miami's black-owned Sir John Hotel. Duos were traditionally based on imagined love affairs between two singers – one male and the other female – but Sam and Dave were never a love affair and threw a stick of dynamite through the door of expectation. Marvin Gaye and Tammi Terrell, and their New York rivals Chuck Jackson and Maxine Brown, shared romantic and descanting lines, harmonising like lovesick gospel singers. Sam and Dave growled like rabid dogs, barking at each other across the stage and performing wild acrobatics. Their stage show was thunderous and their R&B voices tougher than leather. They became known as 'Double Dynamite', the 'Dynamic Duo' and briefly 'The Sultans of Sweat', but as their career boomed and then bust, that early testosterone was replaced with a bitter rivalry. Sam and Dave's ambition took them from Miami's late-night dives to the grandmaster of Florida soul music, Henry Stone, a legend of a man who set up over one hundred independent record labels in his life but became renowned as the owner of Miami's TK Records. Stone's real name was Henry Epstein and, like Jerry Wexler, with whom he built up a distribution agreement similar to the one with Stax, he had been born and raised in a middle-class Jewish home in the Bronx. When Sam and Dave came into Stone's orbit, their explosive stage show was already the talk of the local music scene. Stone mentioned them to Wexler, and together the two of them visited the King of Hearts club. Within a matter of days Sam and Dave had signed to Atlantic and been farmed out to East McLemore. Yet another troubled act was on its way to Memphis.

Sam and Dave's first two Stax singles stiffed, but a third, written and produced by Isaac Hayes and David Porter, was a hit. The rousing and gospel-tinged 'You Don't Know Like I Know' (1966) was tailor-made for the urban R&B charts and for the influential Mod clubs of Europe in the mid sixties. But it was only a taste of what was to come. The next single – the relentless, sexual innuendo-laden 'Hold On I'm Coming' (1966) – was, according to Stax myth, rush-recorded after a throwaway line shouted by lyricist David Porter when he was delayed in the studio toilets. The song effortlessly climbed to the summit of the R&B charts, masquerading as a song about the comforts of love rather than full-on sexuality. Helped by Atlantic's distribution into mainstream stores, it then broke into the pop charts. It became a song that would carry the imprimatur of Stax around the world and has since been covered by a galaxy of stars including Aretha Franklin, Tom Jones, Solomon Burke, Bryan Ferry, Eric Clapton and B.B. King, Martha and the Vandellas, and Bruce Springsteen. Success failed to tame Sam and Dave. Photo shoots, travel plans and radio interviews became a battlefield, and what began as bickering and petty squabbles mushroomed into full-blown stand-offs. For months on end, as their success grew and the demands of being together intensified, the duo only really connected on stage. They ignored each other when they travelled from city to city and often insisted on different dressing rooms and separate tour cars. By February 1968 their most recent hit record, the epic 'Soul Man', which had been released towards the end of 1967, had reached the pinnacle of the charts and was spreading like wildfire across the globe. The concept for the song had come to Isaac Hayes, who had seen graffiti of the word 'soul' daubed on windows and walls during news coverage of the urban riots in Newark and Detroit in the summer of 1967. Hayes told a *Washington Post* journalist: 'If you put "soul" on your door, looters and arsonists would bypass it, like with the blood of the lamb during the days of Passover. And so we extrapolated that as pride – I'm a soul brother, I'm a soul man.'

The term had became a euphemism for blackness and black-owned businesses, and although it had been part of the vocabulary of African-American music for over a decade, the song secured its meaning around the world. Soul became not just a term, but a genre and then a movement. Despite all of their onstage demonstrations of togetherness and their clichéd commitment to 'brotherhood', Sam and Dave were never close, and finally split as a duo in 1970. Both admitted that performing the same hit songs time and again had been a contributing factor but they had precious few options other than to perform their hits, as drugs and fatigue ate away at their reputations. Their pathetic and soul-destroying feud, which had worsened when they were performing in Europe as part of the Stax/Volt tour, sapped their credibility with promoters and impeded their recording opportunities. When Stax and Atlantic parted company in the spring of 1968, it was the beginning of a long and humiliating decline. Because they were signed to Atlantic, whose contracts were now being pored over by new corporate lawyers, Sam and Dave shifted their recording base to New York City, but predictably they never managed to rekindle the unique chemistry they had found in Memphis. Although both brought out solo records, they failed to chart, and as the disputes festered neither found a way to reconcile. They spoke through intermediaries, often lawyers, and on the few occasions when money or a new recording opportunity brought them together again they were uncomfortable shadows of their former selves, refusing even to look at each other on stage. Sam Moore would later claim that they never spoke for over twelve years and did not even have each other's phone number. The pair last performed together on New Year's Eve, 1981, at the Old Waldorf on San Francisco's Battery Street. By then, the show was drained of any real dynamism. Heavier than in their prime, Sam and Dave still insisted on ending with their signature routine, in which the duo danced face to face, reverberating like pneumatic drills. The sequence ended on an exaggerated handshake – one of the most contrived and dishonest acts of harmony in the history of soul music. They walked off stage and never spoke to each other again.

Soul music's dynamic duo came to a final and brutal end in 1988, when Dave Prater died in a car crash. By then he was performing in a bogus Sam and Dave act, having hired a stand-in singer, Sam Williams, to double as Sam Moore. The original Sam fought them in the courts to try to block the new act but his legal suit only injected more acrimony into the veins of a once proud R&B act. A year earlier, Prater had been arrested in Paterson, New Jersey, for selling a vial of crack cocaine to an undercover police officer. His life was spiralling downwards when his car spun off Interstate 75 near Sycamore, Georgia, hurtled sixty-five feet in the air, and ejected Prater to his death. According to the highway patrol, he was impaled in a pine tree. His ignominious end brought one of soul music's most dynamic and troubled double acts to a premature and pathetic conclusion. At last, the fighting was over.

Divine intervention. Snow besieges downtown Memphis, and Dr Martin Luther King's planned march through the city is postponed.

© Seth Rugy/Getty Images

ALBERT KING'S STRANGE MORNING

22 March

Albert King had been drinking for six inebriated hours in a darkened room. He stumbled out to a scene that was both blinding and bizarre. Seventeen inches of snow had fallen overnight and, unusually for a spring morning, downtown Memphis was in lockdown. By mid morning all the city's schools had closed and most stores had failed to open. Roofs and telephone lines had been felled by the weight of heavy snow and thousands woke up to power outages and no way of contacting friends, family or workplace. The major highways in and around the city managed to stay open, but in many cases they were impossible to navigate. Most side streets were blocked and abandoned automobiles lined the streets. The Sanitation Workers Strike only confounded the chaos. Streets were stacked high with rubbish, leaving little snow-capped hillocks dotted along suburban pavements.

When King emerged from the bar-room in the early hours of Friday morning, he blinked through watery red-raw eyes and cursed under his fiery breath. A week ago he had appeared on stage at a fundraiser for the striking sanitation men, but now he yearned to be in a warm bed with Lucy by his side and a day of deep sleep to recover. He was a distinctive figure even in the most flamboyant of company, often wearing spats and a denim bib overall: one part gangster, the other part cotton picker. He had a pencil moustache that he shaved with a forger's care despite the fact that his index fingers were scorched and scarred from stuffing burning tobacco into his old wooden pipe, which he smoked on stage like a demonic granddad. A giant of a man who stood six feet six inches tall, he was nicknamed the 'Velvet Bulldozer' and was known to carry a small handgun inside his bib or suit pocket. Although no one ever saw it, King, a born fantasist, often boasted that he had a sub-machine gun in his tour bus.

King cursed his losses as he trudged home along Beale Street. It was not unusual for him to emerge into the sunlight bleary-eyed, hungover and beaten. He had played craps most of his life and had good fortune and bad. Like so many itinerant gamblers who sang the blues, he had lost more than he had won and fate meant he often lost heavily. According to Memphis legend, he was once forced to pay off a gambling debt with his most treasured possession, his trademark Gibson Flying V guitar, manufactured in 1959 by the legendary company in their sawdust plant in Kalamazoo, Michigan. King had loved the guitar like a girlfriend. Sometimes on stage, as he conjured a sound somewhere between blues and soul, twisting strings with his worn left hand, he could be seen kissing the brown walnut body and caressing the fret as if it were a naked neck. Although he had now secured another guitar – a gift from the Gibson company – King still yearned to be reunited with the original Lucy, and had recorded a song for Stax which was a paean to his loss – '(I Love) Lucy'/'You're Gonna Need Me' was scheduled for release on the morning of 22 March 1968. Stax had set up a day of interviews at their studios on East McLemore and personal appearances at a bar on Beale Street, but most of the engagements were abandoned as the freak weather took its toll.

The Sanitation Workers Strike had lasted for nearly two full months and was threatening to spread to other public service workers.

The snowstorm appeared to be an act of divine intervention; as if the heavens had burst in support of the low-paid workers. More pressure was now unexpectedly heaped on the intransigent mayor, who since his investiture on the first day of the year had been forthright in his stewardship of public services, often demanding the unachievable and spurning reasonable requests to negotiate. Since the death of the two sanitation workers in the thunderstorms of 1 February, there had been several instances when a long strike could have been averted, but Loeb was determined to win at all cost and to drive the strikers into a humiliating climb-down. He consistently argued that the strike was illegal, and, although he always said in public that 'this office stands ready . . . to talk to anyone about his legitimate questions at any time', his words were always more emollient than his actions. On Tuesday 13 February, an International Union official flew in from Washington to meet with the mayor to discuss the core grievances, but Mayor Loeb provoked deeper resentment by threatening to hire new workers unless the strikers returned to their jobs. A small number of trucks left the Department of Public Works depot, but they met with fierce resistance and had to be escorted by the police as they attempted to collect over ten thousand tons of rubbish that was now piled up on the city's streets. According to the labour academic Michael K. Honey, the snowstorm 'seemed providential in some ways but in truth it proved a huge setback to the Memphis movement'. Plans for the march on what the press were calling 'the Day of the Big Snow' were abandoned, and the city was given more time to mobilise against the strike.

The stand-off between Mayor Loeb and the striking sanitation workers reflected a much bigger divide than workers versus the boss. It pitted Memphis's black community against the city and its prolonged history of segregation. On Monday 19 February, the local branch of the NAACP staged an all-night vigil, picketing city hall on behalf of the strikers and widening their local campaign to a city-wide boycott of downtown stores and businesses. Congregations from the city's churches were encouraged to show support for the strike. The Reverend James Lawson, a pastor at the Centenary United Methodist Church and a civil rights veteran, emerged as a key supporter of the strike. Lawson had studied non-violent resistance in India and was a dedicated advocate of the Gandhian philosophy of peaceful protest, the strand of civil rights that had also influenced the Atlanta preacher Dr Martin Luther King. Lawson shared with King a deep-seated belief that as preachers they had to challenge the racial orthodoxies that ruled Memphis and to 'desegregate the minds' of their congregation. As the pace of 1968 gathered, yet another local preacher emerged as a leader of the city's black communities. The Reverend Samuel 'Billy' Kyles, a pastor at the Monumental Baptist Church, had formed Community on the Move for Equality (COME), a collation of Memphis Christians who supported the sanitation workers. Kyles had forsaken a career as a soul singer for the church, having once fronted the gospel group the Maceo Wood Singers and shared stages with Sam Cooke and the Staple Singers. He had also been arrested earlier in the decade for refusing to sit at the rear of a segregated Memphis bus.

On Sundays throughout the spring of 1968, ministers called on their congregations to join a series of protest marches planned for the weeks ahead. The church reached out to the music community, pleading with the city's gospel choirs, high-profile soul singers and blues singers of Beale Street to sing their hearts out for the cause. Stax songwriters Homer Banks and Raymond Jackson reactivated their school gospel choir. Isaac Hayes, David Porter, O.V. Wright and saxophonist Ben Branch all supported the strike, and many more stars from the local soul scene responded to requests from the churches and showed up at an eight-hour gospel marathon at Mason Temple to raise money and morale.

By late February, in a rowdy meeting in the council chambers, packed out by more than a thousand strikers and their supporters, anger overwhelmed the crowd, and police were called to clear the area. It was a prelude to the heightened violence and disruption yet to come. Mayor Loeb complained to the local press that his house was being targeted by striking workers and that windows had been smashed, scaring his wife and family. It was a story that unlocked a whole series of accusations against the strikers. Over one hundred strikers were ejected for staging a sit-in at city hall, students were arrested for picketing high schools in support of the strike, and nine demonstrators were arrested on the corner of Main and McCall and accused of intimidating shoppers during a downtown protest. Burning rubbish across the city was blamed on the strikers, although most of the fires had been ignited by teenagers and some were orchestrated by the Memphis Invaders. Students at Northside High School, near the giant Firestone factory, called for a walkout in support of the striking sanitation workers. More arrests were made at the Democratic Road Public Works facilities when picketers tried to prevent scab lorries from leaving the plant. Yet another activist minister, this time a young man known as the Reverend Harold Middlebrook, had led the demonstration. Middlebrook troubled the authorities more than the older preachers and seemed to be a bridgehead between the church and the city's restless teenagers. He had been educated with Stax musician Isaac Hayes at north Memphis's Manassas High School and he became a youth preacher and community worker at Dr Martin Luther King's Ebenezer Baptist Church in Atlanta. By March 1968, he was still clinging to the creed of non-violence but he'd become close to the charismatic John Burl Smith, a leader of the nascent Memphis Invaders, and led gangs of high-school students in a sit-down demonstration at the junction of Third and Pontotoc. They were arrested en masse for blocking the highway. The national media's interest in the strike took on a new and hysterical tone when it was announced that Martin Luther King would come to Memphis to lead a march in support of the strike. The date was set for 22 March 1968. Pouring oil on already troubled waters and anticipating widespread social disruption, Mayor Loeb instructed the National Guard to initiate riot drills and hostile crowd training exercises.

As Albert King trudged through the early morning snow, the Reverend Jim Lawson made frantic calls to Martin Luther King in Atlanta to stop him travelling. The sudden snowfall was so severe that the march on behalf of the sanitation workers was called off at the eleventh hour, although it was agreed to reconvene a week later, on 28 March. Reverend Lawson joked at the time that Mother Nature had fulfilled Dr King's demands for a general strike but it was a joke designed to keep flagging spirits alive. Lawson had called in every favour he could. A long-time friend of Detroit preacher the Reverend C.L. Franklin, he had managed to secure a half-promise that Aretha Franklin, at the height of her creative powers and then the most famous soul singer in the world, would travel to Memphis to support the strike at a public rally at Mason Temple. But nerves were fraying, and the strike was facing a colossal challenge; the most committed supporters – other public service workers including teachers – had been issued with threatening notices that they would be sacked if they took the day off to support the strike.

In a half-remembered conversation with staff at Stax Records, King had agreed to support the strike, too. In his mind he would headline. King had a habit of stretching the truth, and although he was never a pathological liar, he frequently imagined himself at the centre of things and was rarely burdened by the truth. He often claimed to be a half-brother of the more famous blues guitarist B.B. King, whose father was also called Albert, but it was a fabrication. King claimed that they had shared a similar upbringing in the small town of Indianola, Mississippi, in the Delta region that became the rural nursery of the blues, but they were not related. Early posters promoting Albert King often knowingly fed the distortion, listing him as 'Blues Boy' King to emphasise the B.B. Shadowing his namesake, Albert King even named his dearest guitar 'Lucy' after B.B. King's guitar 'Lucille', and he rarely corrected anyone who made the mistake of thinking he was the real B.B. King or his lost brother. Although it was a small deceit, Albert King was not actually born in Indianola, nor was he actually called King. His social security card reveals his place of birth as the small cotton port of Aberdeen, Mississippi, a slave town hugging the banks of the Tombigbee River, and the name bequeathed by his father was Albert Nelson. He remained Albert Nelson for the first decade of his career and only when B.B. King emerged as a national blues star did he change his name.

The blues had become synonymous with Memphis and its growth from a cotton trading town to a vibrant riverside city. King was part of a rich legacy of fanciful entertainers who dated back to the self-anointed father of the blues, W.C. Handy, a man who managed to turn poverty and suffering into a thriving business. His origins were primitive. His first trumpet was a hollowed-out cow's horn with the tip cut into a mouthpiece, and he grew up making rhythm by scraping a nail across the jawbone of an old horse's skull and playing with broken branches on old milk churns. Handy's primitive instrumentation pointed forward to the jug bands of Beale Street and scattergun bands like Gus Cannon's Jug Stompers, who thrashed out dance rhythms on old pots and jugs, and foreshadowed the powerful percussion that marked out the Stax sound. Handy's first professional outing was in a travelling minstrel show – the plantation burlesque shows that used racist stereotypes to entertain the landed gentry and, later, paying customers. As far back as 1837, there are records of Handy's performances with Mahara's Minstrels on stage in Sacramento, California, charming a mainly white audience, shaking tambourines and clattering old bones. It was when he wrote the genre-defining 'Memphis Blues' – a hymn to the demi-monde of Beale Street – that, according to the Republican politician Jimmy Quillen, Handy 'professionalised' the blues and carved the name of Memphis on the musical map. In a glowing congressional address, Quillen said that the song encouraged 'a million jukeboxes to swell in a million hog-nose restaurants and chitterling cafés . . . It inspired jazz, rock and roll from which soul music came.' But what he did not say was that the blues was predicated on the deep-seated poverty of the southern townships in the aftermath of slavery. Equally, it was aligned to a calculating showmanship in which any of life's setbacks, from blindness to syphilis and crippled legs, were turned into musical material. And every socially deprived environment, from the slave plantation to the prison yard, was evoked in order to bring suffering to the surface. Handy had led the way; then Sleepy John Estes, Furry Lewis, Howlin' Wolf, B.B. King and, eventually, Albert King became his distant and inventive descendants.

According to King's version of his own imprecise personal history, he was one of thirteen children born to an itinerant preacher who left his family destitute. The family moved briefly to Indianola, then with his mother, her two sisters and his rag-tag family he settled in Forrest City, Arkansas. He picked cotton, drove a bulldozer, and worked on highway construction before he became a musician. His first guitar was fashioned out of an old wooden cigar box, a tree branch and a strand of wire. Even when he could afford his first professional guitar, he carried it wrapped in a jute sack which had once held onions. Left-handed, he simply turned his guitar upside down and thereby defied some of the cardinal rules of conventional guitar playing. One of his techniques, bending the strings, became not only a trademark but a guitar trope that was to become a defining feature of blues as it surged forward into rock. Film actor Steven Seagal, an obsessive collector of blues guitars, now owns King's 'Lucy' and once described it as 'the most important blues guitar in the world, a voice from another planet. It has the most amazing tone and all of Albert's energy in it.'

King's first band, In the Groove Boys, was based in Osceola, Arkansas, where he grew up as a teenager. After a brief spell in the early fifties performing with gospel group the Harmony Kings, he finally secured a paid job as a drummer for Jimmy Reed's band. By then, King had moved north as part of the great migration and settled in Gary, Indiana, where he played poorly paid shows in the Rust Belt towns of the North East. But bad luck, aimlessness and a seemingly dated music style worked against him, and he drifted south again, this time to Memphis, where either by chance or clever contrivance he struck up a conversation with Estelle Axton at the counter of the Satellite Records store adjacent to Stax. Always fascinated by the vagaries of record sales, King asked Axton how blues records were selling. They exchanged opinions, and both came to the conclusion that there was still life in the old dog. Axton had regular customers who bought blues records religiously, but they also agreed that the genre had to move on from its sparse Delta roots and embrace the many changes that soul music had swept through black music. First among them was what Stax had perfected – a strong studio backing band that could add substance to songs: a metronome drum sound, solid bass and energetic horns. The conversation moved naturally to the idea that King could front such a session. It was the key to unlocking the most prolific period in his patchy life, and a seam of great records was mined, among them 'Crosscut Saw', 'As The Years Go Passing By' and the towering

'Born Under A Bad Sign', which King often described as his personal autobiography. It was a tale of hard luck and trouble, written by Stax's most personable and morally reliable artist, William Bell, who composed the song in part to cash in on the craze for the signs of the zodiac. Nonetheless, King's blues-soaked version became a worldwide hit and is now a staple of the blues guitar scene, having been covered by Cream, Jimi Hendrix and Etta James. Stax executive Al Bell saw a modernity that gave the time-honoured blues tradition a new lease on life: 'Albert King has taken one extreme, the gut-bucket blues in its rural form, transposed all elements except its reality and added a touch of urbanisation, thus his style becomes contemporary.' And in so doing, King had found a new audience, or what Bell called 'a new breed, the hippies and the European. To them Albert King is the father of modern blues.'

King was possessive about the blues and frequently scolded Stax's younger soul musicians for having deserted what he considered to be the true path of black music. The session musician Sandy Kay witnessed his unique style close up. 'I did Albert King's tracks in B studio with James Alexander, Willie Hall and Michael Toles,' he wrote in his diary about life at Stax. 'Those were the very first sessions cut in B studio – it was recently built, and was actually still under construction. Albert bitched at all of us because we were too young to understand the blues. The air-conditioning didn't work yet and it must have been a hundred degrees in there ... When the session started, Albert was wearing a beautiful pastel suit, matching hat, tie, vest, shoes, handkerchief, *everything*. He progressively took off almost all of his clothes, and ending up sweating rivers in his underwear and socks.'

According to jazz musician Wynton Marsalis, the blues was principally about love gone wrong rather than sociology. This is particularly true of King, who, after joining Stax, fitted easily into their internal songwriting culture, which wrenched tears from a million failed love affairs. 'Everything comes out in blues music: joy, pain, struggle,' Marsalis once said. 'Blues is affirmation with absolute elegance. It's about a man and a woman. So the pain and the struggle in the blues is that universal pain that comes from having your heart broken. Most blues songs are not about social statements.' It was a powerful idea but one that had an upward struggle to be taken seriously; the blues and poverty were so ingrained in the minds of many musicians. The Chicago DJ Big Bill Hill observed that 'the blues had something to do with that bastard of life most black people want to forget. They don't want to be reminded of sad memories.' While that may have been true of the retreating voices of the old bluesmen of the South, it was not true of the new generation of devotees; Janis Joplin, Paul Butterfield, Eric Clapton, John Mayall and even the Rolling Stones idolised the blues, believing it spoke to universal suffering and a new kind of teenage alienation.

King himself became the bad-sign mentor of at least three generations of guitarists, including Clapton, Stevie Ray Vaughan and Rory Gallagher. It was his Stax releases that helped him to connect with a new and vibrant young audience, particularly the countercultural hippies of San Francisco who tapped into the poor, alienated and political undercarriage of blues music. King was booked to open Fillmore West, the showcase for new music in the city's old Carousel Ballroom, which for most of 1968 operated as a laboratory collective of the west coast's most experimental bands such as the Grateful Dead, Jefferson Airplane and Quicksilver Messenger Service. On stage he cut a strident visual style and was often joined by Jimi Hendrix and John Mayall. He returned regularly, and became a Fillmore West fixture with a reputation that spread like wildfire among innovative and informed guitarists.

It was an era when festivals had begun to appear on the counter-cultural map. The long-established Newport Festival, which pioneered folk and jazz, had witnessed its first culture shock in 1965, when Bob Dylan broke with troubadour tradition and played with an electric guitar accompanied by the Paul Butterfield Blues Band. In the summer of 1967, Otis Redding had stormed to success at California's Monterey Pop Festival and instantly transformed his reputation from southern soul singer to international star. Woodstock was only a summer away, and still hidden from view, virtually invisible outside Memphis, a small cadre of local music obsessives were slowly building the Memphis Country Blues Festival, an annual summer event that defied musical categorisation, ranging from deep southern soul to bar-room blues and hardcore rock funk. It laid the first stone in a lengthy building project that would transform Memphis into the most successful 'music tour' city in the world.

Wayne Jackson witnessed the journey close up. The Stax trumpeter once claimed that Albert King, despite his flaws, was the greatest of his kind: 'I think that Albert King was probably the most influential guitar player that ever lived. Every time you hear a rock-and-roll guitar player, he's playing Albert King licks. He's a guitar player who will never die.' But die he did, and in circumstances that were in many ways reflective of his uniquely bizarre life. According to Steven Seagal, King's demise was dramatic. Realising he was having a heart attack, King asked a girlfriend to drive him to a Memphis hospital. She drove to the parking lot, stole his jewellery, and left him to die there, only a few hundred yards from the emergency ward.

SOUL BROTHERS. Young teenagers are attracted to the
downtown protests and join a picket line during the
week that Larry Payne is killed.

LARRY PAYNE'S DAY OFF SCHOOL

28 March

Larry Payne was tall, thin and lithe. Superficially, he was like a young Wilson Pickett, but that's where the similarities ended. Pickett had played in the fast lane of soul music; Payne had yet to have a life. He was barely sixteen years old, an impetuous teenager with no great love of school, and any ambition he did have was restricted by his race and his surroundings. Payne was an irregular pupil at Mitchell Road High School in the Southside, and when he did attend classes it was always with one eye on the door. His parents had separated, and so he spent most of his time waiting for buses and moving between their two homes. Divorce meant a fragmented family but it had one hidden benefit: he had two groups of friends – his schoolfriends at Mitchell and a gang of excitable teenagers on the Fowler Homes Project on Fourth and Crump Boulevard, only ten blocks south of Beale Street, where his mother Lizzie had an apartment. Her home was in the middle of a low-income neighbour-hood, where young people had the streets and not much else, but for Payne, impressionable and desperate to be liked, it was a much more exciting place than learning the states of the union by rote at his school.

Payne liked soul music at a time when the music was changing profoundly. He had taken to the early music of Black Power, especially the Impressions' 'We're A Winner' and James Brown's hit 'Say It Loud I'm Black And Proud', both of which were on heavy rotation locally and unambiguous anthems of black pride. Out in the ghetto projects, a new mood was percolating. For some it was impatience that the pace of change was too slow; for others it was a question of refusing to be deferent. Many black people, particularly the young, were no longer willing to tolerate the bias and hierarchy of the past. The city that Mayor Henry Loeb thought he was in control of was tearing apart at the seams.

Stax were negotiating with a tiny Detroit label called Tuba to acquire the rights to Derek Martin's implicitly political 'Soul Power', a song they subsequently released on their subsidiary label Volt. The B-side, 'Sly Girl', had all the cadences of a Motown dance hit, except for Martin's R&B growl. The first use of the term 'Black Power' as a political slogan was by Stokely Carmichael at a speech in Greenwood, Mississippi, in June 1966, after the shooting of James Meredith. But the term was not yet in everyday usage, and would not appear on a record until late 1968, when an obscure Long Island funk musician, James Coit, released a hectic and hectoring dance record simply called 'Black Power'. Soul was in flux again.

Like many of his age, Payne looked up to older boys, especially those who played fast and loose with life. He hung out with a street gang who the police referred to as the 'Beale Street Professionals', although that was never their adopted name. He had also met members of the Invaders, a group of activists who had leafleted Mitchell High School as part of a city-wide campaign to recruit school students, encourage their support of the Sanitation Workers Strike, and urge them to take more militant courses of action. By early March 1968, the Invaders had a strong base in Riverside and further into the Southside, and were targeting the major high schools in an attempt to influence the curriculum to teach black history in the classroom. A generation had been born that was refusing to accept the glacial pace of civil rights and impatient for change. James Brown, who had played to a rumbustious crowd at the Mid-South Coliseum in January, had been forced to do several encores of 'Say It Loud I'm Black And Proud', a song that had become a street anthem for the emergent Black Power teenagers. But it was neither the Godfather of Soul nor the restless youths of the Memphis Invaders that determined Payne's short life. His fate was to become inextricably bound up in the crusades of the most famous civil rights leader of all time – Martin Luther King Jr.

As Payne ran the streets between Beale Street and the Fowler Homes, John Gary Williams had come home. The Stax soul singer had returned from Vietnam restless and transformed. Since 1964, Williams had been the lead singer with Memphis harmony group the Mad Lads and had taken an enforced break from his singing career when he was drafted into the military. He was keen to return to singing and a career at Stax Records, but a switch had gone on in his mind, and he had witnessed first-hand a war that not only changed him but changed a generation. Williams was not alone. Another member of the Mad Lads, William Brown, the Stax singer-songwriter William Bell, and Raymond Jackson from the Stax songwriting triumvirate We Three Productions had also gone to Vietnam, surviving on basic military supplies and the occasional box of treats mailed out from their local record store by the matriarch of Satellite Records, Estelle Axton. Each week, someone returned home and another was drafted. In the month that Williams returned to Memphis, another contemporary musician was sent to Vietnam. Archie 'Hubby' Turner, a keyboard player at Hi Records and relative of studio boss Willie Mitchell, was drafted into the US Army and despatched to Fort Campbell, Kentucky, for basic training, where the recently conscripted Jimi Hendrix and yet another Memphis musician, Stax songwriter Larry Lee, formed a makeshift R&B band.

Williams arrived home from Vietnam in January 1968 to find the city he had grown up in facing a year of unprecedented political turbulence. The Mad Lads were from Memphis but not of it. Their sound owed more to the northern doo-wop cities of Philadelphia and Baltimore, and they traded in matching suits, shared harmonies and descanting love songs. John Gary Williams, William Brown, Julius Green and Harold Thomas had grown up together and were students at Stax's unofficial academy, Booker T. Washington High School, where they were known initially as the Teen Town Singers and then, briefly, the Emeralds. It was the Stax publicist and sometime songwriter Deanie Parker who helped to shape their unique identity. 'They were young, they were mischievous, and that's where they got their name from. When kids know they are getting under your skin, they turn up the heat, and that's what they did,' Parker claimed. Their name was inspired by their rough hoodlum edges and a nod to local DJ Reuben Washington, whose *Mad Lad* radio show on Radio Station KNOK-970 out of Dallas-Fort Worth reached out to urban teenagers as far away as Memphis. Washington was a local boy and a Stax enthusiast who had been the first to play Booker T. and the M.G.'s 'Green Onions' (1962) on heavy rotation, and was generally credited for its success.

By the mid sixties, the Mad Lads had enjoyed some tentative signs of success with R&B hits 'Don't Have To Shop Around' (1965) (an answer record to the old Smokey Robinson and the Miracles standard 'You Better Shop Around'), 'I Want Someone' (1965) and 'What Will Love Tend To Make You Do'/'I Want A Girl' (1966). None of them crossed over to the predominantly white pop charts but they gave the Mad Lads a strong local following in Memphis, and down into the Deep South.

As the Mad Lads appeared to be prospering, the US military had launched Operation Prairie to attempt to eliminate the North Vietnamese Army. An army recruitment drive swept through the Memphis projects like a gale-force wind. Draft board letters landed at the South Memphis homes of John Gary Williams and William Brown, and the next phase of the group's recording plans was put on hold. Within a matter of weeks, as Williams and Brown were conscripted, new singers were recruited to fulfil live shows, and the original nucleus of the group was despatched to basic training, en route to the battlefields of Vietnam.

Williams served in the malaria-ridden jungles of Vietnam with the 4th Infantry Division. He was often sent on Long Range Reconnaissance Patrol (LRRP) missions along the Cambodian border. From March of 1967 until January 1968 he was in Vietnam during the first weeks of the infamous Tet Offensive, a series of fierce attacks on cities throughout South Vietnam. Although US forces managed to hold off the attacks, half a million troops were besieged in set-piece battles in and around Khe Sanh in Quang Tri province, with damaging consequences. More than 500 GIs died in February 1968 alone. A disproportionate number of the casualties were black and had been conscripted from inner-city neighbour-hoods in Detroit, Chicago and Memphis, as well as the dirt-poor farming communities to the south of the city. News of such heavy casualties shocked the American public and further undermined support for the war.

Williams returned with eye-witness evidence of the chaos of Vietnam. Throughout his service his division faced intense combat. 'These guys were hardcore,' claims Gary O'Neal, an LRRP contemporary of Williams. 'This wasn't run anything like the regular army. There was basically only one rule, do whatever you had to do to survive. Most of the time there was nobody looking over our shoulders, nobody telling us what to do or how to do it, no one giving us any bullshit about uniforms or military procedure. We lived for the mission, and . . . the more time any of us spent in the field, the farther away we got from any type of normal behaviour. To survive out there in the jungle, fighting an enemy who understood the environment, we went native.'

Williams returned a changed man to a city that seemed incapable of change. Memphis had an estimated 90,000 black teenagers; fifty-two per cent of the city's high-school population, they were the core market for Stax records but faced challenging times in the local job market, where the military, unemployment or manual labour were the most common experiences. Almost every black high school in the city witnessed student unrest in 1968. Booker T. Washington High School fought a campaign against local railroad companies after deaths and injuries occurred outside the school grounds, at a spot where seven different rail tracks merged. Trains frequently blocked the crossings for up to thirty minutes at school assembly time, so students regularly clambered over the top of the carriages or, more dangerously, under the wheels of the stationary trains. Rail deaths were racking up. In 1968 local newspaper the *Memphis Press-Scimitar* estimated that in recent years up to 1,700 people had died, mostly in crashes brought about by cars trying to jump the crossings, but schoolkids had also been killed, caught out by the sudden movement of freight trains. Local journalist James R. Reid rode in the cab of Frisco 134, a freight train from Tennessee Yards, and described a scene of terrifying risk. 'As we moved through Memphis,' he wrote, 'we saw car after car, truck after truck, zoom across our path. The killing of motorists at grade crossings has become the greatest concern of the Frisco safety division.' High-school protests were igniting elsewhere across the city. Safety at train crossings was a common complaint, discipline was another, but so, too, was the curriculum and the lack of awareness of black history. This young generation were no longer willing to tolerate their journey from slavery to social discrimination being airbrushed out of history. Prominent among the wave of student pressure groups, social organisations and street gangs were the Invaders, a collection of young radicals in their late teens and early twenties who felt that the Christian ministers for civil rights were too accepting of the slow pace of change. They were described by the police as a street gang, their dynamic name gave that impression, and they were catalogued by the FBI in what was inelegantly called the 'Rabble-Rouser' index, but the Invaders were much more complex than that; they were mostly the young and politicised, students, disenchanted war veterans, welfare workers and the unemployed.

After their discharge from the military, Williams and Brown were told by the current members of the Mad Lads, Julius Green and Robert Phillips, that they no longer wanted Brown back in the group. It was a body blow to the returning veterans, and as a compromise Stax hired Brown to pursue his interest in electronics. He came to be the first black recording engineer in the Memphis studio system. In a stand-off with the new Mad Lads, Stax co-owner Jim Stewart forced them to reinstate Williams, who in turn was glad to be back but less devoted to the group's origins in romantic harmony soul. Williams had been radicalised in Vietnam and now saw his city in a very different light. He befriended other returning veterans, among them John Burl Smith, a Black Power activist with links to the Socialist Workers Party, who in 1967 had formed the Black Organising Project (BOP), an influential street-level political party loosely associated with the Black Panthers, but more commonly known in the city as the Memphis Invaders. Like Williams, Smith had been shell-shocked at the indifference he faced when he came home from Vietnam. 'When I returned, I really wasn't into Black Power,' he once said. 'I was an American who had just served my country, and I was expecting my country to be appreciative.' But he faced bleak opportunities, struggled to find work, and lived in a poorly constructed, federally funded low-rise apartment complex on Hanauer Street in the Riverside neighbourhood, near his old school, Carver High.

Coincidentally, it was Carver High School, with its student body of 2,500 teenagers, that witnessed the worst unrest of the era with riots flaring up there sporadically from February to May 1968. On the most intense day of disturbances sixty-five windows and glass doors were smashed by students protesting on behalf of the Invaders, who had applied to the school to be recognised as an on-campus organisation. The school principal Richard Thompson was reluctant and tried to fend off the Invaders until the disturbances escalated and police were called. The most intense violence followed an incident in the school cafeteria when a female supporter of the Invaders set off a firecracker, deemed by some to be a signal to start the disruptions. A few days before the Carver High School riots, John Burl Smith, John H. Ferguson, Oree McKenzie and Larry Davis (all members of the Invaders) had visited the campus to try to recruit students to what they described as a new Negro theatre unit called the Beale Street Players. It may have been a front for the Invaders but was most likely a legitimate ambition, since both Smith and Ferguson were community workers who focused on youth affairs. The deputy principal, against the wishes of his boss, had in fact welcomed the idea and they were invited back, but their return coincided with acts of violence, and both men were arrested after the police dispersed the crowd with tear gas. Smith and Ferguson were initially charged under an arcane law – refusing to vacate a school property – and later charged with trespassing and disorderly conduct. They were held overnight in jail, having failed to raise the prohibitive bond condition of $50,000. The Memphis chapter of the American Civil Liberties Union (ACLU) took up their case and challenged the scale of the bail money. Smith commented to the local press: 'Who do they think we are – a couple of John Dillingers?'

The Carver High School riots were most likely sparked because a group of students had petitioned the principal, asking for greater rights and student representation, improved cafeteria food and an end-of-term prom. All of their demands were denied, but a seed was sown, and a year later the official wing of the civil rights movement, the NAACP, began a series of protests at Memphis schools called the Black Monday campaign. Students declared themselves absent from school every Monday, parents were encouraged to co-operate, and many teachers joined in, forcing most of the schools in black neighbourhoods to close.

In a subsequent court case John Burl Smith argued his right to be on the Carver High School campus on the grounds that he was a former pupil and, for a period in early 1962, before he was drafted to fight in Vietnam, he had been the captain of the school's football team and had turned up at several sporting events over the years. In the dock he denied being a member of the Invaders and told the court there was no such organisation. It sailed close to perjury but not quite; the group's official name was the Black Organising Project (BOP) – the Invaders was a nickname appropriated by an inner circle from the briefly popular ABC sci-fi drama about alien invaders.

The Memphis Invaders came from across the city, from the blighted ghetto neighbourhoods of the inner city, from the mainly segregated high schools, and from the politically fertile campuses of the southern states. Two prominent members, Curtis Carter and Don Neely, had grown up on East McLemore and were familiar faces at Satellite Records and in the doorways outside Stax. The Invaders had flourished while John Gary Williams was in Vietnam, and by 1968 the group had been infiltrated by the FBI as part of the now-notorious Counterintelligence Program (COINTELPRO). The FBI were experts in covert action and black ops, and by the mid sixties deployed a catalogue of dubious techniques to destabilise political groups, using agents provocateurs, anonymous hate mail, burglary, forgery, defamation and extortion. One popular technique of the time was 'snitch jacketing', in which an FBI agent would set up an activist to make him seem like a police informer, thus undermining trust within radical groups and fostering internal dissent. The Memphis branch of the FBI and the Intelligence Unit of the Memphis Police Department (MPD) had twenty-one different and unconnected sources spying on the Invaders, ranging from paid informers to frightened and compromised young people arrested for minor offences. From February onwards, the Special Agent in Charge (SAC) of the Memphis FBI collated an eight-page communiqué summarising the activities of the Invaders, which was sent to the paranoid and obsessive director of the FBI, J. Edgar Hoover. It painted a picture of low-level local political activism and showed hives of activity at Le Moyne College and Owen College, two historically black colleges that had been set up by church groups to educate freed slaves. The FBI were focusing on a cadre of young Black Power activists who had taken to wearing sawn-off denim jackets with the word 'Invaders' emblazoned on the back, much like an inner-city street gang or a chapter of the Hells Angels. Among them were: John Gary Williams' friend and fellow Vietnam veteran, John Burl Smith; Calvin Taylor, University of Memphis journalism graduate; Coby Vernon Smith, a student at Southwestern College and one of the first two black students at Rhodes College; Edwina Jeannetta Harrell, a student at Memphis State University; and a charismatic but combustible young man with big plans and a distinctive name – one Charles Cabbage.

In March, all of them were listed in FBI documents and considered to be a threat to American society. Concern was raised that the Invaders were targeting Memphis high schools to recruit more members and to bring a more aggressive dimension to local politics, thereby escalating support for the sanitation workers. Young veterans returning from Vietnam were another group that the Invaders successfully targeted. Stax singer-songwriter William Bell and songwriter Raymond Jackson had also been swept up in the conscription drive of 1966. Bell was recruited to the 14th Infantry's mortar platoon and did his basic training at Fort Polk, Louisiana, where he met and befriended one of the titans of the

New Orleans soul scene, the super-producer Allan Toussaint. He was then airlifted to Pleiku, where he saw active service for nearly two years. Before he was flown out, Bell was allowed two weeks' vacation back in Memphis, and he naturally gravitated to his old haunts on East McLemore. He had first recorded at Stax as an ambitious singer with local Memphis group the Del Rios, a featured band at the Flamingo Rooms. His mother warned him that he would end up like 'the rest of these blues bums' and 'would die without a penny', so, under pressure to conform, he studied to be a doctor. Stax knew of Bell's promise and called him in, ostensibly to do backing vocals for Carla Thomas on her first major single 'Gee Whiz'. Another group had been given the job, but they failed to cut it and were sacked. When there was no studio work, he hung out at Satellite Records sharing ideas with Axton, and once watched transfixed as the unknown Otis Redding, doubling as Johnny Jenkins' driver, recorded 'These Arms Of Mine'. Producer Chips Moman talked Bell into recording 'You Don't Miss Your Water' (1961), which has since become one of the defining, most durable ballads in soul music, covered by Otis Redding, the Byrds and Taj Mahal. As Vietnam loomed, Bell recorded two songs that directly addressed the lives of departing soldiers, 'Soldiers Good-bye' and 'Marching Off To War', both released in 1966. A rash of Vietnam soul songs tried to tap into a new and growing market – girlfriends, parents, and family members heading to war – but few made any great commercial impact and Bell's songs soon disappeared from sight. He tried again in the first solemn month of 1968, recording a song for his dead friend Otis Redding. Called 'Tribute To A King', it was a mournful and at times over-literal requiem to the dead star; it attracted some attention but few sales. When success finally came, it had another tangled connection to Redding. Prior to Redding's death, Stax had scheduled the recording of a new duet with his favoured partner Carla Thomas, then a masters student at Washington's Howard University. The song planned for them was 'Private Number', a telephone love song co-written by Bell and his collaborator Booker T. Jones. Soul duets were at their all-time height, and Tammi Terrell's songs with Marvin Gaye had set a standard that few could match. Bell offered to record 'Private Number' himself, after Redding's death, and Stax scoured its own stable of talent for a female partner. Atlantic boss Jerry Wexler argued on behalf of Judy Clay, a former member of the gospel group the Drinkard Singers. Clay had a pedigree that spoke to the era. She had recorded with the white Californian singer Billy Vera in a bid to bring an interracial love story to the charts. Their partnership attracted fascinated attention, but network television shows were reluctant to schedule a black–white duet, fearing it would alienate mainstream audiences. After two indifferent releases, Clay and Vera drifted apart, and she moved south to Memphis to eventually record the song as one of Stax's great love songs, William Bell and Judy Clay's 'Private Number' (1968). It was the first time that Bell had truly shaken off his Vietnam veteran past, and his career as a writer-producer took off.

By contrast John Gary Williams' career had stalled. His greatest work was yet to come, and for much of 1968 the Mad Lads treaded water. Their release 'So Nice' was a throwback to the old doo-wop styles of previous decades, which seemed curiously at odds with Williams' own life as a disaffected veteran and an advocate of social change. Throughout the spring and summer of 1968, anxiety about Black Power and inner-city riots was at fever pitch, and anyone remotely connected to radical politics was harassed, pursued or spied upon. The Invaders taught black history lessons in North and South Memphis communities and Williams often joined them to recount the racism he had witnessed in Vietnam.

The Invaders lacked meaningful resources and moved their base across the city from community hubs to family homes and on again to college campuses, relying on small-scale grants, local fundraising drives and a short-lived protection racket that drew taxes from stores in black arcades across the city. Charles Cabbage, a prominent member of the Invaders, whose brothers followed him into the movement, had ambitions to become a national leader in the burgeoning Black Power movement. A friend of both Stokely Carmichael and H. Rap Brown, Cabbage had graduated from Morehouse College in Atlanta, and while studying there had gravitated towards the Southern Christian Leadership Conference (SCLC), Martin Luther King's Christian-inspired civil rights group. Like many young men of his era and disposition, however, Cabbage had tired of the creed of non-violence and pacifist resistance, and on his return home to Memphis became a street fighter and advocate of Black Power. One of Cabbage's contemporaries at Morehouse was the film actor Samuel L. Jackson, who describes an era fraught with disagreement. 'Morehouse was breeding politically correct Negroes,' he told the *Guardian* newspaper. 'They were creating the next Martin Luther Kings. They didn't say that because, really, they didn't want you to be that active politically, and they were more proud of the fact that he was a preacher than civil rights leader. That was their trip: they was into making docile Negroes . . . And all of a sudden things kinda went haywire on them. I met guys in my freshman class who had already been to Vietnam – they had afros already. Guys that had killed people in a war zone and knew what was goin' on, and had discipline and leadership, those guys got hold of us. And suddenly we were talking politics and finding out how the war was getting run, who was getting killed.'

Briefly, in 1968, Jackson dropped out of Morehouse to join the Black Panthers, while Cabbage returned home to Memphis to immerse himself in community politics and street-level insurrection with the Invaders. Short of funds and unable to even afford a car, the Memphis Invaders were always on the lookout for people who would either sponsor them or support the cause with donations. They approached Stax on several occasions but were rebuffed. They tried to secure grants from the major churches but were regularly sidelined, and so, without operational funding, they tended to take risks. In February, as the high-school protest campaign was under way, the FBI's Domestic Intelligence Division, under the leadership of George C. Moore, recommended that the Bureau extend its counterintelligence programme of spying on black militant groups. With greater resources at their disposal and encouraged by Washington, the FBI recruited another Vietnam veteran, a Military Police officer by the name of Marrell McCollough. His first undercover assignment was to infiltrate the Memphis Invaders. McCollough owned a prized street possession – a 1967 Mustang Fastback – and with that small, but not insignificant, asset at his disposal he was welcomed into the organisation. Within a matter of weeks he was given the grandiose title of Minister of Transport of the Black Organizing Project (Memphis Invaders). It was a catastrophic decision. McCollough, who had enrolled as a student at Memphis State University, was connected to military intelligence, and his real job was to infiltrate and destabilise the Invaders. To cover his tracks, McCollough was not even on the payroll of the FBI, the Military or the MPD; he received his salary cheques from a Memphis utility company, in a convoluted arrangement tied to his electricity bill. It was a well-crafted deception that allowed McCollough to burrow his way deep into the group, participating in drug deals, smoking dope at the Invaders' network of inner-city apartments, and on one occasion he was conveniently arrested for disorderly conduct. All the time, he was reporting to Lieutenant Eli Arkin, a senior police intelligence officer working with the MPD, who in turn had been assigned to collaborate with the FBI's COINTELPRO operations in the city. McCollough was to become a rogue figure in the events of 1968, and as the Memphis Invaders became more deeply entangled in a web of intrigue, his name came to be associated with the dark network of informers working surreptitiously across the city.

It was against this backdrop of intrigue and rising youth militancy that Martin Luther King arrived in Memphis, to lead a march in support of the strike. His flight from Newark New Jersey was late, touching down in Memphis at 10.30 a.m. on 28 March. King was tetchy and hungover. The night before, he had attended a fundraising drinks do at the home of the actor Harry Belafonte and then slept over at the Manhattan home of Albert Logan and his wife Marian, who was a civil rights activist and SCLC board member. They had sat up drinking sherry after sherry into the early hours and latterly drifted into an argument about King's big idea – a Poor People's March on Washington, DC. The Logans were critical of the idea and saw it as a distraction from the movement's core business: challenging discrimination. King became frustrated that his pet project was being argued down so vociferously and he slept fitfully. By the time he arrived in Memphis he was not in a good mood.

Larry Payne had risen early in anticipation of the march. He had read about King's arrival in flyers circulated by the Invaders at his school. His friends at Fowler Homes, the project where his mother lived, had also been talking excitedly about going to the march. Taylor Branch, the Pulitzer Prize-winning biographer of Martin Luther King, described the scenes that unfolded in dramatic detail. 'Pandemonium greeted King at 10:56. Young people engulfed his borrowed white Lincoln . . . the assembled march . . . was numbered anywhere between six thousand and twenty thousand, with estimates clouded by spectators teeming the sidewalks along Hernando Street. At the eye of the demonstration, King . . . recognized the first hint of abnormal tension in faces that pressed against the car's glass . . . Police motorcycles roared ahead of a flatbed press truck loaded with cameras facing backwards, and the huge throng began to stretch out north along a block of Hernando to famous Beale Street, turning left by the park named for W.C. Handy, pioneer of the blues. Next to the statue holding a trumpet, a wreath of fresh flowers marked the tenth anniversary of Handy's death in 1958. Above, officers in police helicopter 201 sighted a clump of thirty students with rocks and clubs trotting west along Beale Street to merge at the turn.'

It was to become a moment of historic significance when two eras met and the spirit of '68 won out. A supposedly peaceful march, led by black America's most revered minister of change had been hijacked. Something strange had happened – driven by rumour more than fact. Earlier that morning, at Hamilton High School, students had refused to join assembly, to show their support for the striking sanitation workers. Unable to control the angry students, the principal called the police, and on their arrival violence erupted, with bricks and bottles being thrown. Oral historian Joan Turner Beifuss recorded witness statements and described a scene of utter confusion. 'Students were trying to enter or leave the school, milling in front, standing in the street. A few desultory bricks were hefted at a laundry truck passing; the back door opened and the clothes fell out. The driver scrambled to reload the truck and get out of the way. A white woman unwarily drove her car onto the back honking her horn to clear the way. Her car was also bricked before the space opened. At 8:30 a.m. a message to headquarters from police helicopter 201 reported that students were massing at Hamilton. Then majestically along the street came a garbage convoy – the trucks and a police escort. Missiles began to fly. Police radioed for aid. Hovering overhead was the police helicopter. Police cars zoomed in and police began sealing off the school area to traffic.' It was a cavalcade of sheer chance. First, a laundry van bearing the logo of the hated Loeb family, then garbage trucks manned by scab labour, and finally a police convoy. An officer radioed back to his control room. 'The situation is now out of hand . . . request permission to break it up . . . request permission.' Bricks rained down on the officers, batons were drawn, and fierce fighting broke out. In the crossfire a fourteen-year-old girl was injured and rushed to hospital. The news spread like a malicious virus, and by the time the story of Hamilton High reached the main march at Beale Street, it was believed, wrongly, that the teenager was dead, killed by a police bullet. The rumour had spread before the truth was out of bed.

At first in twos and threes, and then in much bigger numbers, the students of Hamilton High moved in the direction of Clayborn Temple, several miles away, to swell an already emotional main march. Police were receiving reports that others schools were joining the march – Manassas to the north, Booker T. Washington to the south, Lester High School from the east, and, inevitably, Carver High, the school that had been most deeply infiltrated by the Memphis Invaders. Young people were arriving in unexpected numbers. The march was supposed to convey a righteous anger but it had already curdled into a furious rage. Branch wrote: 'Crashes after the bangs signalled instead the unmistakable sound of storefront windows being smashed along Beale and Main. Moans went up that something was wrong. Young marauders ran through over-matched marshals to attack storefronts ahead of the march, Shainberg's department store, York Arms Company, Perel & Lowenstein – sometimes needing multiple blows to break the heavy plate glass. A helicopter bulletin at 11:24 reported fifteen young people destroying a parked car a few hundred yards to the side and marshals relayed shouted commands to halt the line of the march.'

The march's chief organiser, the Reverend Jim Lawson, told a newsreel reporter that 'at the head of us Beale Street was filled to the sidewalks with people, I didn't quite like that, and we couldn't correct it and when I got about two blocks up the street on Beale I heard what sounded like windows breaking behind us. The next thing we heard was sirens and police men were coming from every direction with tear gas and they started surging down on the lines. I remember one officer came right up in my face and began to curse, someone near me was trying to tell him that this man was a city council man, a city official, and he said I don't give a damn who he is I mean get you and yours out of here now or you're going to get the butt of this gun or a bullet out of it.' Rioting had taken a ferocious grip. Police moved into the crowds, indiscriminately brandishing nightsticks and firing tear gas. Two hundred and eighty people were arrested and over sixty were injured, mostly black. The ministers who had been at the head of the march, including lifelong advocates of non-violence, the Reverends Lawson and Kyles, retreated to Clayborn Temple, eyes stinging with tear gas. Within a matter of minutes, as the police were still attacking teenagers, the state legislature authorised a 7 p.m. curfew and 4,000 National Guardsmen took to the streets of downtown Memphis. At the height of the fighting a news photographer captured an image of broken windows at the Memphis branch of Sears Roebuck. A group of young teenagers are seen struggling with police outside the store. It was a scene of small-scale criminal damage that was soon to become one of the iconic images of Memphis, 1968. But its full drama was yet to be fully understood. In the foreground a teenager is being restrained; to the right of the photograph, a thin, immaculately dressed young man – Larry Payne – watches as one of his friends is wrestled to the ground. Within a few hours Payne would be dead.

Along the route of the march lay the detritus of a demonstration gone wrong: broken sticks, crushed cans and torn posters. Most common among them were the official strike committee posters bearing the now legendary slogan 'I AM A MAN', but among the debris were others: 'BLACK POWER', 'BURN MEMPHIS BURN', and some less than gracious posters designed by high-school pupils that savaged the city's unpopular civic leader – 'MAYOR LOEB EAT SHIT'.

When the riot was at its peak the Reverend Lawson grabbed King and urged him to leave the march, but King protested, concerned that the action would be perceived as his running away. A car was flagged down and the men bundled inside. A police officer on a motorbike escorted the vehicle to an area of the city that was not under siege and negotiated with the management of the Holiday Inn-Rivermont to provide a suite for King and his entourage. The gesture proved to be a double-edged sword. As soon as King checked into the hotel, intelligence officers began to concoct the story that he had fled the violence, ignored the black-owned Lorraine Motel, near Beale Street, and chosen the luxury of a white-owned establishment, occupying the grandest room. Newspapers were briefed and fell into line, accusing King of cowardice.

He woke up the next morning with the reputation of his non-violent movement in tatters. Rather than hide, King called a press conference and faced down the criticism. He reiterated that his intentions were always to avoid violence and he said that the SCLC would return to the city to lead a non-violent march and kick-start their new initiative, the Poor People's Campaign. Later in the day, as King licked his wounds, there was an unexpected knock on the door and three members of the Invaders – Charles Cabbage, Izzy Harrington and Calvin Taylor – asked to meet him. It was a short but fruitful meeting. King vaguely knew Cabbage from his close connections to his alma mater Morehouse College and spoke warmly with him. The Invaders denied they had played any role in organising or even inducing the riot and complained that they had been marginalised from the march by local preachers who disliked their attitudes. They specifically blamed King's friend, the Reverend Jim Lawson, who had purposefully excluded the Invaders from any official role in the strike. As the meeting came to an end, Cabbage made a pitch for financial support from King and the SCLC, and they agreed that for the next march the Invaders would take on marshalling duties and guarantee that teenage demonstrators would be better organised. King was left with one overriding perspective of the Invaders: that they had met him face to face and, unlike many other militant groups he had encountered over the years, they had faced up to their own shortcomings.

As police gained control of the downtown area, Larry Payne and his friends snaked through side streets, carrying their small profits from looting – some clothes, packs of cigarettes and a camera. Just as they arrived at what they imagined was the safe haven of Fourth and Crump, due south of Booker T. Washington High School and directly opposite Fowler Homes where Payne's mother lived, a patrol car spotted them. The youths scattered and ran in different directions. According to a fictitious police report, Payne had been seen trying to loot a petrol station on South 3rd Street and supposedly threatened a police officer with a butcher's knife before escaping from the scene. He was seen again heading home to his mother's apartment through a maze of low-rise houses and was now being pursued by officers on foot. What happened next was the subject of deep disagreement, and divided the MPD and the residents of Fowler Homes into bitter and opposing camps. The police claimed that Payne and others were carrying a television set looted from the Sears Roebuck at 903 S. Third, and so chased the suspected looters into a basement area. Patrolman L.D. Jones said he and his partner, Charles F. Williams, followed the group of youths and trapped Payne. Police then claimed that the teenager emerged brandishing a knife although none of the residents saw the knife in question. News accounts reported that around 12.50 p.m. on 28 March Payne was 'repelled by a blast to the stomach from a 12-gauge shotgun, fired in self-defence by an officer of the law'. Community residents told a different story. 'Larry had his hands up and his back to the door of the storage room. His hands were behind his head when the police shot him,' said one witness. Another said, 'The short, fat policeman shot him. It was a muffled sound, like busting a sack. The gun was touching his stomach. The skinny policeman told him, "You didn't have to shoot him."'

Payne's mother was watching the CBS soap opera *As the World Turns* when a neighbour rushed to her door. 'That's my boy,' I cried. 'I ran out. I ran to touch him. The police would not let me touch him. He said, "Get back, nigger." He put the barrel of the gun right into my stomach. I could feel it.' Lizzie Payne said her last image was of her son lying on his back with both hands outstretched above his head. He didn't have anything in his hands and there was no knife on the ground, she said. The killing was disputed for years to come, but, despite the differing versions, none of the police officers were ever charged. After pressure from the dead boy's family, the police finally admitted that there was no extant evidence and the police gun that killed Larry Payne had been thrown into the Mississippi River. His mother could no longer bear living in Fowler Homes – to pass daily the scene of her son's death was too overwhelming – and so she moved north to Harlem, telling a news reporter, 'That has got the best of my life. It's taken everything out of me.'

Martin Luther King, feeling in some way responsible, and wounded by the violence that had erupted at the march, called Mrs Payne and offered his sincerest regrets. He told her that the next time he was in Memphis he would call to visit the family at Fowler Homes. For reasons now enshrined in history it was a promise he never kept.

'I've seen the Promised Land. I may not get there with you. But I want you to know tonight, that we, as a people, will get to the Promised Land.'

Martin Luther King, 3 April 1968, Mason Temple, Memphis

BEN BRANCH'S SOLEMN PROMISE

4 April

Ben Branch was sitting in a chair in a barber's shop near Firestone Union Hall, North Memphis, unaware that several people, including the Reverend Jesse Jackson and his own mother, were trying to contact him. He had just left the Union Hall after a public disagreement with the janitors, who had told him that the hall had no licence for live music. Branch suspected that the city authorities were in effect banning his band, Ben Branch & the Downhomers, from playing a concert in support of the striking sanitation workers. The no-licence claim smacked of an instruction from on high and Branch knew it to be false; he was brought up locally and had played the hall on numerous occasions, often signing a licence to guarantee payment in advance. Although Branch was born and raised in Memphis, two years previously he had moved north to Chicago to study a postgraduate degree in music. While there he became the Chicago Director of Martin Luther King's SCLC and a leading figure in Jesse Jackson's Illinois-based pressure group

Operation Breadbasket, which was committed to improving the economic conditions of African-Americans. The move to Chicago had given Branch the opportunity of a weekly radio show and a musical outlet that he had never fully enjoyed at home in Memphis. Championed by the irrepressible DJ and civil rights siren, E. Rodney Jones, Radio Station WVON – the one-time 'Voice of the Negro' – dedicated a weekly hour-long show to Branch and to his Operation Breadbasket Orchestra.

On the night before his arrival back home in Memphis, tenor saxophonist Branch and his band had been travelling by plane to Memphis airport when the city was suddenly struck by an electric storm. This was no ordinary storm. The tornados that had engulfed Memphis, Mississippi and Arkansas had destroyed farms, livestock and outbuildings, killed six people and injured over one hundred. It was a storm that became part of Memphis mythology as news spread within the African-American community of Martin Luther King's 'Mountaintop' speech at the Mason Temple, delivered at the height of the storm's electric anger.

The writer Hampton Sides described an Old Testament atmosphere as King arrived in the packed hall. The heat was suffocating, and the audience were using their hymn sheets as makeshift fans in a vain attempt to ward off the sticky humidity. Ralph Abernathy introduced him, 'his words echoing through the vast hall as tornado sirens keened outside'. The Reverend Kyles wrote after the fact: 'That night rain was pounding on the roof, and the rafters shook with thunder and lightning. I remember: the thunderclaps and the wind set the windows banging. Each time it happened Martin flinched. He was sure someone was lurking and going to shoot him. But when he got to the end of that speech and told us he had looked over and seen the promised land, a great calm came over him. Everyone was transfixed.'

'I'm delighted to see each of you here tonight in spite of a storm warning,' King had begun. Then, in a tour de force of public oratory he imagined the worlds he might have been born into, finally returning to the world he would have chosen above all others: the here and now. 'Something is happening in Memphis,' he said in his sonorous foreboding tone, 'something is happening in our world.

And also in the human rights revolution, if something isn't done, and done in a hurry, to bring the colored peoples of the world out of their long years of poverty, their long years of hurt and neglect, the whole world is doomed.' Finally he turned to his own predicament. 'We've got some difficult days ahead. But it really doesn't matter with me now, because I've been to the mountaintop. And I don't mind. Like anybody, I would like to live a long life. Longevity has its place. But I'm not concerned about that now. I just want to do God's will. And He's allowed me to go up to the mountain. And I've looked over. And I've seen the Promised Land. I may not get there with you. But I want you to know tonight, that we, as a people, will get to the Promised Land! I'm just happy that God has allowed me to live in this period to see what is unfolding. And I'm happy that He's allowed me to be in Memphis.'

As King addressed the strikers and their families, Branch's flight down from Chicago had been diverted to Jackson, Mississippi, and then, after another aborted landing, touched down in New Orleans. Only when news of the storm subsiding reached New Orleans, did the plane take off again, this time reaching Memphis. Branch had shared many journeys with King. They had grown up in the same segregated post-war South. Branch had taken his saxophone in a battered case to the Montgomery bus boycotts and had been there at the famous Selma–Montgomery marches in 1965, in support of voting rights. By then he had become a close personal friend of the Chicago contingent's ambitious and self-aware leader Jesse Jackson. It was Jackson who encouraged Branch to leave Memphis, but it was only the promise of a guaranteed postgraduate programme and full-time post with the SCLC that convinced him.

As soon as Branch's plane brought him back home to Memphis he was greeted by old friends and close family members. The Ben Branch Band and its local rival, the Willie Mitchell Band, led by the legendary trumpeter 'Papa' Willie Mitchell, had dominated Memphis nightlife for nearly two decades. Briefly, in the fifties, Branch and Mitchell had both been members of a seminal Memphis band, the Phineas Newborn Sound, the house band at the Plantation Inn, a club across the Mississippi in West Memphis, Arkansas. Apart from their professional success on stage, Branch and Mitchell became mentors to some of soul music's greatest stars. Branch's keyboard player was the young and as yet undiscovered Isaac Hayes, and his featured bass guitarist was the teenage Donald 'Duck' Dunn, who went on to become a member of Booker T. and the M.G.'s and a stalwart of the interracial academy at Stax Records. Dunn had made history as the first white musician to play in one of Memphis's outstanding black bands, setting the unwritten ground rules of musical integration. Mitchell had been a driving force in the city, too. He was the godfather of Royal Studios and the mastermind of Memphis's other great record company, Hi Records, which brought Al Green and Ann Peebles to prominence. Stax executive Al Bell Jr claimed that Mitchell was omnipresent in the city and a force for musical innovation: 'His handprint, thumbprint, footprint, heart print is all over Memphis music,' he once said.

By the age of forty, Branch had played in every significant venue in Memphis, including the Plantation Inn, Club Handy, the Flamingo and Curry's Club on Thomas Street, and had spanned the range of black music from spirituals and R&B to jazz. Like many of his generation, notably producer and blood bank clerk Roosevelt Jamison, he had been forced to juggle two careers simultaneously: educator and musician. Branch had been a student at Douglass High School in Mount Olive, North Memphis, where, paradoxically, his school became an unintended victim of the schools bussing policy. Many black teenagers were bussed out of the North Memphis neighbourhood but few corresponding white kids ever signed up to be bussed into Douglass, and so the attendance roll declined and the school was ultimately closed down. Branch was one of Douglass's star pupils and went on to study at Mississippi State University, returning at the weekends to moonlight at Memphis clubs. His contract – such as it was – required him to play until the last drunken customer had left the building, but then, after a few hours of sleep, he had to rise early to progress his vocation in education. He was a music supervisor in local schools, setting up the Mississippi State Band Directors' Association, an organisation that cultivated instrumentation in the city's black schools. Branch periodically played as a session musician, too; first at Stax, where he was an additional member of the Mar-Keys with Wayne Jackson, Floyd Newman,

Booker T. Jones, Steve Cropper and Donald 'Duck' Dunn. He composed and then played on the instrumental double-sider 'Beach Bash'/'Bush Bash', a relentless sax-led dance song that died locally but was a major hit in Europe, especially on the UK's Mod and northern soul scene. Session work continued when he moved to Chicago, this time with another heritage label, the famous Chess Records, where he shared freelance saxophone duties with Monk Higgins and added beef to songs by vocal harmony groups like the Radiants and the Vontastics. Each Saturday morning, he hosted rehearsals at the University of Chicago's Theological Seminary Rooms, where in February 1968 he met with Martin Luther King and Jesse Jackson. Together they hatched a plan to form the movement's official orchestra – a supergroup capable of playing spirituals, jazz, R&B and soul, and employing the cream of Branch's Chicago and Memphis bands as its nucleus. This new band became known as the Operation Breadbasket Orchestra and Choir, a dedicated civil rights band that became, in effect, the musical wing of Dr King's movement. In 1968 they signed a deal with Chess and settled in Chicago. Branch's capacity for hard work and his restless entrepreneurial spirit stayed with him throughout his life. While still committed to the civil rights movement, he set up Doctor Branch Products Inc., the nation's first black-owned soft-drink manufacturing company, and in 1986 the company signed a $355 million agreement with Kemmerer, the makers of 7Up. Branch spent much of his active working life as president of his own drinks company yet still turned up faithfully for rehearsals and for music education classes.

One of the stand-out songs in Branch's repertoire was an old spiritual called 'Precious Lord, Take My Hand', adapted by the great Thomas Dorsey, the man who first gave gospel music its name and became one of its most devoted exponents. Dorsey, from a tiny plantation town in Georgia, initially broke with his family's ultra-Christian beliefs and toured as a juke-joint blues singer with the provocative name of 'Barrelhouse Tommy', singing lewd and sexually loaded songs to semi-criminal audiences. Like Branch, he moved north to Chicago where he formed the Wildcats Jazz Band, but he struggled to adapt to city life and the cut-throat demands of the early R&B music scene. Dorsey suffered a severe nervous breakdown and returned home to Georgia to convalesce, and after deep reflection on what he saw as a harmful period as a blues singer he reconnected with the church and Christian music. Dorsey reputedly wrote 'Precious Lord, Take My Hand' as he reached out for spiritual strength after his wife and baby son both died in childbirth. Gospel mythology tells of how he locked himself in a room for three soul-searching days, warding off another breakdown by communing directly with the Lord. It was in this painful period of self-realisation that God directed him to write the song. Branch had a rather different interpretation, though, claiming that the song had much deeper roots and was in fact an Alabama slave anthem sung as a spiritual in the cotton fields of the Deep South. Dorsey had embellished it, and with the help of his own publishing company and the mountainous support of Mahalia Jackson, turned the song into a gospel standard. Branch himself had grown up with a scratchy old 78 rpm version in his Memphis home, and could play the entire song as a virtuoso saxophone solo, with only fleeting guest vocals to support him. Having heard the old slave anthem and its numerous renditions, at times in his own Ebenezer Baptist Church in Atlanta, it had become Martin Luther King's favourite song. Something about its legacy, its powerful history, its closeness to despair, and then its bombastic and uplifting Christian drama appealed to his senses, and at times King would weave words from the song into his sermons.

After Branch left the barbershop in North Memphis he took a cab to the Lorraine Motel, a black-owned lodgings on Mulberry Street on the fringes of the Beale Street ghetto and one of the few places in the city where blacks could book a room. He had stayed in the motel numerous times before, and even when he returned to his parental home, his band would check in there. It was also the favoured motel for the travelling entourage of the SCLC. As Branch arrived in the car park near the swimming pool and looked up at the mustard-yellow and blue walls, only a housemaid with a trolley was out on the balconies. The motel was unusually quiet. In Branch's mind it was synonymous with bustle and noise, late-night jam sessions, visiting bands disgorging their stage gear and touring equipment from a fleet of airport taxis, or it was the loud laughter of the Harlem Globetrotters basketball team clowning around the swimming pool. It was in the honeymoon suite that Eddie Floyd had written his greatest hit, 'Knock On Wood', and it was where Stax housed all their visiting black artists. Mable John, Eddie Floyd and Judy Clay were all regular guests, and over the years the motel had been home to Count Basie, Ray Charles, Aretha Franklin and Sarah Vaughan. The motel's owner, Walter Bailey, and his wife Loree, who doubled as the switchboard operator, prided themselves in knowing all the needs and preferences of the visiting stars. Loree and her janitor rearranged Ray Charles' room furniture so that he could navigate the room easily, working to a template that they had agreed with the singer years before. Bailey and his wife tolerated the strange ways of visiting soul singers, delivering late-night liquor to the shameless, and allowing painted ladies to visit rooms long after hours. Loree had spoken of her fears for Joe Hinton, an R&B singer with a bittersweet voice and manicured hands. She took cold milk to his room, as a medical aid, and smeared it on the melanoma scars on his diseased skin. Hinton died of skin cancer later in 1968. Songwriting partners Isaac Hayes and David Porter were a daily fixture at the Lorraine Motel and throughout the humid and sweltering summers preferred to write by the pool or use an air-conditioned room at day rates, rather than bake in the furnace of the Stax studios. On one occasion they reflected on a Coca-Cola advertising sign in the motel grounds and improvised around the motto 'Things Go Better with Coke', which in time became 'Things Go Better', Eddie Floyd's first release on Stax.

King was sharing Room 306 with his colleague Ralph Abernathy. Both had slept late to recover from the thunderous drama of the previous night and the room was in a state of disarray. Open suitcases lay on the surfaces, partially unpacked. The room was strewn with personal effects and half-filled ashtrays, and overlaid by the fug of smoke and Aramis aftershave. A black telephone, which had thankfully stopped ringing since the early hours, was off the hook, and a television, its twisted rabbit-ear antennae always tuned to network news stations, was switched off. On the previous afternoon, King had been served in the forecourt of the motel with an injunction banning another rally in support of the strike. Immediately, a legal challenge cranked into action. An SCLC contingent led by Andrew Young of the SCLC and the Reverend James Lawson of the strike support group COME had gone to the federal court to overturn a restraining order banning further marches. They hoped to convince the judge to protect their right to assemble and to approve a tightly marshalled march the following day. They remained locked in courtroom dialogue for the remainder of the day, and it became clear that after the riots of the recent past, any march would have to be strictly controlled and non-violent. King was adamant that they would need the involvement of the Invaders, whom the SCLC still distrusted but knew had influence over the youth of Memphis. Later in the day, after briefing other staff members back at the Lorraine, the SCLC booked Room 315 to accommodate a cadre of the Invaders, who were due to arrive to negotiate their role if the march was given the go-ahead. A group of Invaders had arrived at the motel, armed and intimidating, in the late morning: Charles Cabbage, Coby Smith, Marrell McCollough, dressed in blue-collar denims, and Charles 'Izzy' Harrington, a squat and pugnacious street warrior wanted by the MPD. Furious that the Invaders had turned up with guns, King was reluctant to be seen in their company and instructed SCLC staffers to communicate with the radicals. In one exchange, Hosea Williams proposed that the articulate Cabbage be put on the SCLC payroll as a way of incorporating the group – a suggestion that was reckless in the extreme. At the time Cabbage was already compromised by the FBI and had charges against him for a string of offences that would have been seized on by the local press as proof that Martin Luther King was giving ground to violent radicalism and consorting with hoodlums. King moved around the motel, lifting the spirits of his staff and chatting with guests, and then called into his brother's room. Alfred Daniel 'A.D.' King had arrived the night before in a Cadillac convertible with his girlfriend Lucretia Ward and the Kentucky state senator Georgia Davis Powers, who in the months before had become King's secret lover.

The King brothers chatted on the phone to their parents back in Atlanta, who had not known the boys were together. They recounted well-worn stories from the past and shared jokes, skilfully avoiding the politics that lay behind the brothers' reunion in Memphis and the violent tension that was building around the strike.

At lunchtime King and Abernathy left Room 306 and headed for the motel's café, where they ordered fried catfish and sat devouring the heaped platefuls with their hands. Both were fans of down-home cooking and preferred the soul food of their childhood to anything more refined. In fact, that night they had been invited to a soul food banquet at the home of the Reverend Samuel 'Billy' Kyles, one of the vanguard of preachers who had risen up to support the strike. After the party, Ben Branch and his band were scheduled to lead an SCLC concert at the Clayborn Temple, in part to raise funds, in part as a musical show of support for the strike.

The King brothers ate heartily and speculated about the two outstanding issues of the day: would the courts overturn the restraining order and allow a peaceful march to progress, and could a deal be struck with the Memphis Invaders, who were holed up in a nearby room, to guarantee a march that was non-violent? Some of King's younger staff members were unconvinced by the Invaders' guarantees and felt they were more interested in securing financial support. They told King they were afraid that violence might rear its head again. He assured them that it was a fear they had to overcome and it was essential that they somehow accommodate the militant youths of Memphis. 'I'd rather be dead than afraid,' he told them.

Then a number of strange and barely believable things began to happen around the motel. An SCLC staffer discovered that the Invaders, armed and brazenly confident, had been charging room service to the SCLC account. They were asked to leave the motel, which they did grudgingly. Ben Branch travelled back to the motel from his mother's home, and the MPD withdrew one of their most senior black detectives, Ed Redditt, from surveillance at the motel. Redditt was notorious among the strikers and their supporters, and was seen by many as betraying his race. There had been threats on Redditt's life from anonymous calls within the African-American community, and so the police withdrew him from tailing King.

Meanwhile, and independently, the only two black firemen in the Butler Street Station near the Lorraine Motel were also withdrawn and suddenly given new assignments. One of the firemen, Floyd Newsum, was a vociferous supporter of the strike and had been at the Mason Temple Rally where King had given this tumultuous 'Mountaintop' speech. Newsum argued against his new assignment but was forced to accede. The outcome – planned or coincidental – was that the only black officers representing public services in the immediate vicinity of the Lorraine Motel had been withdrawn. Around 4.30 p.m., King's attorney Chauncey Eskridge, by then more famous for his court battles trying to keep Muhammad Ali from a jail term for draft evasion, returned from court. The SCLC legal team were ecstatic about a small but significant victory: the march could go ahead but with a route and a set of conditions that would allow the police to contain any potential trouble. A free march had been curtailed but the ban was overturned.

A new energy surged through the motel. King and Abernathy were in Room 306 preparing to go to dinner at the home of the Reverend Kyles. King, who had dry and sensitive skin, took an age to shave and everyone else was assembling in the car park below. Jesse Jackson was there, Ben Branch had arrived with his instruments in tow. King's driver Solomon Jones, who had been provided to him courtesy of a local funeral home, hung out by the open door of his Cadillac, waiting for King's party to descend the stairs. Back in Room 306, King slapped Aramis on his face and headed out to the landing, allowing Ralph Abernathy to use the mirror. The sink was still peppered with King's shaven hairs.

Emerging from the room, King spoke to the throng below. He chatted buoyantly to Jesse Jackson and Ben Branch, who was due to go to an early evening soundcheck for an SCLC fundraising concert later that night (King and his party were scheduled to attend the fundraiser after supper). The driver shouted that it was getting cold and that they should bring overcoats. King agreed and joked about Jackson's new casual hipster look. Jackson had recently abandoned the traditional dark suit for a suede jacket and fawn turtle-neck sweater, and his hair was growing into an afro. Seeing Branch down below in the courtyard, King asked him if he had his saxophone with him: 'I want you to play "Take My Hand Precious Lord", Ben,' he said. 'Play it real pretty, sweeter than you've ever played it before.' King knew by heart the despondent yet hopeful words at the heart of the song: 'When the darkness appears and the night draws near/And the day is past and gone/At the river I stand/ Guide my feet, hold my hand.' As King shared his last words with the saxophonist, a single bullet from a Remington Gamesmaster .30-06 rifle tore through the right side of his face and exited beneath his jaw. He fell backwards against the cinder wall of the Lorraine Motel's balcony, blood pooling around his head.

Dr Martin Luther King Jr was pronounced dead at 7.05 p.m. on 4 April 1968 at St Joseph's Hospital. An autopsy performed by Dr Jerry T. Francisco, the Shelby County medical examiner, concluded that death was the result of a single 'gunshot wound to the chin and neck with a total transaction of the lower cervical and upper thoracic spinal cord and other structures of the neck'. It was later established by a panel of forensic experts that the wounds were caused by the bullet recovered from his body – 'a Remington-Peters, soft-point, metal-jacketed bullet fired from a distance by a high-velocity rifle' – and they concluded that Dr King 'died as a result of one shot fired from in front of him'.

As Father Coleman Bergard, a local priest who had been called to administer the last rites, closed King's eyelids, there was a long peaceful silence. And then the inner cities erupted.

The balcony photograph. Dr King's supporters point in the direction of the shooting. The mysterious Agent 500 is kneeling beside King.

AGENT 500'S BUSY AFTERNOON

4 April

The first person to reach the slain body of Martin Luther King was neither a member of his staff nor a motel employee, and was a man who had many reasons not to be caught in the headlights of history. Agent 500, a twenty-four-year-old African-American secret agent, colloquially known as 'Max', was at the time working as an undercover agent for the MPD, on attachment from US Military Intelligence. Agent 500 grabbed a towel from a nearby laundry basket and tried to stem the gush of blood from King's neck. Two young girls from a gospel choir, who had gone towards King's room in the hope of getting an autograph or a souvenir photograph, stood frozen in shock at the sight of the crumpled body sprawled in front of them. Within seconds, King's closest aides had rushed to the scene and Agent 500 had vanished, taking off down the stairway and out through the courtyard, hidden by the chaos. Ralph Abernathy had been in the bathroom of Room 306 slapping aftershave on his face when he heard the shot. Andrew Young, the

SCLC's executive director, had arrived at the scene after his day of intense courtroom wrangling to secure the right for another march. Hosea Williams, another SCLC executive, was with him, and Jesse Jackson, then the SCLC's man in Chicago, was nearby, already climbing the external stairs. On the balcony itself, the Reverend 'Billy' Kyles stepped back in disbelief, and so it came to pass that King's faithful deputy Ralph Abernathy pushed his way through the scrum of bodies. Senator Georgia Davis Powers, who had driven through the night from Kentucky to be with her lover, was alone in a downstairs room; so, too, was King's younger brother A.D. In another room were the scattered clothes of Detroit soul singer Mable John, then recording an album track at the Stax Records studio. She has since claimed that she had been asked to vacate the fated Room 306 at the request of the management to allow King to have his favourite room. It was just one of innumerable claims, counter-claims and coincidences that surrounded the shooting. Either conscious of the status of those gathering around the dying King, or more likely anxious about his visibility at the scene of the assassination, Agent 500 handed the now blood-soaked towel to Ralph Abernathy, shielded the two young girls from the trauma of the dying man, and quietly faded into the background.

Agent 500 was a short, stocky African-American man known as Marrell McCollough, who had grown up in brutal poverty in Sugar Ditch Alley, a shanty town blighted by open sewers in Tunica, Mississippi. He had served as a military policeman in Vietnam where his tours of duty overlapped with Stax singer William Bell and the Mad Lads vocalist John Gary Williams, the singer whose commitment to social change had taken him into the inner sanctum of the Memphis Invaders. McCollough had arrived in Memphis in February as part of the multi-agency operation called 'Lantern Spike', a top secret endeavour to monitor, infiltrate and disrupt the Sanitation Workers Strike. After his service in Vietnam he was identified as someone with skills that could be used by the secret state, and he was recruited to the 111th Military Intelligence Brigade, then based at Fort McPherson, Georgia. He had three towering advantages: he was young, black and streetwise. At the time, Military Intelligence employed nearly 800 army officers and over 1,500 civilians in a bewildering array of clandestine or semi-official roles. McCollough was one of only sixty-seven black undercover officers, most of whom had been recruited with the express purpose of deployment on secret projects monitoring civil rights or infiltrating emergent Black Power groups.

As the Sanitation Workers Strike intensified, McCollough was assigned to a top secret unit of four hand-picked officers working for the Domestic Intelligence Unit (DIU) of the MPD. His first assignment was to infiltrate the inner circle of the Invaders and insinuate his way into the social lives of the city's young militants. It was a role he took to with alarming success, and within a matter of weeks, as previously mentioned, he had been promoted to the grandiose role of Minister of Transport of the Black Organizing Project/Memphis Invaders, on the grounds that he was one of the few young men with a car in a sprawling city notoriously difficult to navigate by public transport. Coby Smith, an Invader who befriended McCollough, claims he was a very 'accessible person' who did him favours and picked him up most mornings. 'We're talking about some poor youngsters in a very poor town,' Smith later told a Congressional Assassinations Committee. He testified that he had come to know McCollough after an introduction by the Riverside faction of the Invaders, who rated him highly. 'We didn't have anything. We didn't have any money. We got around the best we could, which was usually to bum a ride. In fact, the police would sometimes have to give us a ride. The ones that were watching us would sometimes give us a ride.'

Agent 500 returned from Vietnam at a critical moment in the rise of the surveillance state. As a cover for his activities, he had registered as a student at Memphis University but rarely visited the campus – he often claimed that prior to joining the Invaders he had been a warehouseman. From his modest rented home at 1445 Clementine Road, tucked away in obscurity near the faceless construction sites around Highway 240, McCollough travelled with the Invaders by day and drank with them at night. He would then sit up into the small hours, filing daily intelligence reports and feeding them into a bewildering array of agencies, ostensibly to the local MPD's Red Squad, and through them to Military Intelligence, and then onwards to the FBI's COINTELPRO programme – the pernicious and highly confidential response to the summer of inner city riots in 1967. 'The purpose of this new counterintelligence endeavour,' the FBI's own communiqué claimed, 'is to expose, disrupt, misdirect, discredit, or OTHERWISE NEUTRALIZE the activities of Black Nationalist hate-type organizations and groupings, their leadership, spokesmen, membership, and supporters, and to counter their propensity for violence and civil disorder.' Responsibility for COINTELPRO's successful implementation in the South was the Memphis police chief Frank Holloman, a former FBI operative who had worked for over twenty years for the Bureau, much of it in J. Edgar Hoover's Washington office. Holloman had directly approved Agent 500's assignment.

Hoover's pathological hatred of Martin Luther King was an open secret in Washington. By the mid sixties he had poured substantial resources and manpower into a nationwide surveillance programme which probed into the lives of King's political allies, the finances of his church, and, most scandalously, into the minister's adventurous sex life. The FBI field office in King's home town of Atlanta, Georgia, held voluminous paperwork on his activities filed under the codename 'Zorro' (taken from the popular television series of the late fifties), the secret identity most agents habitually used when they were discussing King. The surveillance had become personal and vindictive. Hoover was of the view that King was not only a threat to the established order but a hypocritical philanderer whose gospel exhortations were at odds with a string of sexual liaisons with married women. At a poisonous press conference as far back as November 1964, Hoover had lashed out at King's criticism of the FBI by describing the civil rights leader as the 'most notorious liar in the country'. The campaign against King degenerated into prurience when FBI officers installed microphones in a room at the Willard Hotel in Washington, DC, and recorded King having sex with an unnamed woman. A few months later, in the days before King was due to be honoured with the Nobel Peace Prize in Oslo, the FBI anonymously dispatched an edited copy of the surveillance tapes from a mailbox in Tampa to his wife. The intent was obvious:

to ruin King's marriage and undermine his reputation. The package contained a venomous letter proposing that King should consider suicide rather than risk the humiliation of his sexual secrets being made public.

Harry C. McPherson, a White House special counsel and Lyndon B. Johnson's speechwriter, claimed that the aftermath of the summer of riots had created the perfect conditions for the FBI's expansion. The words 'law and order', he wrote, were simply the new 'code words for racism'.

Hoover had seized his chance to delve into the lives of black activists with the hypocritical zeal of a voyeuristic patriot. He once described Martin Luther King as 'a tomcat with obsessive degenerate sexual urges' and believed King was 'an instrument in the hands of subversive forces seeking to undermine our nation'. The FBI flooded the White House with daily intelligence reports on Black Power activists to the extent that President Johnson's staff felt overwhelmed by the volume of evidence – much of it fanciful and questionable, and, according to historian Kenneth O'Reilly, 'short on facts and long on rhetoric'. The tangled wires of surveillance and whispered evidence gathered in covert operations had exposed divisions within government, too, pitting Hoover's FBI against the US attorney general Robert Kennedy. The Washington editor of the *Nation*, David Corn, described the ethics of law enforcement as a 'titanic clash' between Kennedy and Hoover, whose distrusting relationship had festered into one of the great power feuds of American politics. According to Corn, it went beyond personality or politics and was 'in a way a fight over the meaning of justice in America'.

Marrell McCollough had become a secret agent as much by chance as ambition. On his demobilisation from Vietnam, like many before him he had moved from the military police to a civilian role, but during his interviews he had emerged as a strong candidate for the needs of the time. It was not simply that he was black, he was also an affable man with streetwise instincts and extremely good communication skills. The MPD had come under pressure to demonstrate that it was an employer open to black recruits and one willing to promote talent from the African-American community. It was a time of minority recruitment and one when young people had become fascinated by a wave of popular culture that glamorised the role of undercover agents – an era of secrecy and suspicion. Network television had struck a rich vein of success with themed television shows featuring spies and secret agents. FBI detectives starred in movies and primetime shows, among them *The Man from U.N.C.L.E.* series (1964–1968), the James Bond franchise, *Mission Impossible* (1966–1973) and the comedy parody show *Get Smart* (1965–1970). Those shows in turn begat a wide range of theme tunes – the Ventures' 'Hawaii Five-0' (Liberty), 'Mission Impossible' by Lalo Schifrin (Dot) and the Detroit instrumental 'Undercover' by Bongalis (MS Records) – that gave instrumental credence to a world of disguise, subterfuge and undercover operations. Ironically, the Invaders had taken their name from an ABC science-fiction series in which a young architect turns secret agent to fight a secretive group of alien invaders. Throughout the sixties a rash of pop and soul songs glorified the undercover cop, many of them major hits in the ghettos: Edwin Starr's 'Agent Double-O Soul' (Ric-Tic Records), Little Hank's 'Mister Bang Bang Man' (Sound Stage 7), Smokey Robinson and the Miracles' 'Come Spy With Me' (Tamla Motown) and Gene Faith's 'Call The FBI (My Baby's Missing)' (Power Exchange). One soul record stood out from the crowd and led inevitably back to Memphis. Luther Ingram & the G-Men's original version of 'I Spy (For The F.B.I.)' (Smash) was recorded in New York City in the mid sixties and was unfairly trumped in the charts by a cover version of the same song, an international modernist anthem recorded by Jamo Thomas, an aggressive Chicago-based soul singer. Despite seeing his original recording usurped by Thomas, the talented Ingram, an elegant gospel-trained singer from Jackson, Mississippi, found himself sucked into the dark criminal subculture of sixties soul when he encountered two formidable and physically intimidating men – Johnny Baylor and Dino Woodard – who within weeks would arrive in Memphis in a blaze of both guns and questionable glory.

* * *

Even within a few hours of King's death, McCollough was distancing himself from the aftermath of the assassination and being economical about what he told others. He was soon back among the low-income apartments, arcade stores and community centres where the Invaders hung out, saying nothing. He spent some of his days casually calling in at soul shops across the city, including Satellite Records at Stax and the Mack at 883 Porter, an emporium for Black Power paraphernalia, fashion accessories and the latest soul vinyl. It was in late July, on one of his regular visits to the 'black arcades', that McCollough began to hatch a plan to entrap the Memphis Invaders militants in a carefully orchestrated drugs bust.

He planned the bust with one of his closest allies in the world of Memphis surveillance, Lieutenant Eli Arkin of the MPD's Red Squad, a dark-haired schemer with a heavy moustache and darting eyes, along with another police lieutenant Tom Hall, a man with a cropped military haircut, jowly chin and the look of better days. McCollough knew in advance that on 2 August there would be a Friday night drugs party at two adjacent brown-brick apartments in a low-income housing project at 1644 Hanauer, near Carver High School. McCollough knew in advance that John Burl Smith, the key target, would be there, and that there would be drugs on the premises. On the day, three syringes, a number of marijuana joints, a bottle of Luminal, forty-six phenobarbital pills and an item described by the police report as 'an oriental water pipe' were seized. On a simultaneous raid on the premises of Smith's neighbour Lizzie Jones the police found a gallon jug of liquid barbiturate, phenobarbital and two .22 calibre pistols. Four Invaders were taken into custody, including Charles 'Izzy' Harrington (20), who was described as an area co-ordinator of the Afro-American Brother-hood and was one of the delegation of Invaders who met with Martin Luther King at the Rivermont Hotel in the aftermath of the abortive rally that had led to the death of Larry Payne. McCollough was arrested along with Smith and three others – Oree McKenzie (18), the cousin of Mad Lads singer John Gary Williams, Verdell Brooks (20), and a woman, Jewell Davis (18). To protect McCollough's cover, he was taken to the station and charged with disorderly conduct and possession of legend drugs (those that can only be dispensed with the permission of a licensed physician) without a valid prescription. Conveniently, in a Memphis police press briefing, McCollough's Christian name was given as Marion and his surname erroneously misspelled. He was described coyly as an 'affiliate' of the Invaders, but the press were briefed that he was not on the payroll of their umbrella group, the Neighborhood Organizing Project. The charges against him were eventually dropped and his identity as an undercover officer carefully protected. In a court appearance of some bravado, Smith denied the charges, claiming he did not smoke tobacco let alone marijuana, and that he had never used a syringe. Smith normally wore a denim jacket with Invaders emblazoned on the back, but on trial he showed up in a razor-sharp grey suit and blue tie. The Vietnam veteran, who had served four years in the air force, rose up in the dock to protest his innocence and rolled up his sleeve to demonstrate to the jury that he had no needle marks, no collapsed veins and no obvious signs of intravenous drug abuse. After four and a half hours of deliberation the jury found Smith guilty and he was jailed for eleven months and twenty-nine days in the Shelby County Penal Farm.

No one can be certain about the circumstances that brought Marrell McCollough to the balcony of the Lorraine Motel on 4 April. He had spent the morning ferrying two SCLC officials around town – James Orange and James Bevel, who found him personable enough – and then drove them back to the motel where he rejoined the Invaders in their room. What is strange, and remains unexplained to this day, is Agent 500's curious activity on the day in question. During the afternoon of King's assassination, he was with a group of Invaders at the motel thrashing out a marshalling plan that would ensure that the civil rights march planned for the following day would be non-violent. After King's executives discovered that the Invaders were armed – and putting room service on the SCLC tab – they were asked to leave the premises. The Invaders dispersed. But by 5 p.m. McCollough was back in the immediate area, this time, incredulously, at an MPD meeting at Jim's Grill on Main Street, below the shabby rooming house where the fatal shot came from. With McCollough were two other police officers, one of whom was Lieutenant Earl Clark, the MPD expert sniper. Agent 500 had moved unobtrusively around the motel building, surveying the pool and glancing up and down Mulberry. Soon after the furtive meeting with his police colleagues, McCollough returned to the Lorraine Motel and hung out in the busy car park. He was there when the shot rang out. McCollough stayed with the MPD for a few unsettled months after the assassination, and then disappeared back into the murky world of military intelligence, returning to Fort McPherson. In 1974 he joined the CIA and may have been deployed in the African republic of Zaire to track down black militants, including the honorary Black Panther and former student leader Stokely Carmichael, once described by the FBI as having the 'necessary charisma to be a real threat'. Carmichael had recently married the African singer Miriam Makeba and travelled with her to Africa to see Muhammad Ali's heavyweight title fight against George Foreman, the Rumble in the Jungle. Among the claims and counterclaims whirling around King's assassination, what is indisputable is that Agent 500 was a first-hand witness to the assassination of Martin Luther King and a key player in the subterfuge that enveloped Memphis in 1968. McCollough's presence in the area around the Lorraine Motel is just one among many unexplained occurrences, leaving open the prospect that either strange things happen, or that a full-blown conspiracy reaching into the most secret corners of the surveillance state was in place.

With the benefit of hindsight, the movements of Agent 500 are at best extraordinary; they have since formed part of a civic case brought by King's widow accusing the MPD of being involved in a conspiracy to kill her husband. In summary, what is now accepted as fact is that sometime in the afternoon of 4 April, Marrell McCollough had driven a small contingent of Invaders to a pre-arranged meeting with executives of the SCLC. A room had been booked at the Lorraine Motel, on the balcony to the south of Dr King's room, number 306. The meeting was ostensibly to secure the Invaders' agreement that they would join a marshalling group that would guarantee a peaceful march through downtown Memphis, to help re-establish King's status as a leader of non-violent protest. Just after 4.30 p.m. McCollough made his excuses and briefly left the motel, crossing Mulberry Street on foot and emerging near the entrance to Jim's Grill, a bar on South Main Street, which was a regular haunt of off-duty Memphis police officers. According to eye-witness reports, McCollough regularly joined a small group of up to five men, including police officer Lieutenant John Barger and MPD sharpshooter Lieutenant Earl Clark. This small cadre of officers, and their meetings at Jim's Grill, have featured consistently in conspiracy theories surrounding the assassination. Whatever the true sequence of events, by 5.45 p.m. McCollough had returned to the Invaders' room at the motel and rejoined discussions. Only a few minutes later, there was a bang on the door and a motel staff member informed the group that they would have to vacate the premises, as their bill was no longer being underwritten by the SCLC. These instructions have become the subject of significant disagreement. Some have claimed that the orders came from Jesse Jackson, who was in the area near the swimming pool pacing around, irritated by the presence of the Black Power radicals. Others believe it was Andrew Young who pulled the plug on the subsidised room. Others claim the instruction came from King himself. He supposedly felt betrayed and undermined and was incensed that the Invaders were heavily armed, bringing guns to a meeting that was supposedly about guaranteeing non-violence. Rather than argue or cause a disturbance, the Invaders, including Charles Cabbage, Coby Smith and, behind them, their Minister of Transport McCollough, aka Max, aka Agent 500, walked down the stairs towards the forecourt. They were still on the motel premises when the fatal shot struck. Instinctively, Agent 500 rushed back up the stairs to assist King. Some have since claimed it was a human reaction to a tragedy; others that it was what a serving police officer would be expected to do. Many more have rushed to the more sinister interpretation that Agent 500 was somehow implicated. A favourite theory is that he had gone to give a silent signal to a sniper squad, who were hidden in a bushy area opposite the motel. The mysterious sniper squad, if they ever really existed, then vanished from sight.

It is now the settled conclusion that it was lone gunman James Earl Ray, a racist criminal from Alton, Illinois, who killed Martin Luther King. Ray had escaped from the Missouri State Penitentiary in April and, in a bizarre journey across America, snaked his way to Memphis where he fired the fatal shot. Like the deaths of John F. Kennedy and Malcolm X, the conspiracy theories have yet to subside, but if they have even the thinnest vestige of credibility then officers from the MPD, agents of the FBI and shady operatives from Military Intelligence colluded in the killing. In that murky scenario Agent 500 had a front-row seat.

Memphis photographer Ernest Withers.

ERNEST WITHERS' BLOOD VIAL

4 April

Ernest Withers had known Martin Luther King most of his adult life. It was a moment of compulsion that took him up the external stairs of the Lorraine Motel to the exposed corner where King had been shot. Congealed blood still lay thick on the concrete floor. Withers crouched down and, using a small shard of glass, scooped some of King's spilt blood into an old photography vial that he had found amongst his camera equipment. It was to stay in his refrigerator at home for decades to come.

Withers was a native of Memphis. He had attended Manassas High School beneath the soaring white smokestack of the Firestone Tire & Rubber Company and briefly considered working there during the war, when the plant produced rubber life rafts and gas masks for the military. But a much better opportunity opened up when, leveraging his interest in amateur photography, he secured a traineeship at the Army School of Photography. Withers was a keen sports enthusiast who followed Negro League baseball and heavyweight boxing bouts and often took his camera along with him. On his demobilisation from his unit at Fort Bliss, Texas, he followed advice from boxing legend Joe Louis, who in the post-war period ran a ghetto recruitment campaign on behalf of the United Negro and Allied Veterans of America, an organisation set up to support returning military personnel. In days of heightened paranoia, the organisation was labelled as subversive, and Withers was suspected of being a communist. Ironically, Withers was already showing an interest in small-scale capitalism and had begun selling photography services to new mothers and married couples in the side streets along Chelsea Boulevard, often going door to door with his portfolio. He briefly became one of the first black officers of the MPD, but it was a distraction from his real passion and he left to set up the Withers Photography Studio on Beale Street, a Memphis institution which provided wedding and graduation services to the local black community. Even as a young man, Withers' distinctive frizzy hair, his cumbersome kit strapped across his chest, and the gargantuan Graflex camera he carried with him, made him a familiar figure around Beale Street. By the early sixties he had became the photographer of choice for Stax Records and he took instructions from Jim Stewart and Estelle Axton to provide standard studio shots of the label's first generation of stars: Carla Thomas and her father Rufus, local saxophonist Floyd Newman, and the self-styled 'happiest man in the world' R&B pianist Ivory Joe Hunter. It was local and low-cost, but with time the commissions took on a more pressing and glamorous urgency, and the studio opened early in the morning and often closed long after midnight. Otis Redding needed new photographs but was due to fly to Europe; the Mad Lads had a new release but they were playing that night in Birmingham, Alabama, and singer William Bell had to be photographed in his army uniform then in casual dress. Withers juggled all the requests for Stax but also stayed in touch with the offices of the Southern Christian Leadership Conference in Atlanta as the caravan of civil rights unfolded.

He was a formidable witness to the history of civil rights and his camera captured some of the most momentous moments on the journey of social change. He was beaten up and jailed in Jackson, Mississippi, after a sit-in where civil rights students tried to break the segregated soda fountain stalls at Woolworths. Beaten, insulted and smeared in ketchup, the non-violent protest led to mass arrests. He documented the trial of the murderers of Emmett Till, an African-American teenager who was lynched in Mississippi after reportedly flirting with a white woman. His body was dumped in the town of Sumner, where a murder trial lasted for five claustrophobic days in a tiny courtroom.

Withers was witness to the Montgomery Bus Boycott campaign in the fifties, when African-Americans refused to ride city buses to protest segregated seating, and he was an approved photographer at the funeral of Medgar Evers, the civil rights activist who was murdered by a segregationist in June 1963. Withers' photographs had a candour that stemmed from his use of a normal-focus lens and from his confidence with the events he was witness to: he was in every respect an insider within a movement that had every reason to be suspicious of the white-owned national media. The photographs he took of the integration of Little Rock High School, a set-piece dispute over desegregated schooling, were taken not from the vantage of the armed Arkansas National Guardsmen but from the hopeful perspective of a group of black teenage girls arriving at the school gates in their bobby socks and dirndl skirts. Proximity to the movement also brought him close to Martin Luther King, who he frequently photographed in private moments, off-stage and away from the glare of the news media. It was his relationship with King and the Southern Christian Leadership Conference staff in Atlanta that made him both useful and vulnerable to the FBI. At some stage in 1958, in the aftermath of the desegregation of Little Rock High School, Withers was approached by an agent of the FBI. It was casual at first, and then in 1961 William H. Lawrence, a thin-faced spook who wore elegant black half-framed spectacles and who ran the Bureau's Memphis field office, requested that Withers be recruited as a PCI (FBI-speak for a Potential Confidential Informant). Initially, Withers received a poor recommendation from the MPD, which he had left in strained circumstances. According to the police, he had taken an irregular payment from a city bootlegger, but Withers always claimed it was a means to an end, to pursue his dream of owning and operating a photography studio aimed at the African-American community. As the heat of desegregation intensified and the civil rights movement challenged discrimination in housing, education and the workplace, Withers' insider knowledge became ever more valuable. From 1964 the FBI held a '170' file on the photographer ('170' was the classification for a contact who could provide information on organisations and individuals holding 'extreme political views'). The events of 1967 turned the screws on Withers. Martin Luther King's now famous speech, 'A time to break the silence', at the Riverside Church in New York City encouraged the civil rights movement to oppose the war in Vietnam, and summer riots besieged Newark and Detroit. It was then that the FBI published its COINTELPRO communiqué, committing its network of agents to infiltrate black militant organisations. In early 1968, FBI agents visited Withers' studio on Beale Street. According to his critics, the meeting dragged the photographer deeper into betrayal; according to his family, he was threatened, damage was done to his workplace, and the agents demanded information about photographs he had taken over the years. Many featured Martin Luther King and his staff, but many more, stored in boxes, stacked on shelves and hung as negative strips from kitchen pegs, documented the rich history of Memphis music, a treasure trove from the infancy of rock 'n' roll to the height of southern soul.

There was a still of the stick-thin Elvis Presley posing with R&B crooner Brook Benton resplendent in a plaid dinner jacket at the WDIA Goodwill Revue at the Ellis Auditorium, on the corner of Poplar and Front Street. There was a bizarre photograph of Rufus Thomas dressed in an eccentric Native American headdress posing with a coolly bewildered Elvis, a photograph that crystallises the different and co-existing music scenes in the city. There was a print of Howlin' Wolf standing in a fruit market with his aching electric guitar surrounded by prunes, watermelons and canned vegetables in Arkansas, circa 1950. There was a photograph of Ike and Tina Turner at Club Paradise, Memphis, in 1962; Tina's in a gold lamé dress, aggressive at the microphone, as her razor-sharp husband prowls jealously behind her. It is a photograph latent with the spousal abuse that was to surface in years to come. There was a box containing prints of Big Ella at Club Paradise, bursting out of her shimmering party frock as she screams into a hand-held microphone. And there was a now iconic photograph of James Brown at the Mid-South Coliseum in 1965, kneeling on stage and clutching a collapsed microphone stand, his skin shimmering with sweat and his eyes on the verge of stage tears.

For much of the fifties, Withers had been the unofficial photographer in residence at the Hippodrome on Beale Street. It was there that he photographed B.B. King, implausibly dressed in spats and summer shorts, playing to an overspill audience. It was there that he shot the stunningly glamorous R&B queen Ruth Brown, her glossy dress billowing above golden high heels and her diamante earring decorously framing a perfect period kiss curl. A young and flamboyantly dressed crowd look up at her with awe. And it was there that he captured a hectic and fired-up Lionel Hampton, in a crumpled zoot suit, with his drumsticks in mid-flight banging out a beat for a delirious audience. Stacked on his desk were proofs of the soul singer Johnnie Taylor, a stunning vocalist from across the Mississippi River in West Memphis, Arkansas, who in the aftermath of Otis Redding's death was becoming Stax's most formidable male singer. His new single 'I Ain't Particular' had just hit the stores and his stellar worldwide hit 'Who's Making Love' was about to be recorded at East McLemore. Withers had just completed another Stax commission, portraits of a white teenager called Johnny Daye, whom Otis Redding had discovered in Pittsburgh while on tour. Redding's recommendation had brought Daye to Memphis but his mentor's death resulted in a stillborn career. Daye was recording the ballad 'Stay Baby Stay' at Stax when King was killed and, despite a short period as a backing singer for the R&B giant Bobby Bland, returned home to Pittsburgh bitter and penniless.

Withers had been the creative eyes of civil rights and the Memphis music scene until the FBI came knocking. Sometime in 1967, after King's denouncement of the war in Vietnam, Withers' studio was visited by agents. They turned over his darkroom, demanded to see photographs, and forced Withers to give information on some of the people photographed with King at rallies across the southern states. The interrogation lasted over an hour and the FBI took a batch of photos away with them, including some wholly innocent pictures of young singers from the Stax studios. From 1967 to 1970 Withers provided more photographs, basic biographical information and scheduling details of King's itinerary to agents Howell Lowe and William H. Lawrence, both of whom had been trained in domestic surveillance. Many of the photos he provided fell under the COINTELPRO programme, images taken within the Memphis mosques of the Nation of Islam and the broader Muslim community and many more of Martin Luther King and the non-violent campaign he had pioneered. Withers provided information on a wide range of prominent Memphis figures, from street-corner militants to those on educational campuses, including the irrepressible Lance 'Sweet Willie Wine' Watson, a member of the Memphis Invaders. He had photographed the ministers who had supported the Sanitation Workers Strike, including Bishop G.E. Patterson and the Afrocentric Professor David Acey of the University of Memphis. According to documents released under the Freedom of Information Act to the daily newspaper *The Commercial Appeal*, in a landmark ruling, Withers' reports to the FBI increased in regularity during the Sanitation Workers Strike. It was a time when King's reputation was also undergoing a profound change. According to Professor Michael Eric Dyson, King was becoming too powerful for some. 'The more he protested poverty, denounced the Vietnam War and lamented the unconscious racism of many whites, the more he lost favor and footing in white America,' he wrote in his book *I May Not Get There with You*. King had become a figure of near-obsessive focus and increasingly bitter resentment. 'In many ways King was socially and politically dead before he was killed. Martyrdom saved him from becoming a pariah to the white mainstream.'

Over time he compromised others, handing over photographs of a group of local Catholic priests who supported the strike, and implicated a US Civil Rights Commission worker, claiming he was a supporter of Black Power groups and someone close to the Invaders.

Prior to his death, before the full extent of his role as an FBI informer was exposed, Withers offered a partial defence. Throughout 1968 until King's assassination, Withers had FBI agents 'regularly looking over his shoulder and questioning him'. Clearly compromised by the pressure he had come under, he made the decision to avoid any of the private or inner-circle meetings he had always had access to. 'I never tried to learn any high-powered secrets,' Withers said. 'It would have just been trouble . . . [The FBI] was pampering me to catch whatever leaks I dropped,' he told a gathering at an exhibition in Norfolk, Virginia. 'So I stayed out of meetings where decisions were being made.' He also conceded that there was another reason: meetings meant poor and unmemorable photographs.

King's assassination had triggered an intense photographic reaction. Withers was there with his cameras draped like a ring of onions round his neck. An FBI surveillance squad with long-distance lenses was surveying the car park outside the Lorraine Motel from a nearby high building and a young black South African documentary film-maker called Joseph Louw was working there on a documentary film on civil rights. He hoped to use the film to raise awareness of non-violent resistance in America as a way of provoking opposition to the apartheid regime back home in Johannesburg. Louw was relaxing in Room 309, a few doors along the corridor from King, when he heard the shot ring out. He grabbed his stills camera and began frantically to take shots of the scene. Unable to develop them in his room, he talked Withers into opening up his studio. The two photographers rushed a few blocks to Beale Street past an eerily quiet John Brown's Pool Room, where hustlers usually hung out in doorways or shared bets round the tables. Inside the darkroom they patiently watched the shallow rippling tray. One of the images that came to life was to become one of the most iconic photographs of all time. It showed a group of men, mostly colleagues of Martin Luther King, standing over his dying body and pointing in the presumed direction of the assassin's vantage point. Their arms are raised in unison. Ralph Abernathy, Andrew Young and Jesse Jackson had instinctively pointed to the rear of a decrepit rooming house on South Main. The next day the image led front pages around the world, but what few, if any, noticed at the time was another man bent over King's body – Marrell McCollough, the undercover operative known as Agent 500.

When Withers returned to the crime scene from his studio, he climbed the outside stairway at the motel and knelt down to scrape the congealed blood. Only he can know what his motive was. Unknown to even his closest friends, he was the informer codenamed 'ME 338-R(Ghetto)', who since the start of 1968 had received regular pay cheques from the FBI. But he was also a hugely creative man with deep roots in civil rights and a great love of the music of his hometown. For those who are unforgiving about his betrayal, Ernest Withers' small vial of blood was a final and degrading insult, and for those who can imagine a troubled man caught up in the intimidation and deceit of the era, it was a desperate attempt to stay close to a man who had shaped history: to see him still as a dear friend.

Who's Making Love? A studio shot of
Stax recording artist Johnnie Taylor.

JOHNNIE TAYLOR'S SEXUAL DILEMMA

April

Johnnie Taylor had never considered sex a dilemma. Chasing women was never his priority in life and when anyone, especially a visiting journalist, asked about his love life he talked warmly of his girlfriend, and how happy they were together. Ironically, Taylor hated the song that made him famous – 'Who's Making Love' – and from the outset struggled even to mention it by name, calling it 'that song' or 'the boogity boogity song'. He would confess his doubts to Bettye Crutcher, one of the songwriters, and she would reassure him, touching him warmly on the knee in a motherly kind of way.

Taylor had heard on the tangled and unreliable Stax grapevine that there were concerns about the song: it was too racy, potentially career damaging, and risked being banned by radio stations. Mable John, the Detroit singer whom Taylor looked up to as an authority, told him it was doubtful that Berry Gordy of the Motown Corporation would ever green-light such a song, that it was too frank and too feisty. Gordy, the morally conservative boss of Motown, was then of the belief that romance sold records but sex did not. He warned his own singers that overt sexuality was holding back black music, confining it to late-night ghetto bars and chasing away the mainstream.

The theologian Michael Eric Dyson, when writing about the late Martin Luther King, described the underlying feelings in the song as something like a 'civil war inside', a clash of values that nags away in the minds of southern men. It was a tension so powerful it had helped to shape the rise of R&B music and eaten away at the soul of almost all of black music's greatest male singers: Sam Cooke, Solomon King, Marvin Gaye and, eventually, Al Green. Religious men captivated by sex and love. Now the 'civil war inside' had begun to infect Taylor – how could he possibly sing this song and remain faithful to the traditional values he had grown up with?

Johnnie Taylor was conflicted. He knew it was a great song – that much was obvious to anyone who had ears – but a nagging doubt was to stay with him for months to come, and it touched on areas of life best left alone. According to Rob Bowman, in his authoritative history of Stax, producer Don Davis had to bully Taylor through the recording process. 'Johnnie really bitched about doing the song,' Davis claimed, and to spur the singer into action, he threatened to give it to other vocalists. 'I just kept harassing him, really. "I'm just going to give the song to Sam and Dave, you can forget it." That was a big challenge to his ego.' The song had a uniqueness that Taylor had not heard before, even if its controversial storyline still worried him, so, with a heavy heart, he went into the Stax studios one sultry spring night and belted out 'Who's Making Love' with all his formidable talent. And so it passed that a song about betrayal and illicit sex, with its choral refrain 'Who's making love with your old lady? While you are out making love', became Johnnie Taylor's biggest hit, and possibly the best song he would ever sing. It raced to number five in the *Billboard* Hot 100, dominated the R&B charts for months, and sold over a million copies in the tense summer of 1968. It was Stax's biggest-selling record of the year and gave the studio self-belief that Otis Redding's death could finally be laid to rest.

Johnnie Taylor had been a child genius on the gospel circuit in his native Arkansas. Although he had long since crossed over to secular music he still had lingering doubts about turning away from the church. Not everyone in his family had agreed with his move from gospel to soul music and they never would. Then there was the legacy thing. He had been a member of some of the finest gospel groups – first, the Highway Q.C.s, who had sung at the Reverend King's Ebenezer Baptist Church in Atlanta and included Lou Rawls and Sam Cooke as members. Then Johnnie had been hand-picked to replace the late Sam Cooke in gospel giants the Soul Stirrers. There were no greater accolades in gospel and no tougher spiritual standards to live up to. At the age of seventeen, Johnnie Taylor was already on a gilded stairway to heaven, signed to Cooke's indie label SAR Records where he recorded a charming love song about fortitude and tolerance, 'Rome Wasn't Built In A Day' (1962). It had a simple message and one that was in every sense compatible with Christian teachings. But after Sam Cooke's mysterious and unseemly death – he was shot dead during a late-night dispute with a female hotel manager in Los Angeles – SAR folded and Taylor moved to Memphis to join Stax Records, refashioning his image not through the cadences of gospel but as 'The Philosopher of Soul', a name that played on his thoughtful and reflective personality. In an industry known for its sexual misadventures and promiscuity, Taylor was remarkably loyal. He married his girlfriend Gerlean Rockett in 1970 and remained married to her until his death in 2000. Even in death, he remained faithful; he was buried next to the only other woman in his life, his mother Ida Mae Taylor, in a cemetery in Kansas.

By May, Taylor had listened to several demo versions of 'Who's Making Love'. Homer Banks sang it to him in a corridor at Stax. Bettye Crutcher, tall, elegant and alluring, sat down with him in a quiet room and explained the song's innocent origins. She had previously written another Taylor record, 'Somebody's Sleeping In My Bed' (1967), which he had recorded months before. It was mildly suggestive, but this new song took the theme of sexual infidelity much further than he was comfortable with. Then, after a week of badgering by good people and reassurances by others, Taylor, not wanting to let anyone down, agreed that he would sing it. Success was immediate, and landed Crutcher a much coveted BMI award for composition. She received the award on the same night that John Lennon was honoured for 'Hey Jude', a song set against the backdrop of Lennon's divorce from his first wife Cynthia but which magically captured the anti-war zeitgeist of 1968. Unintentionally, Crutcher's multi-award-winning 'Who's Making Love' had something tangential to say about the year, too, and particularly the last dramatic months of Dr Martin Luther King's life.

Worries that the song might fall foul of a radio ban or city-wide censorship proved unfounded but the anxieties were real enough. Of all the cities in America, Memphis had one of the worst reputations for heavy-handed censorship. The Memphis Censor Board had been formed as far back as 1921 to 'censor, supervise, regulate, or prohibit any entertainment of immoral, lewd, or lascivious character, as well as performances inimical to the public safety, health, morals, or welfare'. Their powers stretched to every area of entertainment, but the greatest sensitivities were in cinema and the recording industry. One of the city's most notorious censors, Lloyd Binford, had banned films by Charlie Chaplin, calling him a 'London guttersnipe' after hearing stories of Chaplin's passion for young teenage girls. He also banned any films starring Ingrid Bergman because she had left her husband and shacked up with Italian director Roberto Rossellini. When announcing the ban on Rossellini/Bergman's landmark 1949 film *Stromboli*, he refused to permit 'the public exhibition of a motion picture starring a woman who is universally known to be living in open and notorious adultery'. Binford was an unreconstructed segregationist who used his power to oppose any cinematic depiction of racial equality. In 1945 he blocked a stage show of the hit musical *Annie Get Your Gun* at Ellis Auditorium because there were black actors in the cast 'who had too familiar an air about them'. Mayor Loeb, the scourge of the sanitation workers, was also an ardent supporter of strict censorship, and Binford's legacy lived on in Memphis long after he himself retired. In the post-war period, as Memphis blues mutated into rock 'n' roll, the city police routinely smashed records they received complaints about. Four hundred copies of three blues recordings –

'Move Your Hand, Baby' by Crown Prince Waterford, 'Take Your Hands Off It (The Birthday Cake Song)' by Billy Hughes and 'Operation Blues' by Amos Milburn – were ritually destroyed by order of Carroll B. Seabrook, then chief of the MPD, after a complainant heard them on a jukebox in a downtown bar. Well into the sixties, R&B music was still considered to be a corrupting influence. Billie Holiday's song 'Love For Sale' was banned because it supposedly promoted prostitution, and in 1966 a mass burning of Beatles records was orchestrated by southern radio stations outraged at John Lennon's quip that the Beatles were more famous than Jesus.

Despite his anxieties about singing what was to become his greatest song, Johnnie Taylor remained faithful to pure emotional soul across his entire life. His career saw him signing for the greatest pure soul labels of the post-sixties era, first Stax, and then the short-lived Beverly Glen in Los Angeles, where he was a label mate with Bobby Womack and Anita Baker, and finally Malaco Records of Jackson, Mississippi – the self-styled 'Last Soul Company' – where he shared duties with Bobby Bland, Z.Z. Hill, Denise LaSalle, Shirley Brown, Dorothy Moore (of 'Misty Blue' fame) and Benny Latimore. His other great hit 'Disco Lady', despite the unpromising title, was a near-perfect up-tempo soul song devoid of the worst synthetic excesses of the disco era.

Johnnie Taylor's 'Who's Making Love' would become one of the most influential soul records of the era, digging down into one of the time-honoured themes of southern music: marital infidelity. Its reach was all-pervasive, breeding answer-records, rivals and reprises by a generation of deep soul artists. The self-assured Bettye Crutcher wrote some of the best of them, including 'Somebody's Been Sleeping In My Bed' (1967); Ted Taylor's self-lacerating betrayal song 'I'll Hate Myself In The Morning' (1976), composed with the peerless Sam Dees; and eventually Barbara Mason's 'From His Woman To You' (1974). Mason, a mainstream soul singer who recorded in the Philadelphia independent scene for Arctic Records during the late sixties, had signed to Buddha Records, where she toughened her persona, singing about infidelity with an uncommon frankness on songs like 'Bed And Board' and 'Shackin' Up'. In a style that was hugely innovative and daring for a black woman, she would interrupt her singing to deliver straight-talking 'raps' about romance direct to the other women in the audience. The style, which became synonymous with singers like Shirley Brown and Millie Jackson, reflected changing attitudes to sexuality and power, and, perhaps unsurprisingly, appealed in the main to female audiences. In 1975 the brilliant Shirley Brown recorded Crutcher's 'It's Worth A Whippin', an agonisingly honest song that unusually fronts up to female betrayal and is sung from the perspective of a woman who finds deeper love outside marriage. Songs of betrayal and infidelity became commonplace, and enrich southern soul in particular. While they did not begin with Taylor's 'Who's Making Love', his success emboldened others. Doris Duke's 'If She's Your Wife, Who Am I?', Ann Peebles' 'Feel Like Breaking Up Somebody's Home' and Jean Stanback's 'The Next Man' were just three among many that captured an era of changing attitudes to sexuality, women's assertiveness and infidelity.

Bettye Crutcher, in particular, challenged lyrical convention and stimulated a new candour in soul music. She was born into a city unaccustomed to black women with such forceful attitudes. 'I guess I was writing when I was about seven or eight,' she said in a rare interview with *Soul Express* magazine. 'I wrote little poems, and that was kind of an outlet for me. I was never an athlete kid, so writing has always been a friend of mine. As I got older, I wrote just as a hobby, and a friend of mine came by one day and said, "I can't believe you're writing like this and you're not doing anything with it." I said, "When the stack pile gets too high, I just throw it out."' A friend dared her to take some of her childhood poetry and stories to her audition at Stax, and she did, explaining to the seasoned songwriter David Porter how she fashioned songs from nursery rhymes and turned childhood lyrics into often demanding adult love songs. 'Somebody's Sleeping In My Bed' was a play on lines taken from the fairy tale 'Little Red Riding Hood', and 'Who's Making Love' was influenced by a record she had first heard in childhood – 'Who Takes Care Of The Caretaker's Daughter' – a 1925 radio hit by novelty jazz singer Whitey Kaufman and his Original Pennsylvania Serenaders. The song was reactivated by Bobby Darin and Johnny Mercer in 1961 when Crutcher was a teenager, and it was their versions she knew best. Homer Banks, her co-writer, has also cited the same influence, although he claims that he had heard Frank Sinatra singing the song on network television (it was more likely Bobby Darin).

Bettye Crutcher divided opinion. She was a capable singer who preferred composition and has variously been described by those who worked with her as 'pushy' and 'lazy'. Whatever the truth, she was not hugely prolific, but the songs she did write soared above the average. At last Stax had someone who was willing to tackle 'the civil war inside'. She wrote honestly about infidelity and the rampant levels of betrayal in relationships, sometimes drawing on her own life, but just as often on the lives of her friends and family. 'Call Me When All Else Fails', 'Up For A Let Down' and 'Walk On To Your New Love' all spoke of betrayal, connivance and failed love. She soon became part of Stax's best in-house writing team – We Three. 'There were two young writers, Homer Banks and Raymond Jackson, who were kind of writing together,' she recalled. 'Homer is like a think-tank and he's the ideas man. He would always come to me to finish the song, because he always wanted a female point of view, which I really liked about him.' Crutcher had a firm set of personal values, which often rubbed up against the more religious singers at Stax. She was a convinced secularist who believed her songs were about love in the real world – a world that was cruel, unforgiving and, most of all, changing. She infamously fell out with Mavis Staples of the Staple Singers for insisting that the gospel singer did not improvise religious references in one of her songs. She had, rather courageously, stopped a recording session to tell Staples to stop referring to Jesus or the Lord. It led to a tense stand-off between two very determined women. Staples ended the studio session prematurely, refused to record any more of Crutcher's songs and was never produced by her again. Bettye for her part continued to plough a path in secular soul music, one that dug deeper and more honestly into the complex world of the bedroom and rarely, if ever, looked back to religion. In time the We Three writing team – Crutcher, Banks and Jackson – became a fully fledged production company and record label called We Produce. They released records by the Temprees, cover versions such as their hectic interpretation of the standard 'At Last' and the Crutcher-inspired 'Follow Her Rules And Regulations'. We Three came to a pitiful ending in October 1972, when Jackson accidentally set fire to himself while trying to ward off rats under his home. He packed gasoline-soaked rags into a hole beneath the house unaware that he had spilled gasoline on his clothes. When he lit the match, flames engulfed him, and Jackson, who had served without incident in Vietnam, suffered seventy-five-degree burns and was rushed to a local Memphis hospital where he subsequently died.

Although it was unknown at the time, Martin Luther King's tragically short adult life was also troubled by the so-called 'civil war inside'. He shared with Johnnie Taylor a joyous Christian upbringing that valued the gospels above secular soul music, but when it came to personal and sexual fidelity, he fought a long losing battle. Coretta forgave her husband a lot, not least his obsessive pursuit of civil rights and the consequential absence from home, but she was never fully aware of the extent of his dalliances. Coretta, a gifted soprano and confident pianist in her own right, had mapped out a career as a jazz and gospel singer, but abandoned any notion of being a professional musician when she married King on the lawn of her mother's home in Marion, Alabama. She devoted the remainder of her life to her family and to her husband's memory, with a depth of devotion that her husband had fallen far short of.

Back in 1964, after the passage of the Civil Rights Act, and irked by King winning the Nobel Peace Prize, J. Edgar Hoover developed an unhealthy obsession with King's private life. In one of the most abhorrent acts in the era of surveillance in American society, Hoover instructed one of his deputies, William Sullivan, to concoct a letter as if it had been written by a disillusioned King supporter.

In view of your low grade, abnormal personal behavoir [sic] I will not dignify your name with either a Mr. or a Reverend or a Dr. And, your last name calls to mind only the type of King such as King Henry the VIII and his countless acts of adultery and immoral conduct lower than that of a beast.

King, look into your heart. You know you are a complete fraud and a great liability to all of us Negroes. White people in this country have enough frauds of their own but I am sure they don't have one at this time anywhere near your equal. You are no clergyman and you know it. I repeat you are a colossal fraud and an evil, vicious one at that. You could not believe in God and act as you do. Clearly you don't believe in any personal moral principles.

King, like all frauds your end is approaching. You could have been our greatest leader. You, even at an early age have turned out to be not a leader but a dissolute, abnormal moral imbecile. We will now have to depend on our older leaders like Wilkins, a man of character and thank God we have others like him. But you are done. Your "honorary" degrees, your Nobel Prize (what a grim farce) and other awards will not save you. King, I repeat you are done.

No person can overcome facts, not even a fraud like yourself. Lend your sexually psychotic ear to the enclosure. You will find yourself in all your dirt, filth, evil and moronic talk exposed on the record for all time. I repeat – no person can argue successfully against facts. You are finished. You will find on the record for all time your filthy, dirty, evil companions, male and female giving expression with you to your hidious [sic] abnormalities. And some of them to pretend to be ministers of the Gospel. Satan could not do more. What incredible evilness. It is all there on the record, your sexual orgies. Listen to yourself you filthy, abnormal animal. You are on the record. You have been on the record – all your adulterous acts, your sexual orgies extending far into the past. This one is but a tiny sample. You will understand this. Yes, from your various evil playmates on the east coast to [redacted] and others on the west coast and outside the country you are on the record. King you are done.

The American public, the church organizations that have been helping – Protestant, Catholic and Jews will know you for what you are – an evil, abnormal beast. So will others who have backed you. You are done.

King, there is only one thing left for you to do. You know what it is. You have just 34 days in which to do it (this exact number has been selected for a specific reason, it has definite practical significant [sic]). You are done. There is but one way out for you. You better take it before your filthy, abnormal fraudulent self is bared to the nation.

To disguise the letter's origins and to distract from any suspicion that it had been composed at the heart of the FBI in Washington, Sullivan sent an agent to Miami where the false hate mail was sent in a package to King's home in Atlanta. King's love life was unquestionably reckless, and at odds with his status as a religious leader, but what is less well known is the range of relationships he was playing off against each other in his last fateful days in Memphis.

On 3 April, King's Eastern Airways flight into Memphis was late, having been delayed on the ground in Atlanta after a credible bomb threat. On their arrival in the city, the SCLC delegation were met by board members of COME, the support group backing the sanitation workers. The Reverend Jim Lawson had allocated an activist called Tarlease Mathews to accompany King and act as his chaperone. A funeral services company, R.S. Lewis & Sons, owned by a local NAACP activist, provided a limousine and a trusted driver, Solomon Jones, at no cost to King. COME refused any support from the MPD, who they considered hostile to both the strike and to King's movement, and asked a police detail to leave the airport. Mathews had a stand-up row with police detective Ed Redditt at the airport and left him in no doubt that his presence was unwelcome. Already sporting the beginnings of an afro, Mathews was something of a local personality in Memphis – a tenacious and charismatic individual. In her teenage days, she had been arrested at the Memphis City Zoo for entering the grounds on a night designated for whites only. She subsequently filed a historic lawsuit against her arrest that in effect ended discrimination in public places in Memphis, most notably the zoo and a string of well-heeled suburban golf courses. By 1968 Mathews, now in her early thirties, was married with three young children. She came with an impeccable curriculum vitae in civil rights. She was a board member of the NAACP, an honorary probation officer and an advisor to the juvenile court, specialising in difficult and unruly black teenagers. Mathews ran her own beauty salon in South Memphis, and in a gesture of solidarity offered the sanitation workers free haircuts for the duration of the strike. King had already heard of her by reputation but they did not know each other well. Over the course of their first day in Memphis, according to various conflicting accounts, they became close enough for Mathews to invite King and his fellow SCLC executives to her Binghamton home for a steak dinner. This was immediately after he had delivered his stirring 'Mountaintop' speech to the strikers. What took place that night became a matter of serious litigious dispute. In the first edition of his patchy and not wholly reliable autobiography, *And the Walls Came Tumbling Down*, published in 1989, Ralph Abernathy made the sensational revelation that Mathews and King disappeared into a bedroom and had sex, staying in the room together until they re-emerged at 1 a.m. Although admitting to being charmed by King, Mathews felt slighted by the accusations. She was a married mother, had a reputation as a proud civil rights activist in her own right, and in her version of events accusations of a sexual liaison undermined her reputation. In 1993, under her chosen African name, Adjua Abi Naantaanbuu, Mathews sued Abernathy, his publisher Harper & Row and the book's editor Daniel Bial, seeking a total of $10 million in damages. She demanded the book be pulped and republished without 'the defamatory material'. The dispute ceased to have much relevance after April 1990, when Ralph Abernathy, the man who had lived in the gigantic shadow of Martin Luther King, died. At his funeral, Coretta King sat majestically in black, as if widowhood was her calling. Abernathy's personally scripted eulogy was read out – two brutally honest words – 'I tried'.

The allegation relating to Tarlease Mathews was not the only one; far from it. King fended off numerous insinuations and did indeed have a string of lovers. His repellent and destructive FBI files catalogue a string of extramarital liaisons that could quite easily have been accompanied by the voices of deep southern soul. It was a life populated by other women, by mundane motel rooms and by the choral refrains of Johnnie Taylor's 'Who's Making Love'. King was not naïve to the contradictions and often spoke about 'the civil war inside him' – the battle between honesty and deception, between promiscuity and fidelity, and between passing lovers and a devoted wife. The night before his assassination, when King returned in the early hours to his room at the Lorraine Motel, Abernathy claims that another woman, an unnamed second lover, was waiting for their return – a woman from the SCLC secretariat who had travelled with him on the delayed flight from Atlanta. She was supposedly in love with King but, feeling edged out of his life, had packed her bags and, after one last fight with Abernathy about King, left the motel early.

And then, most significant of all, was 'the senator', King's real extramarital love. Senator Georgia Davis Powers, the grandniece of a slave, was born in a two-room cabin near Springfield, Kentucky, and rose to become the state's first black senator. She had driven north to Memphis with A.D. King and had taken up residence in Room 201 at the Lorraine Motel, where the door remained unlocked and ajar for King to discreetly enter. By 3 a.m., after leaving Mathews' home and supposedly arguing with the second woman, King joined Davis in her room. The following day, Davis was brushing her hair at the mirror in her room when the bullet struck King down. She later confided to Ben Kamin, in his landmark book *Room 306: The National Story of the Lorraine Motel*, that 'someone was pointing to the second floor. I looked up to my left and gasped. One of Dr King's knees stuck straight up in the air, and I could make out the bottom of one foot.' She climbed the stair and saw in another room Andy Young and Ralph Abernathy, 'their faces grim, feverishly telephoning for an ambulance'. When the ambulance eventually arrived she instinctively went to climb in the back. It was Young who suggested that it may not be the best idea and guided her away from the vehicle. The job of ringing King's wife back in Atlanta fell to Jesse Jackson.

By April America's doomed war in Vietnam had reached a point of crisis. Opposition on the home front was no longer confined to students and counterculture radicals: it was now a mainstream occupation with daily news bulletins and editorials in many of the major newspapers asking searching questions of the war effort. A familiar Vietnam training chant among black GIs ended with the taunting words 'Jody's got your girl and gone'. It was a primitive rap chant, part of the African-American culture of insults known as 'the dozens'. As young men tried to undermine or unsettle their colleagues with put-downs, a new fictional character emerged from the fertile landscape of war – his name was 'low-down Jody Ryder' and he became one of the central figures in the story of southern soul. Jody, whose surname was a thinly veiled hint at his infamy, was a loathsome character who specialised in seducing married women. Supposedly excused military service because of a bogus disability, he prowled the ghetto streets and nightclubs in pursuit of women whose husbands or boyfriends were on active service in Vietnam. Jody was a by-product of the 'civil war inside' and soul music's lyrical fascination with sexual betrayal. Jody's greatest moment came via Johnnie Taylor, who by 1968 had secured an unwelcome reputation as soul music's man of sexual candour. Taylor's second major hit, 'Jody's Got Your Girl And Gone', was a 1970 Stax release written by the respected Detroit producer Don Davis, who by then had relocated in Memphis. Jody songs had been percolating in the minds of soul lyricists since the late sixties. The Chicago-based duo Mel and Tim, who were later to move to Memphis to join Stax, released 'Mail Call Time' (1969), a song about black GIs waiting in line for letters from home, in which Jody features as a threat to lasting love. A rash of Jody songs came thick and fast, each new release characterising him as an even darker and more scheming sexual predator than before, and one to watch out for: Dallas vocalist Bobby Patterson's 'Right On, Jody' (1971); Sonny Green's 'Jody's On The Run' (1971); and Skip Jackson and the Shantons' 'Promise That You'll Wait' (1970). But it was an otherwise unknown southern soul singer from Greenville, South Carolina, Ann Sexton, who was to record the most challenging variation on the Jody theme on the locally distributed Impel Records. Its message was that some self-assured women were no longer willing to wait around for their soldier-lovers to return, and for many Jody was a better option. The underground hit 'You've Been Gone Too Long', which refrained the words of Taylor's hit 'Jody's Got Your Girl And Gone', broke with the perception of women as compliant lovers twiddling their thumbs and waiting faithfully at home. Sexton, a cousin of the famous Motown artist Chuck Jackson, signed to John Richbourg's Seventy-Seven Records label, part of the southern giant Sound Stage Seven, but her greatest record was one with no budget and no expectation. 'You've Been Gone Too Long' was an instant classic that again signalled changes in the way female singers imagined relationships. Turning her back on a boyfriend who's been away too long, she takes off with Jody. It was the greatest song that Bettye Crutcher never wrote.

The day after Martin Luther King's death, as Memphis woke up to the carnage of overnight rioting and the stigma of being America's most hated city, Tarlease Mathews drove to the R.S. Lewis Funeral Home, where King's first memorial service was held. The sons of the owner – Robert Jr and Clarence Lewis – had worked diligently through the night, warding off their own tears as they groomed King's body and rebuilt his damaged face. To give them inspiration, they played recordings of King's greatest speeches. Mathews leaned over the coffin, kissed his forehead and whispered a few prayers to herself. She passed away in 2008 refusing to dignify gossip or in any way compromise King's reputation, or indeed her own.

Time magazine wrote: 'In Memphis, before it was carried south toward home, King's body lay in state in an open bronze casket, the black suit tidily pressed, the wound in the throat now all but invisible. Many of those who filed past could not control their tears. Some kissed King's lips; others reverently touched his face. A few women threw their hands in the air and cried aloud in ululating agony.' King's widow was flown by private jet from Atlanta and, in honour of her husband's last campaign, she walked silently through downtown Memphis with the striking sanitation workers, local ministers, loyal supporters, onlookers, mourners and a contingent of the staff of Stax Records. The author Hampton Sides described it eloquently: 'The march was beautiful, pitch perfect, decent. It moved forward without incident, a slow river of humanity stretching more than a dozen city blocks. Arranged eight abreast, the mourners silently plodded past department store windows that had been carefully cleared of lootable items . . . and which were replaced with discreet shrines honouring King. Coretta marched at the front, with Abernathy, Young, Jackson and Belafonte. There were clergymen, black and white, and then labour leaders and garbage workers. Farther back could be found such celebrities as Sammy Davis Jr, Bill Cosby, Ossie Davis, Dr Benjamin Spock, Isaac Hayes and Sidney Poitier.'

King's body was then transported home to Atlanta, where a memorial service was held at the Ebenezer Baptist Church. Thirteen hundred people attended. Mahalia Jackson sang King's favourite hymn, 'Take My Hand, Precious Lord' – the song he had asked Ben Branch to play for him seconds before he was shot. A private family funeral followed with King's casket loaded onto a simple wooden farm wagon and pulled by two local mules along four miles of urban roads from Ebenezer Baptist Church to King's old school, Morehouse College. Over 100,000 people lined the route and the symbolism was not lost. King's final promise was that the poor would descend on Washington, led by mule trains to create a city within a city, to bring their stories of poverty and deprivation to the seat of power.

Georgia Davis Powers was one among the many mourners. The secret lover of Dr Martin Luther King followed the funeral cortège quietly with a friend, outwardly grieving like those around her but inwardly agonising as she watched the dead leader's widow at the head of the cortège. In her memoirs written many years later she finally admitted her true feelings: 'How could I not have *seized* the moment,' she said of her first romantic encounter with King, 'no matter what my fears, no matter what the obstacle? When we were together, the rest of the world, whose problems we knew and shared, was far away . . . He trusted me, and I him, not to talk about us.' But she was not naïve about King's other liaisons, and, assuming one of the classic roles of southern soul – the other woman – she confronted them head on. 'Others have speculated about Dr King's relationships,' she wrote. 'I have no knowledge of affairs he might have had with other women; that was not what we talked about when we were together. I only know that our relationship began as a close friendship between two people sharing the same dream, working for the same goals, and it crossed the lines into intimacy.' Davis, whom King elegantly referred to as 'the senator', was haunted the remainder of her life by his last utterance to her. As they walked to her room along the motel balcony, he whispered words that not only spoke of the fleeting preciousness of intimacy but of King's dark foreboding about his own life: 'Senator, our time together is so short.'

The vicinity of the assassination. *Top left*: Jim's Grill, which opens to the back of the crime scene and becomes a hive of conspiracy. *Top right*: the rear of the rooming house where the shots apparently come from. *Bottom left*: the entrance to Canipe's Amusement Company where a police officer protects the bundle containing the murder weapon. *Bottom right*: the Lorraine Motel from the car park.

GUY CANIPE'S RECORD STORE

April

Guy Canipe ran a struggling record store at 424 Main in the street parallel to the Lorraine Motel. A fifties jukebox obstructed the glass doorway, and although it didn't entirely block the entrance, it was an object that had to be navigated as you made your way into the shop. Canipe sold second-hand slot machines, remaindered stock, and old deleted records from companies across the southern states for twenty-five cents a throw. If you bought an entire box he would do a deal, but in the main he sold singles and, less often, LPs which did not fit easily in the racks. He was a businessman but not a rich man; he made most of his modest income repairing old amusement machines, jukeboxes, pinball tables and slot machines. He had a pile of old one-arm bandits stored at the rear of the shop and periodically sold Antique Mill Five Centers to bar-owners or collectors. Among his stock of records was a living history of Stax's failures: the records that might have been and the ones that never stood a chance. He sold copies of Wendy Rene's 'Bar-B-Q', an infectious party record that missed out in the rush for feelgood pop like the Chiffons and the Ronettes. He had a small boxful of a 1962 record by the Canes, 'I'll Never Give Her Up (My Friend)', a forgotten song written back in the dying days of doo-wop by Chips Moman and Steve Cropper that lost out to better known harmony groups like the Moonglows and the Drifters, and he had a mountain of copies of Rufus Thomas's early records. Thomas had called in one day looking for a refurbished jukebox so Canipe had a snapshot taken of the two of them lounging by a reconditioned Wurlitzer. It was decaying now but was still stuck proudly to the cash register with a strip of Scotch tape that had parched in the sunlight. Canipe's Amusements was a strictly cash-only store, no credit, no loans and no paying up over instalments. According to those who knew him, Canipe was a cautious man, with a distinct drawl as if he was from Texas or the southern edges of Oklahoma, but, whatever his origins, he had diverse tastes and liked any form of music as long as it made him money.

He let his customers play the stock before buying on a small turntable at the rear of the store, but there were strictly worded notices preventing misuse; careless scratches were not good for business, and records removed from their original company sleeves sold less well, so he was fastidious about how the records should be returned to their rack. Unintentionally, Canipe had created a mausoleum of sorts, a resting place for the debris of fifties consumerism, teenage pop, primitive rockabilly and rocking blues from the days before Otis.

It was the middle of a quiet and profitless afternoon when two African-American men, Julius Graham and Bernell Finley, came into his store to look at his new stock. Canipe knew them from previous visits and left them to rummage at the back of the store as he attended to repairing a Wurlitzer 1800. It was deathly quiet. The store darkened towards the rear, which led on to an unkempt area of overgrown bushes and wild hedgerows down onto Mulberry Street and the Lorraine Motel. He periodically glanced over at the two men, looking at the size of the pile of records they had set aside, trying to convert them into cash in his mind. They seemed to be methodically searching the crates of records – for God knows what – and Canipe knew from past experience that it was best to just let them search.

Suddenly, Canipe heard a loud thud and saw a man throwing something into the shop doorway. He shouted out, and the surprise of his voice attracted Graham and Finley at the back of the store. Canipe ran to the door and his two customers followed him. All three saw a man running south on Main Street. He was of 'neat appearance, around thirty years old and wearing a dark suit'. The man climbed into a white Mustang, screeched off and disappeared before any of them could take note of the number plate. In the doorway Canipe saw what looked like a shabby old bedspread or industrial rag wrapped around what appeared to be a broom handle or, possibly, a rifle. The bundle had been dumped in a hurry and the man racing away in the white Mustang was the only man who could have thrown it there. Within less than a minute an officer from Shelby County Sheriff's Department arrived and immediately contacted MPD headquarters, who told him to seal the area and stand sentinel, but under no circumstances to interfere with the items. Canipe returned inside his store, and since the two record hunters were required to stay for questioning, they went back into the shop to continue their search.

The bundle contained much evidence to implicate the escaped prisoner James Earl Ray in King's murder, including, among other items, two cans of Schlitz beer, the 8 April edition of the Memphis newspaper, *The Commercial Appeal*, a plastic bottle of aftershave lotion, a .30-06 rifle with a serial number matching that of the weapon James Earl Ray had purchased in Birmingham, Alabama, together with ammunition and a pair of binoculars. There was also a portable radio with an identification number scratched off it. When the FBI eventually deciphered the number, it was revealed to be Ray's Missouri State Penitentiary inmate number.

For nearly a year, since he had escaped from prison hidden in a bakery van, Ray had been living an erratic and peripatetic life, using different pseudonyms and seemingly stalking King. He was an obsessive racist who had developed a deranged compulsion to kill King, but the rifle provoked a grand narrative now familiar to American assassinations: was Ray a lone gunman or the patsy in a grander conspiracy? Another question remained unanswered: to what extent did local news media aid James Earl Ray by circulating details of King's itinerary? The newspaper found in Canipe's doorway carried a front page story about Dr King, one that placed him at the Lorraine Motel at lunchtime on 3 April. Ray's fingerprint was found on the front page of the newspaper.

In less than two hours of frantic calls, the bundle that was to become a major source of evidence was removed from Canipe's doorway and taken to the downtown offices of the FBI. Special Agent Robert Jensen, a respected Danish-American officer, made an inventory of the contents and then prepared their dispatch to the FBI headquarters in Washington, DC, where a team of forensic experts awaited the evidence. Canipe, Graham and Finley were eventually allowed to leave the store and return home, on condition that they would be visited again by detectives from the MPD to give fuller official witness statements. When the investigating officers arrived at the shared home of Julius Graham (40) and Bernell Finley (24) at 804 North Fifth Street near Chips Moman's American Sound Studio, they were curious about why two men of different ages would be cohabiting. But when they inspected the premises what they found was not a domestic home but a small warehouse of records stacked neatly along the walls, and a table of dispatch materials – wrapping paper, cardboard sleeves and rolls of Sellotape. The two men were running a mail order company supplying Memphis records to dealers and collectors around the world. They had found customers far beyond Memphis that Guy Canipe could only dream of. Graham gave officers the best witness description of the fugitive, but by then James Earl Ray was long gone, travelling across state lines, dumping his white Mustang car at a housing project car park in Atlanta and then travelling north by Greyhound to Detroit and onwards to Canada, where he assumed yet another false identity and flew to London. After a two-month manhunt, Ray was arrested at Heathrow airport on 8 June and extradited to Tennessee. With powerful evidence stacked against him, he eventually pleaded guilty to the first degree murder of Dr King and was sentenced to ninety-nine years.

According to Hampton Sides' account of the immediate aftermath of King's assassination, 'the city of Memphis began to prepare for racial apocalypse'. Riot squads were on emergency alert, and across the city people were already discussing where they were when they heard the news of King's death.

Stax publicist Deanie Parker later told the magazine *Wax Poetics*: 'I was on my way to work when I heard the news over the radio. The sky got dark and the wind picked up instantly – it looked as though the world was coming to an end . . . Driving through Memphis, it was almost as if they'd put up traffic barricades – the streets were empty and there was a stillness. Nobody wanted to talk above a certain decibel. We didn't want to admit the unthinkable: that it happened *here*. By the time I got to 926 East McLemore, everybody was glued to the final news, praying and hoping that it wasn't really true.'

The Staple Singers were en route to Memphis to take part in the now legally permitted march in support of the strike the following day, and were just leaving their hotel room in Nashville when the news flickered onto a television screen. Walter Cronkite, the doyen of American broadcasting, delivered the tragic news that their friend and spiritual leader had been killed. The Staples had known King for years and had shaped their early career around the folk music of civil rights. Their early inspirational songs such as 'Freedom Highway', about the Selma marches, and 'Why (Am I Treated So Badly)?', a song sung from the childlike perspective of the Little Rock Nine, the black kids excluded from school in Little Rock, Arkansas, had both been directly about the freedom movement and written with King's campaigns in mind. Jesse Jackson once described the Staple Singers as 'unabashedly freedom fighters', and they considered King their spiritual mentor. Pops Staples cancelled their Nashville concert and the group travelled as planned to Memphis to find the city in a state of nervous breakdown. It was not a wasted journey. They returned once again to the Lorraine Motel, which was a crime scene but still open for business. After a round of meetings with Al Bell they ended their relationship with Epic Records and signed a contract with Bell. Steve Cropper, a Stax veteran, yet remarkably only twenty-six years old, became their creative producer.

At the time the news of King's death broke, Bell was at the Stax studios on East McLemore recording a Vietnam protest song, 'Send Peace And Harmony Home', by a young gospel singer Shirley Walton. According to Bell, 'She couldn't get into the song – the passion wasn't there. Then, on the sixteenth take, Homer Banks came in the studio and said, "Hey, Dr King just got killed." This was as the tape was rolling. Shirley started singing, and tears just poured from her eyes. We did a limited edition release on that and gave copies to Mrs Coretta King and the family and had it read into the Congressional Record. Afterwards we destroyed the master, because the idea wasn't to exploit the song.'

The singer-songwriter William Bell was out driving. 'I remember all of the lights in downtown Memphis were green in one direction, which was odd, but I didn't know what had happened,' he told *Wax Poetics* in a historically rich requiem by writer Andria Lisle. 'When I got to Stax, they were all talking about it, and I realized that's what was going on when I passed through downtown. We were all in shock. In the aftermath, when all the looting started, David Porter, Isaac Hayes, and I went on the radio and pleaded for calmness and for the people to not destroy the neighbourhoods. The thing that hit me the most was that Stax was one of the few buildings in the area that was left untouched. The neighbourhood held Stax Records in high esteem.'

Around 8 p.m., as tensions rose, the police received a call threatening that an explosive device had been planted at Warners Theater at 52 South Main Street. The building was evacuated, a seat-by-seat search was carried out, but no bomb was found and the incident was reported as a hoax. By 10 p.m. the theatre had opened for business again but customers were thin on the ground. Memphis producer Willie Mitchell was due to leave the city for a concert in Texas: 'The next day I had to go to Dallas for a gig, but there were riots all over town,' he told Andria Lisle. 'The National Guard came in, but folks were burning up shit all over downtown! I wanted to make my gig, so I left some neighbourhood winos to take care of the place. I just picked 'em up on the street, bought 'em a case of wine, and locked 'em in the studio! Man, I was scared when I drove back across the Mississippi River after my gig – I'd heard on the news that they were burning down buildings all over Memphis. I turned on Lauderdale, and I could see the front of the building. Then I saw that the door was still locked. I went in, and everything was miraculously still here. All of the winos had passed out, except for one who was sitting in a chair making sure nothing bad happened. I gave those drunks some more wine and let 'em go home again!'

Isaac Hayes, always politically engaged on the fringes of the civil rights movement, joined a group of friends and formed the Memphis Black Knights to combat police brutality, job discrimination and inadequate housing for blacks. The organisation, like many at the time, had its origins in a North Memphis teenage street gang before garnering the support of DJs at radio station WDIA. As the gang members grew up and became more aware of local needs, they transformed into a community activist group. Hayes and other Black Knights who had studied at Manassas High School, a school with a formidable music history, were part of a delegation that lobbied the mayor against curfews. In the aftermath of the troubles, Hayes performed at a benefit concert at Hunter College in New York for the Soledad Brothers, a group of prison protestors in the California penal system. 'I contributed my talents to that because they *were* political prisoners,' he told *Rolling Stone* magazine. 'This is where I'm at. I'm not the turn-the-other-cheek kind of person, no. But I believe in using tact and intelligence.'

Bettye Berger, a local artists' agent, was by then president of her own company, Continental Artists Attractions, representing Joe Tex, B.J. Thomas and the Bar-Kays. She was at home at the time and had planned to go shopping at the Whitehaven Plaza near Elvis Presley's Graceland mansion. 'But there wasn't a soul there,' she remembers. 'The city was eerily quiet. I had a plane full of artists coming in, the first big money for my agency, and everything was cancelled.' It was a critical time for one of her best artists, Joe Tex, who was in Memphis to record a beer commercial for the San Antonio Pearl Brewery. At the time Tex, who was signed to the Nashville soul label Dial, had only recently converted to Islam and was unsure whether he should be recording a beer commercial or indeed whether he should be hanging out with the notorious

Wilson Pickett and a young and reckless Bobby Womack. It was an ominous atmosphere and the session was eventually cancelled. Bettye Berger remembers: 'Tanks were rolling down Lamar Avenue, which was scary. It was just a sad, sad day.'

The sad, sad day erupted into a violent night. Riots flared in over a hundred cities across America. In Memphis, the military and the police circled neighbourhoods on and around East McLemore, assuming it would be a likely trouble spot. Looting and wanton destruction began in earnest as thousands of young blacks took to the streets. At first the violence was low-level – windows smashed, liquor stores looted and bricks thrown at passing cars – but then the sky lit up with a satanic rage. A building supplies company on North Second Street was torched. As firemen tried to fight the blaze at O.W. Ferrell's yard, police carrying sub-machine guns tried to ward off mobs of protestors. Flames leapt over three hundred feet into the air and as the inferno swept through reinforced roofing and a tyre store the smoke became thicker, darker and hellish. Dense pungent black clouds engulfed the skyline and jets of gasoline flames darted up into the air. Walls of boxes stored at the rear of Leone's Liberty Cash Grocery at 485 Vance were set alight, burning through electricity cables and endangering a nearby apartment block. There were reports of theft, but by comparison with previous urban disturbances they were small in number – as if stealing property was less important than destroying it. It was a riot that was subtly different to the summer of 1967; as if a young generation had come onto the streets of the city not for material gain but to teach Memphis a lesson. The police were better organised, too, and much had been learned from previous disturbances. Rather than act as a source of antagonism, police units often hung back to allow small incidents to run their course. The city arranged for street lights to be switched off, knowing that darkness was less attractive to onlookers than the illumination of shop windows and the theatrical glare of busy intersections. They shot at neon advertising signs to discourage crowds and were instructed to refuel at commercial gasoline stations rather than waste time returning to base. Although the MPD's despised tactical units were on the streets, they were under strict instructions not to aggravate relatively small incidents. Heavy-handed policing had been the spark that had ignited riots in Newark, Cleveland and Detroit in the previous twelve months, and the MPD, at least superficially, had learned its lesson. Tactical patrol units and paramilitary National Guardsmen were called and marshalled under the control of Colonel Hollis Williams of the battle-hardened 3rd Brigade of the 30th Armored Division. Again, the instructions were to be visible but to hold back and ignore smaller attacks on corner liquor stores, in order to be ready for serious rioting: pathetic drunkenness was tolerable but mass armed insurrection was not. The National Guard were rushed to Springdale and Howell in North Memphis, where police cars were shot at, and further reports came in that police officers were isolated in the Johnson and Tillman area and were at risk of serious injury. Only then were tactical units instructed to act. Unit 16 was directed to assist the isolated patrolmen, who had become separated from their vehicle by an encircling mob. As soon as the officers were rescued the tactical unit was told to retreat from the streets, take up a disguised position east of Crump Boulevard, and await further instructions. The hope was that the flames of anger would recede with the night.

The compromised mayor, Henry Loeb, was driving to a speaking engagement at Ole Miss, the famed University of Mississippi. His car was heading south on Highway 51 when he saw a car occupied by Sheriff William Morris and stopped to ask him about a phone call he had made to the mayor earlier in the day. Thus it was by sheer chance that he found out that King had been shot. He instantly made the decision to cancel his speaking engagement. Loeb was now at the very heart of a darkening drama. Death threats had flooded into his office and into the editorial teams at most of the major newspapers. By refusing to settle with the sanitation workers and encouraging scab labour to take to the streets of the city, Loeb had made himself one the most despised men in the city. Although he had played no part in the death of Martin Luther King and has never featured even in the most outlandish conspiracy theories, many felt that he had created the circumstances that made the assassination possible. Seriously at risk, Loeb agreed with the police that his family should be moved from their suburban home to a secret safe house. Tables from around his office were turned over by staff and used as makeshift shields by the windows. Anxiety greeted every phone call and every knock on the exterior doors. A heavily armed Praetorian Guard made up of police officers and private security encircled the beleaguered mayor and shadowed his every move. The name Loeb was dirt. Throughout the night, anyone who shared his surname, including distant relatives, were threatened on the phone, and his brother's chain of laundry stores, which had been targeted by strikers earlier in the year, were laid to waste. The Invaders put out instructions through their grapevine of supporters that Loeb laundries were a legitimate target, more valuable to the cause than attacking convenience stores and stealing packs of cigarettes.

Mayor Loeb, aware of his toxic reputation, felt it was his moral duty to go on live television to make public service announcements. Driven more by a misplaced sense of civic duty, rather than ego, he was taken by police guard around Memphis's local television stations, fully cognisant of the fact that for many he was the problem not the solution. Loeb had not eaten all day, and when the tour of television stations was over he suggested a late-night meal. But every café, bar and restaurant in the city was closed under the terms of curfew he himself had ordered. Loeb ended his night of hell curled up in his bunkered office eating a dry salami sandwich bought from a police station vending machine. The power he had once craved was now reduced to pathetic ineffectualness. Within a matter of days Loeb's trademark forcefulness capitulated and his opposition to the Sanitation Workers Strike crumbled. The union branch Local 1733, unbeaten and unbowed, had won, and jubilant members ratified the agreement with the city at a meeting held on 16 April in Clayborn Temple. The strikers cheered, stamped their feet, and hugged one another in a prolonged victory demonstration. The celebration, however, was tinged with sadness as it was recalled how Martin Luther King was assassinated while in Memphis to aid the strike. 'Let us never forget that Martin Luther King, on a mission for us, was killed in this city,' Jerry Wurf, the international president of the strikers' union the AFSCME told the hushed meeting. 'He helped bring us this victory.'

John Gaston Hospital had its busiest night ever as minor casualties from the riots and the gravely ill lined the crowded corridors. Many companies, even those geared to night work, had closed, and very few openly disobeyed the curfew, which was scheduled to last until 5 a.m. the following morning. Isaac Hayes told local Memphis journalist Andria Lisle, in her impeccable oral history of the night *I Know a Place*, that Stax staff had called city hall and the local police to get permission to work through the curfew. 'The National Guard was lined up and down every street, because there was rioting all over town. He said, "One of them almost shot my buddy Benny Mabone when he opened the studio door. This soldier levelled on him – he was a young kid, and he didn't know any better. [Benny] was like, "No, no, we're in the studio, man. We got permission. Drop your rifle." Deanie Parker worked on, as did many other staff members. She told Lisle that she was furious about the curfew. "I thought it was overkill," she said. "Of all the places in the community, Stax was an integrated organization . . . The curfew interfered with the lifestyle we enjoyed here, which was so atypical of Memphis. The National Guard set up their bivouac right on the corner, but Bettye Crutcher and I decided to defy them, so we stayed in the studio. We did take some things seriously – we carted out all of the master tapes, because we were afraid of looters. Someone torched Jones' Big Star right across the street, where David Porter used to sack groceries. Later that night we got scared, because we didn't know how we were gonna get out of there and go home."'

Mrs Loree Bailey, the fifty-two-year-old wife of Walter Bailey, the owner of the Lorraine Motel, had collapsed in the immediate aftermath of King's assassination. She knew King well and had prepared his room on countless occasions. On hearing the fatal shot and seeing his crumpled body, she retreated back into the motel's staff living quarters and collapsed with what was a suspected cerebral haemorrhage. A doctor claimed that 'the shock had been too much for her'. Unconscious, she was rushed to the Baptist Hospital where she died having never regained consciousness, the second and forgotten fatality at the Lorraine Motel that night. She was buried a few days later at the city's New Park Cemetery.

In Washington, wearied by the war in Vietnam, President Johnson called an emergency meeting of his key staff. He had only recently announced his intention to retire and not seek re-election. Although he privately despised King for opposing the war and publicly opposing his policies, he was astute enough to know that the assassination had potentially catastrophic repercussions that could damage race relations for decades to come. LBJ stood solemnly on the White House lawn broadcasting to the nation and beyond to the international community. He invited all Americans to search their hearts and to abandon the path of racial division, to 'reject the blind violence that had struck down Dr King'. His words fell on deaf ears. Within walking distance of the White House, rioting was already encroaching on Capitol Hill. According to local newspaper *The Washingtonian*, the riot had its epicentre in DC's downtown ghetto areas. 'At the busy intersection of 14th and U streets in Northwest DC – the heart of the District's black community – the news arrived on teenagers' transistor radios.' This was the area of the city where soul music had thrived. It was the home of the famous Howard Theater; the neighborhood that had once housed DC's most gifted vocalists, from Marvin Gaye to Sam Moultrie; the neighborhood where Al Bell and Eddie Floyd had set up their independent soul label before they were drawn inexorably to Memphis; and the ghetto which had once been the creative hub of the doomed Shrine Records, an independent soul label whose inventory perished in the riots. According to reports, 'people began to gather at the intersection, which was near the Washington office of King's Southern Christian Leadership Conference. Rioters, many of them teenagers, smashed windows, looted stores, and started fires. They tossed Molotov cocktails into buildings and threw bottles, bricks, and rocks at firefighters who tried to put out the blazes. The mood was part anger, part exhilaration.'

The crime writer George Pelecanos, a child witness to the DC riots, watched the exhilaration morph into a self-destructive loss. 'The people who lost the most,' he claimed, 'were the people who lived in those neighborhoods. H Street was black Washington's shopping corridor. You had Sears, Morton's, Woolworth, and they employed thousands of black Washingtonians. All those jobs were gone, and people had no place to shop. Nobody went downtown any more. They were afraid.'

Back in Memphis, on the morning after King's assassination, Frank R. Ahlgren, editor of *The Commercial Appeal*, announced a $25,000 reward for information leading to the capture of the killer. It came with the veneer of public service but was at best opportunistic, at worst guilt money. The paper had pilloried King in editorials and published scathing cartoons prior to his death. The editor was an unwavering supporter of Mayor Loeb in his opposition to the strike and complied with FBI and police requests to place stories critical of civil rights. But, in fairness to the paper, it published a strident front-page editorial that raged against violence and described the killing as 'a tragedy for Memphis'.

Meanwhile, the hunt for James Earl Ray intensified. Within days the FBI were focusing a strand of their investigation on a bar called the Grapevine Tavern on Arsenal Street, St Louis, owned by Ray's brother John Larry Ray. The bar had opened recently, on New Year's Day 1968, and had quickly become a magnet for criminals, disaffected Ku Klux Klan members and supporters of George Wallace, the segregationist politician and American Independent Party candidate, whose headquarters were on the same block. James Earl Ray had been an ardent supporter of Wallace's presidential campaign, and the presence of Klan members hanging out at the Grapevine gave the investigation team serious pause for thought. There was a bitter irony in this line of enquiry. Although the FBI had always kept a close eye on Klan activity, much of their recent focus via the COINTELPRO programme and the Memphis-based Operation Lantern Spike focused on black militant groups like the Panthers, the Blackstone Rangers and the Memphis Invaders. The files on Martin Luther King held in Atlanta under his code name 'Zorro' far outweighed those on local Klan activity. In a desperate bid to bring balance to their efforts, the FBI targeted Klansmen everywhere, heaping intense pressure on the Mississippi Klan especially, who had a history of bomb-making and were active in blowing up synagogues and killing black activists. A Georgia lawyer, Jesse Stoner, the founder of the National States Right Party

(NSRP) and publisher of the fascist newspaper *The Thunderbolt*, was an early Klan suspect (later he was to become James Earl Ray's attorney). Stoner, who ran for governor in Georgia in 1970 and once described Hitler as 'too moderate', had often called for King's assassination, but he had an airtight alibi on the night of the murder: he was being shadowed by FBI agents as he addressed an NSRP chapter at a Klansman's barbershop in Meridian, Mississippi.

It was into this febrile atmosphere that a young singer, Linda Lyndell, arrived in Memphis. She may have been one of the most talented and least fortunate singers who ever set foot in the city. Lyndell's reputation preceded her. Her real name was Linda Rowland and she was born and raised in Gainesville, Florida, where she became a gifted child singer on the southern gospel circuit, often the only white girl in a black choir. By her mid teens she was singing in a garage band, the Rare Breed, a campus band from University of Florida, and a house band in Gainesville's first strip bar, Dub's cocktail lounge. Lyndell converted to R&B and toured regularly with some of the most sexually ferocious groups of the era, including southern soul balladeer Gene Middleton, the Ike and Tina Turner Revue and James Brown's Famous Flames. Memphis mythology has it that she was recommended to Stax by Otis Redding prior to his death, but Lyndell had performed on stage with numerous Stax acts, including the Bar-Kays and Sam and Dave, and had been a preferred pick-up artist when Stax acts toured her native Florida. Lyndell was strikingly good-looking and had a voice that could shift in texture from satin to gravel. In an industry that was still notoriously conservative about soul music, she fulfilled a latent fantasy, that somewhere in America a white girl would emerge who could sing like Aretha and look like Nancy Sinatra. Lyndell offered that possibility. One Stax promotional photograph, taken at midnight, shows her in a sultry pose, wearing a tight satin catsuit and saturated in neon lights. Behind her is a drive-in motel and a 1967 Pontiac GTO. You don't have to be a master semiotician to read the signs of strident sexuality.

As a young woman Lyndell met a Florida DJ, David 'The Demon' Newman, from Jacksonville, who was a cousin of vocalist Jackie Moore and a talented songwriter in the South. It was Newman who recommended her to Stax. Her debut single, written and produced by Newman, was called 'Bring Your Love Back To Me', and it was released on Volt Records, coincidentally in the week of Redding's death. The song stiffed. Then, in 1968 she returned to Memphis for a second studio session, this time recording the stunning 'What A Man', a driving R&B classic later recorded by the rap team Salt-N-Pepa. In the week of its release, in part driven by the sexually provocative images of a young white woman working in a black idiom, she started to receive death threats from a Ku Klux Klan branch in northern Florida. The threats came first in poison pen letters and then by sinister phone calls. Posters of her appearances were defaced and Stax received threatening packages stuffed with Klan literature. Understandably traumatised, Lyndell retreated, turning down lucrative bookings and not pushing the song hard enough promotionally. She eventual left the music scene and returned to her native Gainesville to escape the glare of the recording industry.

On 8 April 1968, an estimated 42,000 silently marched through Memphis led by Coretta Scott King, the executives of the SCLC, union leaders and Stax staff members including Isaac Hayes and John Gary Williams of the Mad Lads. It was a sombre funereal occasion but some banners demanded that the intransigent Mayor Loeb settle the strike. Embarrassed by the aftermath of the assassination, Loeb had very slightly shifted ground, and negotiators had reached a deal that allowed the city council to recognise the union and guarantee a better wage. The deal brought the strike to an end, but the union had to threaten another strike several months later, to press the city to follow through with its commitment. The 1968 strike was won, but it had left a sorry legacy that split a divided city even further.

King's assassination fractured already tense racial relationships in Memphis and put intolerable strain on Stax's once enlightened policy of studio integration. Many said then, and have since, that the events of 1968 irrevocably changed the atmosphere. Al Bell's promotion up through the ranks of the company and into the role of shareholder alienated some and angered others. Bell told the writer Robert Gordon that King's death had strengthened his will to drive an era of black empowerment at the company. 'What hit me with Dr King's death was that it was time to start moving with economic empowerment.' But Bell also admitted that others felt differently, struggling to take anything positive from the times, and that a kind of collective pain settled on Stax. 'Dr King's murder changed our lives and our way of living, but at Stax it didn't change how we interacted with each other,' he told writer Andria Lisle. 'It's difficult to articulate how it affected us, but if I had to narrow it to one word, I would say "pain". Everybody – Black and White – was sad. Remember, we went to the Lorraine Motel and the Four-Way Grill together, we ate together, swam together, and slept together. Everyone could relate. Then, all of a sudden, the White people working at Stax were concerned about the Black people on the outside who wanted to hurt them because of their skin color.'

It's a well-worn truism that grief is like a fingerprint, unique and highly personal. Some claim that the pain came with a divisiveness that had not really been visible at Stax before. Isaac Hayes, who had joined many of King's campaigns and led the Stax delegation at his funeral, pushed for equal employment at Stax. Hayes claims that he told Jim Stewart, 'This company primarily caters to the R&B market. You've got to represent us – you've got to have more Blacks in here working in other jobs besides the musicians. I got him to hire a Black secretary, Earlie Byles, and Al Bell got a Black secretary, too.' But what neither Bell nor Hayes admitted was that their advocacy of greater black ownership and the drive for greater recruitment of black staff left many white people within the company feeling exposed and vulnerable. Producer Steve Cropper and the bassist Donald 'Duck' Dunn, both Stax loyalists, admitted to feelings of vulnerability and insecurity about how to react to the new mood.

'I was devastated,' agent Bettye Berger said. 'Here we'd built up relationships with people working together, playing together, loving each other, and worshipping together, and I thought it was going to be ruined. I didn't feel any different, I just felt sorry. I felt guilty, too. I wanted to walk up to everybody and apologize. Right afterwards, I went to some NAACP meetings – Rufus Thomas's wife sold me a membership. I got some bad vibes there. That bothered me, but it didn't kill me.'

Jim Stewart tried hard to cling to what made Stax unique. He told a reporter that its specialness was bound up in a mythologised era of racial harmony: 'Because we've learned to live together at Stax Records, we've reaped many material benefits. But most of all we've acquired peace of mind. When resentments break out all over the nation, we pull our blinds and display a sign that reads: "Look what we've done together."' It was romantic but true, and it had come perilously close to being snatched from the studios of Memphis.

Most people agree that King's death bored deep into the minds of the creative staff at Stax. Some writers wanted to bring more anger into their lyrics, others felt more of a sense of loss. Isaac Hayes said at the time: 'My whole world collapsed; I couldn't create or do anything. It took me a year to get back in full form.' Booker T. Jones, among the most introspective of people at Stax, felt the death all but ended their bond with the Lorraine Motel. 'It wasn't just that it happened in Memphis,' he once said. 'It was an institution for us. And so it couldn't have been closer had he been shot at 926 McLemore.' William Bell, who had spent the first part of the sixties in Vietnam and had long harboured the idea of setting up his own label, moved to Atlanta where he founded the critically respected Peachtree Records. 'I didn't have the heart to stay in Memphis,' he said solemnly. 'Booker T. and I left together. He went to L.A., and I came to Atlanta.' He felt a sense of personal bereavement that he was escaping the city he had grown up in. Memphis had tested William Bell to the limit, and when he packed his bags he said forlornly that he couldn't imagine why he would ever come back.

Guy Canipe's store lasted a few years longer but it, too, closed, a victim of the owner's age and a fading interest in reconditioned jukeboxes. The doorway lay dormant for many years as Main Street festered, and the only use it served was as a shelter for drunken panhandlers escaping from the winter winds. It would be decades before it would find a new purpose. Remarkably, it is now the gift store for the National Civil Rights Museum, a centrepiece tourist attraction for those many millions of pilgrims who want still to witness the place where King died.

In the courtyard of the Sorbonne in Paris, 30 May 1968, where students and teachers have been in occupation since 13 May.

BOOKER T. JONES AND THE PARIS RIOTS

30 May

It was by a series of bizarre coincidences that Maoist revolutionary students came to influence the life of Booker T. Jones. When the phone rang at the Stax offices, no one had ever heard of Jules Dassin, but the phone call triggered an assignment that would take Jones to the heart of Europe, into a cauldron of intense political upheaval, and lure Stax into the high-wire world of commercial cinema. Nothing Jones had witnessed in his young life in Memphis – even the riots in the aftermath of King's killing – came close to matching what he was about to see in Paris.

Booker T. Jones was the closest Stax music had to a prodigy: the son of a high-school science teacher, through his protected child-hood he mastered a wide range of instruments before embarking aged fourteen on the life of a professional musician, working in nightclub bands and sitting in on Stax sessions that at times were strictly adult-only. Like Little Stevie Wonder at Motown in Detroit, Jones was a precociously gifted kid who could take his place alongside the most seasoned of professionals. His mother worried about the cynical and hard-bitten environments he sometimes worked in but encouraged him to be the best. It was a remarkable achievement in child-rearing; Jones became one of the precious few child stars who survived the journey with his ego and emotions intact. The CBS publicist and jazz aficionado Bob Altshuler wrote fulsomely of the young Jones on the sleeve notes of the 1962 album *Green Onions*: '[His] musical talents became apparent at a very early age. By the time he entered high school, Booker was already a semi-professional, and quickly recognised as the most talented musician in his school. He was appointed director of the school band for four years, and in addition, organised the school dance orchestra which played for proms throughout the Mid South. In the classroom, he concentrated on the studies of music theory and harmony . . . Booker's multiple activities earned him a coveted honour, that of being listed in the students' *Who's Who of American High Schools.*'

Booker T. Jones Jr, blessed with a name inherited from his father and from the great Negro educator, came to the attention of Stax's Jim Stewart while still at Booker T. Washington High School, a place that he joked had in part been named after him. He took occasional work as a studio musician, appearing as backing instrumentalist on many sessions, hauling around a huge variety of instruments with him, knowing he could do a decent or a spectacular job, depending on what was required on the night. Jones was only in tenth grade when he first stepped into the studios of what was then Satellite Records in South Memphis. He had been hired on a one-day cash-in-hand contract to play the baritone saxophone on 'Cause I Love You', a song written by Rufus Thomas and his daughter Carla. But the big break came in the early months of 1962, when Jones adapted a traditional twelve-bar Memphis blues and disrupted it with his nagging organ sound, to co-create 'Green Onions', one of the most famous instrumentals ever recorded. Although his parents had sparked his obsession with music, buying, salvaging or borrowing instruments to widen his range, it was always conditional on completing his education, and, unlike almost every other rising star in the cut-throat world of R&B, he followed the path of Carla Thomas – who attended Howard University in Washington at the height of her success – and interrupted the very real prospects of global fame to complete a degree at Indiana University. To maintain momentum, he returned to Memphis at weekends to record at Stax, where he was a featured instrumentalist behind the major recording artists of the time, including Otis Redding and Wilson Pickett. According to all his extant educational reports, Jones thrived at Indiana University and managed to balance two distinctly different lives: he joined the university's symphony orchestra as a trombonist and rehearsed amidst the gothic beauty of the Bloomington campus, and then shuttled back to Memphis to play organ in the Stax studios among the boarded buildings and decaying stores of McLemore Avenue. On his graduation, Jones had numerous offers to play with professional orchestras, but he defied his tutors, turning down the grand halls of classical music in favour of the grittier world of R&B, and rejoining his own group, the M.G.'s. Although he played almost every instrument in the orchestral range, it was the Hammond B-3 organ with which Jones became synonymous. Journalist Marc Myers claims that it was Booker T. who 'transformed the Hammond B-3 organ from a gospel instrument featured primarily behind jazz and blues saxophonists to a rock-soul keyboard that influenced several generations of rock and soul musicians'. The Hammond was a ghetto centrepiece, made famous first in churches, then gospel concerts, but it then betrayed the Good Lord and moved into R&B nightclubs and featured on scratchy jazz releases, most famously by Jimmy Smith and Brother Jack McDuff. For years, the instrument was associated with cheapness and availability, and sold in low-budget stores and pawnshops on Beale Street. The organist John Medeski once described the Hammond organ as 'the poor man's big band'. But for all its associations with the ghettos of the early sixties, Jones and his cultured control of his keyboard transformed its image yet again, and with Stax's increasing reach his relentless hard-edged organ attack came to define a subgenre of soul music which Geoffrey Stokes in his book *Rock of Ages* described as *pure* Memphis – 'spiritually . . . midway between New Orleans and Detroit'. It was a sound that would infect clubs across the world, driven by youth culture, the Modernists and amphetamine soul.

Stax session musician Sandy Kay, who came to the company at a time when the Detroit vocalist Darrell Banks was recording an album, was in awe of Jones. In his diary he described watching every small gesture he made. 'One of the things I remember is how much I wanted to get to know Booker. I wanted to play music with him, I wanted him to teach me to play better. But it was difficult because he was around so infrequently. That was a disappointment to me. Several times, I'd sit quietly in his office, watching him at his desk writing string charts – directly from his head to the paper, not even referring to the piano to try out the lines or harmonies. That totally amazed me. Booker was, and still is today, a rare combination of a schooled, educated musician, and also a "feel" player that can get down into a groove effortlessly. If this sounds like a case of hero worship, maybe that's because it is.'

It was the juddering and edgy urban sound pioneered by Booker T. Jones that Jules Dassin wanted to capture for *Uptight*, destined to become one of the most controversial and seminal films of its time. Dassin had long harboured a desire to remake and modernise John Ford's classic film *The Informer* (1935). A Paramount executive, nervous about a remake of a political film, supposedly said, 'I'm crazy, but we'll do it,' and allocated a budget of two million dollars. The events of 1968 heightened Dassin's passion and sharpened his focus, and he began to imagine a remake of the film with a black cast, shifting the theme of betrayal away from the original context of Irish republicanism to the politics of Black Power and insurgent groups like the Black Panthers and the Memphis Invaders. Not fully aware of this radical shift of thought, the funders at Paramount continued to reluctantly support the film. It was never a priority for the company and fell off the studio's radar. Using his Paris apartment and working surreptitiously from a rented home on Fifth Avenue in New York, which his new wife Melina Mercouri had rented during her stint on Broadway, Dassin immersed himself in black politics, culture and music. He was keen to cast the young black actor Ossie Davis in a leading role, but he was tied to a tight filming schedule in Mexico and recommended his wife, the emergent black actress Ruby Dee. She ultimately starred in the film but, more importantly, became the authentic voice in the scripting process. Dassin wanted a film that would burn with the passion of the ghetto. Dee convinced him not to set the film in a fictional Harlem or a grieving Memphis, but in her home town of Cleveland, Ohio, in a notorious neighbourhood called Hough. Her logic was simple. Hough had been the site of destructive riots in the summer of 1966 but was rarely the backdrop to feature films. Hough was also home to one of the great desegregated nightclubs of the era, Leo's Casino, where the Supremes, Marvin Gaye, John Coltrane, Ray Charles and the Temptations had headlined. The club had nearly been engulfed by the riots, and as Dee recounted the story to Dassin, he became obsessed with finding a soundtrack to the film. Dee and Dassin played music incessantly throughout the scripting sessions, and although they had no specific plans to recruit Booker T. and the M.G.'s, they agreed that it was worth commissioning Stax to provide musicians who could oversee the soundtrack. When the request first came to the McLemore studios it was directed to Al Bell's office, who in turn recommended Jones, sensing that his multi-instrumental skills were best suited to shaping a soundtrack. Although Jones had worked in almost every conceivable area of contemporary black music he had never scored a film. Through Stax's new connections in Hollywood, Jones flew there briefly to meet the urbane master of musical soundtracks, Quincy Jones, who taught him about sequencing, layering and playback techniques. After an intense round of tutorials Booker T. and the M.G.'s then flew on to Paris for an initial period of post-production.

With Memphis shell-shocked by the assassination of Martin Luther King and the city still on high alert, Jones boarded the plane for Paris believing he was leaving social turmoil far behind. He imagined a Paris of high culture and had even planned to visit some of the city's great symphony halls. He was genuinely taken aback that his plans were thrown into disarray. Paris, a city used to political upheaval, had become engulfed by well-organised cadres of Maoist-inspired students and hardened strikers, who had taken to the streets and were on the brink of winning control of the city in a rebellious time now known simply as May '68.

On his first few nights in Paris, Jones stayed with Dassin and his wife. Looking out the windows at the troubled arrondissement below, Jones watched the Paris uprisings close up, as students built barricades, fought with riot police and led mass demonstrations through the streets. According to an anonymous student's eye-witness account of the first days of the Paris uprisings, 'the rue Gay-Lussac still carries the scars of the "night of the barricades". Burnt-out cars line the pavement, their carcasses a dirty grey under the missing paint. The cobbles, cleared from the middle of the road, lie in huge mounds on either side. A vague smell of tear gas still lingers in the air. At the junction with the rue des Ursulines lies a building site, its wire mesh fence breached in several places. From here came material for at least a dozen barricades: planks, wheelbarrows, metal drums, steel girders, cement mixers, blocks of stone. The site also yielded a pneumatic drill. The students couldn't use it, of course – not until a passing building worker showed them how, perhaps the first worker actively to support the student revolt. Once broken, the road surface provided cobbles, soon put to a variety of uses.'

As Paris burned, Jones soon learned that Dassin and his wife were committed political activists and fully in support of the striking workers and enraged students. Melina Mercouri was a fervent opponent of the Greek military junta and became the international face of Greek resistance in exile. As a consequence of her public stance, she was stripped of her citizenship and her property in Greece was seized. But her determination and the influence she had on Dassin was electrifying. As they navigated their way through barricades to the editing suite Jones was given a running commentary of the events and the many factions that had taken to the streets. It was in marked contrast to his first European visit when he had been a featured act on the famous Stax/Volt European tour of 1967, appearing at the Olympia Theatre in Paris, supporting Otis Redding. For very different reasons, Dassin and Mercouri were living in forced exile in Paris, and were passionate that the film they wanted to make would become the first feature film to reflect the waves of anger that were surging through America's inner-city ghettos. They told Jones they wanted a soundtrack of the streets, the Stax sound, but infused with urgency, anger and the hope of change. It was the beginning of a project that would remain controversial for decades yet to come, before its true creative ambitions burned out.

Jules Dassin was a Jewish New Yorker who had been an actor in ARTEF, the militant Yiddish theatre company that emerged against the backdrop of the Depression of the thirties and was one of the great forces of progressive ideas in Manhattan's Lower East Side. He moved into cinema, first directing short films and then becoming one of the pioneers of film noir such as *The Naked City* (1948) – 'a painstaking procedural thriller whose principal character, filmed wholly on location, was New York City itself' – and *Thieves' Highway* (1949), an intense modern thriller set unusually in the rural farmlands of central California. Dassin's career was seriously derailed in the paranoid fifties when he was identified as a communist by the now notorious McCarthy witch hunts and blacklisted from working in the film industry. He relocated first to London and then to Paris, defying the American ban, and after a lengthy hiatus directed the multi-award-winning film *Rififi* (1955), remarkable for its lengthy and much copied opening heist sequence, where not a word is spoken. In Paris Dassin met and married Melina Mercouri, who had recently been exiled from her native Greece. At the height of the coup d'état there, Mercouri had been performing on stage on Broadway and immediately began a spirited vocal campaign to reinstall democracy in Greece. Nightly throughout 1968, she raged against the generals and received standing ovations from crowds who barely knew there was a military junta in her homeland. It was Mercouri who pressurised Dassin into challenging his status as a banned film-maker in America, and through a series of intermediaries he managed to convince Paramount to develop and seed-fund his remake of John Ford's *The Informer*. The story of betrayal, in which an Irish rebel acts as an informer and sells out a close friend in order to gain passage to America, obsessed Dassin. He, too, had been betrayed – to McCarthy's House Un-American Activities Committee (HUAC) in 1948 – by the tragic Edward Dmytryk, who, facing exile and impoverishment, eventually named those in

Booker T. Jones and The Paris Riots   171 the film industry, including Dassin, he knew to be members of the Communist Party.

Responding intuitively to the assassination of Martin Luther King, Dassin headed to Atlanta and filmed part of the official funeral cortège and then travelled on to Memphis and Cleveland, where he filmed the aftermath of rioting and the burnt-out ghetto buildings. As he travelled from city to city, like a guerrilla film-maker, he gathered raw documentary footage that would add edge and authenticity to the finished film. In one scene a group of radicals are watching television coverage of King's funeral and the script picks up from the solemn images. 'The man from love got his head shot off,' says the character Jeannie, played by Janet MacLachlan. 'And all those people learned nothing,' says the organisation's co-leader B.G., played as an austere Afrocentric militant by a rising star of black cinema, Raymond St Jacques. 'Death is a fast teacher. They'll learn, it's clearer now.'

Uptight opened to mixed reviews. Most critics could see its intent to create a breakthrough film that was dramatically honest about ghetto politics and the insurrectionary Black Power activists, but there was criticism for some of the acting, mostly focusing on the melodramatic and odd performance by the emotionally tortured informer, a character called Tank played by Julian Mayfield. Like Dassin, Mayfield was a leftist intellectual who was at the time under FBI surveillance suspected of communist agitation. Mayfield's performance was a frustrating flaw in the film that Dassin himself recognised. He had tried to secure the services of the talented young actor James Earl Jones as Tank, but he was unavailable and the compromise of casting a friend always irked Dassin.

The phlegmatic Roger Ebert was one of several prominent critics who saw real value in the film, but in his regular column in the *Chicago Sun-Times* he questioned the motives of its backers, stating that 'it's remarkable that a major studio financed and released this film'. What he did not know was that Paramount did everything in its power to dump the movie. Scared off by its themes and its frankness, they got cold feet and refused to order up enough prints. The cinemas that were keen to show it struggled to get access to the film and many more movie chains, intimidated by its content, simply ignored it. The publicity budget was risible. Interest from European territories, especially France and Germany, failed to convince Paramount that it was worth backing. Whatever their real motivations, the studio's reluctance to get behind the film has since been interpreted as censorship by default. Ruby Dee, the co-writer and producer, remains convinced that Paramount tried to pull the film from distribution and washed their hands of its controversial ideas. Nonetheless, with each passing year, the reputation of the film grew and mutated, and by the nineties, all but impossible to track down, *Uptight* took on a cult status and its underground reputation soared.

For all its invisibility in the past, *Uptight* became a 'forgotten classic', the forerunner of the black urban thriller, the genre of films that subsequently became known as blaxploitation movies. As for the soundtrack, it survived independently. Jones for his part was unimpressed by the basic sound facilities in Paris. After completing the film track he returned to Memphis and re-recorded the music at the Stax studios. Most of the tracks were composed to fit the urgent pace of the movie and were mostly instrumentals, but periodically Jones called on the services of the gospel-trained vocalist Judy Clay to front some of the tracks. Clay had recently enjoyed widespread success with 'Private Number', a duet with William Bell, and Stax were keen to find her opportunities as a solo singer. Jones himself sang on one track, but the biggest success from the entire *Uptight* project was the film's relentless refrain, a Hammond-led instrumental that became known as 'Time Is Tight'. On commercial release in early 1969 it reached number six in the *Billboard* Top 100 pop charts and became Booker T. and the M.G.'s biggest hit since 'Green Onions'.

Curiously, as Booker T. Jones worked on the soundtrack in an editing suite in troubled Paris, another character soon to sign to Stax was working only a few streets away. After travelling the world, the black bohemian Melvin Van Peebles had temporarily settled in Paris, where he was producing plays, directing short films and recording obscure music. Within a matter of eighteen months, on the back of a lucky break with one of his French shorts, he would embark on the next great chapter in African-American cinema, the self-funded and innovative *Sweet Sweetback's Baadasssss Song*. Born in Chicago, Melvin Peebles was a beatnik with a restlessly creative streak who had studied literature in Chicago and read street poetry in Amsterdam. He adopted the Dutch name 'Van' and became known thereafter as Melvin Van Peebles. He had travelled extensively, married and then divorced a German photographer, Maria Marx, and worked for a spell on the San Francisco cable cars. He affected a revolutionary pose, wore berets and utilitarian work wear buttoned up like Chairman Mao, and smoked gigantic cigars in the style of Fidel Castro. He was invited to Paris by Henri Langlois, the eccentric founder of La Cinémathèque Français, who introduced him to the French auteurs of the day such as Jean-Luc Godard and Claude Chabrol. With the shambling but well-connected Langlois as his mentor, Van Peebles started to produce low-budget shorts in Paris and then embarked on his first feature film, *La Permission*, or as it became known in the USA *The Story of a Three-Day Pass*, a film based on his own novel and derivative of the French new wave in that it was shot entirely in black and white. Coincidentally, Van Peebles used many French freelance film technicians who then went on to work with Dassin on the post-production of *Uptight*. With a French feature to his credit and a coterie of France's best known directors singing his praises, Van Peebles managed to secure a US release for the film in the spring of 1968, and subsequently bagged a three-picture deal with Columbia Pictures. According to his own version of events, Van Peebles then converted the retainer from Columbia into the seed-funding for another project, the seminal *Sweet Sweetback's Baadasssss Song*. With limited funding he improvised a shooting schedule, making up scenes as they moved from location to location. Van Peebles hired a crew who would work cheaply and yet were confident with sound and cameras, a crew unburdened by the studio system or union practices. He turned to the porn industry for his technicians and made up the script as he went, shooting the entire film over an intense nineteen days. He post-produced with a loan from Bill Cosby and dubbed a self-composed soundtrack, in part performed by a then unknown and homeless Earth, Wind and Fire. Melvin and his son Mario both star in the film, which features a set-piece scene in which Van Peebles and a young Black Panther beat up an LA cop with his own handcuffs after a false arrest. The scene was endorsed by the Panthers, whose notoriety brought it even greater publicity. So, too, did its restless editing style, which was punctuated with radical jump-cuts and montage sequences. Closer to an underground art film than studio blockbuster, it opened in only two cinemas, but word of mouth carried it much further, and the original no-budget film grossed over $4.1 million, making it the most profitable film of its era. Suddenly, black films had become financially viable and the race was on to bring even more to the screens. Stax picked up the musical rights to the film and released 'Sweetback's Theme' as a single, but it was the album that breathed life into future music by becoming a seminal source for the first generation of hip-hop artists.

Meanwhile, a routine meeting in New York in the summer of 1968 kick-started the third and most triumphant of Stax's trilogy of blaxploitation films: the daddy of the genre, *Shaft*. At the time, a Cleveland-born journalist Ernest Tidyman was completing a pulp novel called *Flower Power*, a racy book about the latest youth cult, the hippies. At an editorial meeting with his publisher Alan Rinzler, then the editor of Macmillan's mystery department, a better idea surfaced. Rinzler was relatively new to the industry and unrestrained by its conventions. A Harvard graduate, who by his own admission was 'living on the Lower East Side, writing terrible plays and loading trucks as a fur freight despatcher in the garment business' only a year before, he was determined to make a success of commercial literature. It was a meeting fizzing with ideas but dominated by a major literary controversy, the publication of William Styron's slave novel *The Confessions of Nat Hunter*, which, despite winning the Pulitzer Prize for Literature in 1967, was roundly attacked by black intellectuals for perpetuating myths about black rapists and victimhood. Tidyman and his publisher discussed the whole notion of the poor victim and became excited about turning the concept on its head by creating a character bulging with ability, who could become a black literary hero. Together they began to imagine a smooth and athletic Harlem detective whose name became John Shaft. Tidyman made it a priority and quickly knocked off a detective thriller called *Shaft*. Predictably, on the back of Melvin Van Peebles' commercial success with the first breakthrough black movie, the film studios had abandoned their normal anxieties and were hunting high and low for an unpredictable commercial film that could appeal to what they described as a new 'urban' market. A detective novel with pace and a clear plotline suited all their needs, and the novel *Shaft* was bought up by MGM, with Tidyman writing the screenplay.

Initially, Isaac Hayes, by then a successful recording artist off the back of two important and commercially successful albums – *Hot Buttered Soul* (1969) and *Black Moses* (1971) – harboured the thought of moving into acting and offered himself up to director Gordon Parks Jr for the title role of John Shaft. Hayes had been working with the Detroit producer Don Davis on the origins of what became *Hot Buttered Soul* in the last days of 1968. It was a disruptive album which has since become a landmark in the evolution of soul. Four tracks, each substantially longer than the traditional three-minute pop song, used strings in a way that paralleled the movie soundtrack, but then brought in urban synthesisers in ways that foretold the chase sequences in *Shaft*. The opening track is a drug-laced version of 'Walk On By', not in the classic style of Dionne Warwick's love song but as if it was scored by Curtis Mayfield and a streetful of junkies, and then boldly followed by a borderline unpronounceable track that used the Sanitation Workers Strike as the basis for a modern love song: 'Hyperbolicsyllabicsesquedalymistic'. 'We absolutely changed the landscape of popular music with those albums,' Al Bell said. 'We helped make it possible for artists like Marvin Gaye, Curtis Mayfield, Stevie Wonder and Michael Jackson to achieve the kind of greatness that they reached.'

After the critical acclaim of *Hot Buttered Soul* Hayes assumed the persona of 'Black Moses' and, using the challenging language of post-slavery, described a kind of musical emancipation that arose from a period of depression and extended mourning after King's assassination. He described this reawakening as something akin to self-discovery: 'I'm not chained any more. It's a new freedom. I'm free.' In another exchange he touched on the one area of self-realisation that set him apart. Despite endless approaches, Hayes was always reluctant to endorse mainstream politicians, preferring to focus on what he called 'the misery of the ghetto' and the unfinished business on the streets of Memphis. Of all the superstars who emerged from Stax it was Isaac Hayes and, of course, John Gary Williams of the Mad Lads who came closest to reflecting the distressed communities of Memphis in song. The global success of *Shaft* took Hayes into a stratospheric level of fame that no one at Stax – not even Otis Redding – had witnessed before. On the night of his Oscar nomination, a local Memphis journalist Larry Williams spoke to Hayes by phone a few hours before the ceremony was broadcast across America. Williams described him as 'detached as black coffee' but quietly superstitious and anxious not to talk about the Academy Awards directly. A part of Hayes' reluctance was brought about by a disappointing night at the Grammy Awards, where he dominated the nominations but only managed to win one consolation award. It was an emotionally bruising experience and one he did not want to repeat. When the Oscars came round it was a golden year, with *Klute, The French Connection, The Last Picture Show* and *Shaft* all in the mix. Hayes was nominated in two categories: Best Original Dramatic Score, where he lost out narrowly to Michel Legrand's 'Summer Of 42'; and Best Song where he dominated the category with the movie's title tune, the triumphant 'Theme From *Shaft*', which Hayes himself described as 'a shot heard around the world'. Only the third African-American to win an Oscar, after Hattie McDaniel and Sidney Poitier, Hayes walked tentatively on-stage at the Dorothy Chandler Pavilion wearing a petrol-blue suit trimmed in white mink. He was uncharacteristically nervous at the podium and could only mumble a few words of thanks, dedicating the Oscar to his grandmother, Mrs Rushia Wade, who was sitting in the audience next to his now empty seat. She had raised him as a child and was his guest of honour at the ceremony. Hayes had been born into a shockingly poor dysfunctional family and raised in a tin shack in Covington, Tennessee, forty miles north of Memphis. He was abandoned by his father when only eighteen months old. After his mother died prematurely in a mental asylum in Bolivar,

Tennessee, he was formally adopted by his grandparents and raised in Memphis from the age of six. Poverty and deprivation had hounded Hayes throughout his young life. According to the black music magazine *Wax Poetics*, 'Hayes's humble beginnings – from sleeping in abandoned cars and dropping out of school because he didn't have decent clothing to watching his sister and grandmother get sick from hunger – would haunt him through adulthood.' The memory of a mother incarcerated, screaming and then sedated in a psychiatric hospital had given him a deep-seated anxiety that his mother's illnesses might be hereditary. Deanie Parker, Stax's head of publicity, once said, 'When I first met Isaac, he had two shirts – one red Ban-Lon and one yellow Ban-Lon – a pair of khaki pants, and one pair of shoes that didn't have laces. He lied his way up into Stax, saying he could play this and that. He was learning all the time, he had a symphony in his head.'

His halting performance at the Oscars was in marked contrast to his return home to Memphis, where a spontaneous groundswell of excitement grew and thousands who had seen him live on television mobbed the airport. Hayes and his grandmother were escorted through the crowds by police officers who parted a pathway through a congested concourse. He held the Oscar aloft in one hand like a sporting trophy and protected his grandmother with his other arm as she smiled at the crowds, tiny and bespectacled and with her gospel coiffure still immaculate from the night before. There can be no more sentimental image in the entire history of soul music than Hayes oozing machismo in dark glasses and a sawn-off denim jacket, Memphis Invaders-style, shielding his grandmother in a gesture of unconditional love. Mrs Rushia Wade finally shed a tear of joy when her grandson was met by local dignitaries at the airport and given the special award of Honorary Colonel and Aide-De-Camp of the Governor of Tennessee. The archaic award – steeped in the history of the civil war – was in marked contrast to the frantic urban street music of *Shaft*, but Isaac Hayes dutifully accepted and then told them he planned to take the next day off and just 'walk the streets of the black community, and thank the people personally'. One of the deepest discriminations in the history of Memphis had been broken. The city's highest honours, until then always gifted to whites, were bestowed on a bald ghetto superstar with a strident sense of his own emancipation, who went by the name of 'Black Moses'.

On the blackboard in Al Bell's office in Stax is a list of tasks, and to the upper right his vision of a new era for the label written in chalk – 'A Soul Explosion, By People, For People, 'Cause People Buy Stax-Volt Records'.

AL BELL'S
BIG THERMOMETER

May

Al Bell's thermometer was a thing of crude beauty. It was grafted onto the office wall with all the cut-out elegance of a daycare centre, and Bell measured it day and night. What excited him most was when the temperature rose to the point where it broke through the measuring gauge and threatened to explode. Then he could announce to the assembled staff in the voice of an eccentric doctor that Stax was gripped by fever. He even named this new wave of activity as the 'Soul Explosion'. The office thermometer was something more than a corporate sales chart, it was a visible symbol of Stax's performance on the marketplace: the new releases, the records they had out there that were still selling, and the new directions in what had become a fast-changing and unpredictable market. 'I took a poster board and drew a thermometer, and filled it at the bottom with red ink. As sales increased, I would increase the mercury,' he told writer Robert Gordon. 'And at the top of the thermometer, I had it explode out into what I called Heaven. And that was after we had achieved our goal.'

The thermometer had arrived at a critical moment in the evolution of soul music. The genre was expanding in a hundred different directions. The bubblegum soul that Motown had perfected from their factory in Detroit was far from exhausted and groups like the Supremes and the Temptations still dominated the charts. But new impassioned forms of soul music enriched by social commentary were finding their voice, and for the first time in their narrow-minded history, the movies were beginning to show a passing interest in a black audience. Nonetheless, the distant past still exerted a powerful influence on sales: gospel was thriving and there was still a market for big voices. Although Bell was not convinced that Stax had found a serious replacement for Otis Redding, Johnnie Taylor was emerging as a serious contender, and Aretha Franklin was at the height of her powers, albeit out of Stax's reach – signed to the detested Atlantic Records.

Bell's biggest challenge was not just to second guess the capricious-ness of musical tastes but to rebuild Stax after their devastating fallout with Atlantic. Nor was it simply about building a new roster of artists; he had to become the architect of a new distribution network that could reach deep into the ghetto record stores and look beyond their core market in the southern towns, breaking consistently into the cosmopolitan markets in Washington, New York and Los Angeles. As Bell went about the daunting task of rebuilding a Stax empire that had been denied some of its biggest names, he was tasked with another urgent shift of focus: to navigate away from recording one-off catchy singles and break into the more lucrative albums market. Change was everywhere, social, economic and creative.

Bell was in many respects the perfect leader for changing times. Born Alvertis Isbell in Brinkley, Arkansas, in 1940, he grew up in a rusting railway town situated halfway between Memphis and Little Rock, the state capital of Arkansas. He came of age as a teenager in the formative years of R&B, in the days of the single turntable, when, with his boundless imagination, he imagined running a radio station from his teenage bedroom. By force of his formidable personality, he began to secure bookings as a high-school DJ and guest slots on local radio stations. Bell's teenage years coincided with dramatic events in the history of civil rights, especially the desegregation of schooling in Little Rock that shaped his beliefs. In 1957, when Bell was still only seventeen years old, the battle to desegregate Little Rock Central High School, once a bastion of white supremacy in the city, became a worldwide cause célèbre. A baying mob of over a thousand white protestors gathered along the intersections of 14th and Park, overlooking the faux-gothic grandeur of the high school, to prevent nine young black students from entering the building, in violation of a series of new laws which outlawed segregation in the education system. It was a stand-off that turned violent and political. The Little Rock controversy escalated to the White House, provoking an exchange of heated words between Arkansas state governor Orval Faubus and President Eisenhower, who had instructed the National Guard to protect the children and their parents. Images of paramilitaries lined up against small children carrying their school bags and fearfully holding their parents' hands travelled the world and brought Faubus and the culture of segregation into international disgrace. Al Bell witnessed it all. At the time he was a DJ at high-school dances and proms across the Little Rock schools' system, and the scenes nagged at his conscience, encouraging him to join the civil rights movement. When he graduated from high school, he enrolled at college and his first salaried job was at Radio Station KOKY, Little Rock's first urban soul station, where he assumed the now familiar role of jive-talking shaman: 'This is your six-feet-four bundle of joy, two hundred and twelve pounds of Miss Bell's baby boy,' he rapped, inducing the listeners to fall in love with the music and seducing them with his charm.

In a disarmingly honest interview with Andria Lisle in *Wax Poetics*, Bell talked about his young life: 'Back in Arkansas, I worked for a white man who owned a grocery store and a fruit stand. I heard all the time, "Niggers can't do nothing but sing and dance." At first it bothered me – then I realized that singing and dancing is a multi-million-dollar industry. I lived in a segregated community that was permeated with racism, but when I DJ'd every morning, students from Central High School and Dunbar – its Black equivalent – would congregate and dance while I played records on the air. When the school crisis took place . . . I got a chance to see the attitudes of the European-American community. So in 1959, I'd dropped out of college in Little Rock and joined the SCLC [the Southern Christian Leadership Conference] leadership workshops, which were held in Midway, Georgia. At the time I carried a switchblade knife, and I was quite prolific in handling it. I went to Midway with that knife in my pocket. I didn't have the passive resistance philosophy – if you attacked me, you could expect some kind of response. We were on a march in Savannah when a White gentleman said, "Nigger." His spit hit my clothes, and before I could think, I pulled my switchblade out, broke rank and went after him.' According to Bell, he lost control and retaliated, pursued through the crowd by SCLC leaders Hosea Williams and Ralph Abernathy, and was admonished for breaking one of the cardinal rules of the strictly non-violent SCLC. Bell claims that Martin Luther King spoke to him directly and criticised him for brandishing a knife: '"Alvertis, you have some of the better qualities of Marcus Garvey," he said, "but all those things must come later." I replied, "Jesus had Peter with him – *he* carried a sword, so what's the problem with my knife?" I respected Dr King, even though I didn't totally believe him. I continued to support him because I loved him.' Bell's disagreements with King's movement were not simply about violence but about a deeper underlying philosophy, a principle that led him to befriend Jesse Jackson and feel closer to the Chicago branch of the SCLC. Bell and Jackson had grown restless, unconvinced by silent protests and passive-resistance marches, and both believed that change was bound up in ownership, growing black businesses and extending job opportunities for young African-Americans.

Bell's career as a staff member of SCLC began in 1959 and was short-lived. Although he continued to support King in public, he wanted to pursue the politics of economic emancipation. One of his earliest disputes with Stax was that the company was profiting from black music but was essentially white-owned. In sharp contrast to their northern rivals Motown, a company that was firmly in the grip of Berry Gordy and his formidable sisters, Stax remained in the control of a white southern family, Jim Stewart and his sister Estelle Axton.

Bell briefly worked as a DJ in Memphis in the early days of the sixties and was one of a throng of personalities who met around the counters of Satellite Records, angling for the best new releases for his show. Despite his unbridled self-confidence, Bell's first attempt at running his own business was an abject failure. He moved from Little Rock to Memphis and on to Washington, where he set up a poorly distributed independent record label called Safice, an old-school soul label that released records by the Mystics, Roy Arlington and Bell's long-time friend, Eddie Floyd. Floyd was a gifted vocalist who had left his native Alabama as part of the great migration north to Detroit and there he joined one of soul music's great unheralded groups – the Falcons – sharing vocal leads with the impetuous Wilson Pickett and Jo Stubbs, the brother of Levi Stubbs of the Four Tops. Lost amidst the overabundance of competing talent in Detroit, Floyd eventually followed Bell to Washington and then on to Stax, where their careers ignited.

It was on the campus at Washington DC's Howard University that Bell brazenly introduced himself to Carla Thomas, who was studying there at the time. He talked her into cutting some demos with Eddie Floyd at Bell's radio station. Sold on their talent and determination, Carla Thomas mentioned the demos to her father Rufus and through him Bell was introduced to Stax. The offer of a job followed within weeks. He had been hired as Stax's first full-time promotions officer, to plug a gap in the company's workforce. By 1965, possibly earlier, the team at Stax had become sceptical of just how much Atlantic were promoting their product. 'Business-wise we were getting lost in the shuffle,' Steve Cropper admitted. 'If a promotions guy walks into a radio station and he's got six Atlantic records and one Stax record, what's gonna happen?' Bell was hired to bring that era of dependence to an end. His most obvious skill was in communications. His connections with DJs and radio stations across the country, particularly in the Delta region, were second to none. Furthermore, he had highly developed public-speaking skills, shaped by radio broadcasting and his days as a young political advocate at the SCLC. Articulate, self-confident and unrestrained by his initial lowly status at the company, Bell quickly became a senior employee and, ultimately, the driving force at Stax Records. His meteoric rise within the company was at best divisive: for some he was a passionate and inspirational leader; for others he had tipped a delicate balance and brought the creed of black ownership to the forefront of the company.

The extent of Bell's influence was colossal and his passion for change burned like a torch. Until his arrival no one had tried to make sense of Stax as a significant force in African-American music. It had evolved and grown piecemeal, driven by its doomed distribution deal with Atlantic and the honey-dripping promises of Jerry Wexler. Bell filled a vacuum – he influenced artists' development, oversaw the move to albums, drove the growth of a diversified portfolio of subsidiary labels, and jettisoned the homely old label design of dancing 45 rpm discs, replacing it with a more strident and streetwise design, the now iconic snapping finger. Booker T. Jones likened him to Otis Redding: 'he had the same type of energy. He'd come into the room, pull up his shoulders and that energy would start. He would start talking about the music business or what was going on and he energized everywhere he was. He was our Otis for promotion.' However, according to one Stax veteran, 'he not only bore grudges, he nailed them to the office wall'. In a gesture of calculated revenge Bell encouraged the former gospel group Jeanne and the Darlings to record a derivative version of Sam and Dave's hit song 'Soul Man' – the outcome was a stripped-back funk song knowingly called 'Soul Girl'. Jim Stewart loved its latent energy, but most of all he loved its coded vengefulness and the idea that Stax, through its subsidiary label Volt, was giving two fingers to Jerry Wexler and Atlantic. A resentment was building that would not subside until long after 1968 was over.

To begin with, Bell spent the vast majority of his time on the road. He had identified Chicago as a breakout market, noting its huge urban sprawl, strong radio stations that played black music, and its political network via Jesse Jackson and Radio Station WVON (the self-styled 'Voice of a Nation') where DJ and programme director E. Rodney Jones and an excitable Stax enthusiast by the name of DJ Butterball helped with promotion.

His days were spent sweet-talking DJs and bludgeoning store owners into stocking Stax records, but by 1967 he had recruited a small staff of regional promoters and returned full-time to Memphis. For a while, he shared an office with Jim Stewart, and they struck up an unlikely partnership – the garrulous and at times bombastic Bell and the quietly anxious company owner. 'What was precious about working in that one office with Jim and spending so many hours with him was his determination to record and release authentic music,' remarked Bell. Stewart's dedication to Memphis blues artists and to the old ways took Bell by surprise. His appearance and his innate conservatism made Stewart easy to parody. He looked like someone who had mistakenly stumbled into the studio until the recording started, and then Bell saw in him a passion and determination that defied his appearance. Stewart was a relentless taskmaster, sometimes driving the studio band the M.G.'s into long and unforgiving nightshifts, railing at them for overcomplicating songs. His greatest asset of all was a Stax trademark: keep it simple.

Simplicity was Stax's hidden virtue. Every Monday morning Bell established a short and highly focused creative meeting for all available staff. He asked what people had heard out at the weekends, in bars, clubs and on radio. Anything surfacing in the R&B or pop charts was assessed and then copied, and any new trend in the industry was hastily embraced. With the new label design, Bell fashioned a bold and overarching concept – 'The Sound of Memphis'. It was derivative of Motown's 'Sound of Young America' and came over as intensely arrogant to some of the other studios across the city, but it shouted of Stax's ambition and new-found self-confidence. Within a few months of the new logo, and with the backbone of a new distribution network in place, Stax released a string of successful singles, including Johnnie Taylor's 'Who's Making Love', Eddie Floyd's cover version of the old Sam Cooke classic 'Bring It On Home To Me' and one of Stax's most successful records ever, William Bell and Judy Clay's 'Private Number', a love duet that unashamedly crashed into a market previously dominated by Motown's Marvin Gaye and Tammi Terrell and Wand's Chuck Jackson and Maxine Brown.

'Private Number' reached the Top Twenty in the American R&B charts, but more persuasively it stormed the charts in Europe, peaking at number eight in Britain, where it became a nightclub classic. Yet it was not Judy Clay's first attempt at a love duet. Controversially, at Atlantic, she had been paired with a white singer, Billy Vera, in what was touted as America's first interracial pop couple. The idea backfired. Badly. Many radio stations refused to playlist their song, there was a blanket television ban on appearances, and most of the nation's press avoided what was perceived by many as risky subject matter. The contentious coupling was exacerbated by a virulent rumour that Clay was pregnant with Vera's child; in fact she was pregnant by her husband, the jazz drummer Leo Gatewood. To add insult to injury, the duo's best song, 'Storybook Children', was eventually performed on network TV by all-white couple Nancy Sinatra and Lee Hazlewood. Frustrated by the racist attitudes still prevailing in the mainstream, Clay was dealt a second blow. She was signed to Stax, and Vera to Atlantic, and the war between the two companies eventually broke up their partnership. Judy Clay, like Don Covay and Wilson Pickett, was seen as a 'difficult' artist and her prickliness in the recording studio, driven as much by perfectionism as much as pettiness, left her short of allies. Despite the cult status and popular success of 'Private Number', she was eventually released from her contract, the first of a series of setbacks that blighted her career. According to her son, whom she bore during the controversy, failure in the industry scarred her emotionally for the rest of her life. Clay had once sung with the most formidable of all the gospel groups, the Drinkard Family, which produced Cissy Houston, sisters Dee Dee and Dionne Warwick, and provided the nucleus of the supergroup of backing singers the Sweet Inspirations. Clay watched as their careers evolved and it hurt. 'I can't communicate to you how much of an issue it was to my mother to not have her career,' Leo Gatewood Jr said, on his mother's passing in 2001. 'It was an overriding theme in our house, so much so that as a child, I would try not to let her see any award shows, because she would openly cry. She'd see somebody like Patti LaBelle or Aretha on TV, and try to comment. But you could see it crushed her. That never changed.'

Underlying finances at Stax were still precarious and in a way always would be. As Estelle Axton and Jim Stewart shopped around for a new partner who could close the gap left by the severance of their deal with Atlantic, Bell played a prominent new role as broker. There had been several near-misses, but deals with MGM, MCA and ABC had all driven into the sand, and so Bell recommended that Stax hire the services of one of black music's major sorcerers, Clarence Avant, an industry stalwart who was formerly the manager of R&B titan Little Willie John and jazz star Sarah Vaughan. Bell and Avant had met at the annual National Association of Television and Radio Announcers (NATRA) convention held in Atlanta in August 1967. The convention was a landmark event in the soul calendar – 'where DJs came to argue'. Five hundred disc jockeys and most of the independent label owners attended the event at the newly built Hyatt Regency, where the organisers had made the decision to shine a light on the burgeoning southern scene and particularly on the rising tide of Otis Redding. It seemed that soul music was splitting along regional lines. The massive northern cities of Chicago and Detroit were now rivalled by the southern cities of Memphis and Atlanta. It was a turning point in the industry and a moment for reflection on the hard racially divisive realities. Up to 500 radio stations across America targeted largely African-American communities, but only four of them were black owned. According to one extant report, 'a revolt is slowly building up among more than 1,500 Negro disc jockeys from coast to coast, who are "fed up" with the slave conditions under which many of them work . . . Secret sessions are being held between them to decide on a course of action to win for themselves a bigger share of the pie.'

Many of black entertainment's biggest stars, including Sidney Poitier, Bill Cosby, Nina Simone, Jackie Wilson and former Motown singer Kim Weston, were also in town. At NATRA's opening Friday-night dinner hosted by RCA Records, Dr Martin Luther King delivered the keynote speech. Reflecting on a summer of riots, he rehearsed sentiments that he would repeat on television and at the SCLC in Atlanta five days later. 'I refuse to allow myself to fall into the dark chambers of pessimism . . . The futility of violence in the struggle for racial justice has been tragically etched in all the recent Negro riots . . . There is certainly something painfully sad about a riot. One sees screaming youngsters and angry adults fighting hopelessly and aimlessly against impossible odds. And deep down within them, you can see a desire for self-destruction, a kind of suicidal longing.' His speech inspired Florence Greenberg, the founder of the New York R&B labels Scepter and Wand, who was there representing Dionne Warwick, Chuck Jackson, Tommy Hunt and Nella Dodds. Upon her return home to New York, she penned a personal note of thanks to King and enclosed a donation to his cause. But King's speech about the futility of violence was met with mixed feelings; it was far too cautious for some in the room. African-American politics were increasingly fragmenting along violent and non-violent lines. Student firebrand H. Rap Brown arrived at the convention to try to convince soul music's most versatile DJs to embrace a more militant message, and to become voices for change in ghetto communities. By the time of the next NATRA convention, held in August 1968 in Miami, violence would erupt and drive a wedge through the industry that damaged soul music and demonised the genre for some record labels.

As Bell and Avant drank together in 1967, they talked about the deals that Stax might strike. At the time, Avant had just concluded a deal incorporating Venture Records in California, the first joint venture between African-American artists and a major record company. Impressed, Bell enlisted his help to broker a deal with yet another conglomerate in a move that brought Stax under the control of an irrepressible and eccentric mogul known as 'The Mad Austrian' – the boss of Gulf & Western, 'Hurricane Charlie' Bluhdorn. Bluhdorn was a force of nature who acquired businesses as if they were toys (150 over his lifetime). *Vanity Fair* described him as 'rapacious, combustible, and passionate, a man who routinely made the impossible happen as he built his Gulf & Western empire'. He was a man obsessed with deals. 'Some people like golf, Charlie liked to acquire things,' Jack Valenti, the Motion Picture Association of America president, once said. 'Making a deal to him was one orgasm after another.'

Back in 1965, in the midst of Otis Redding's most prolific year as a barnstorming R&B singer, Stax's Volt subsidiary had released the so-called 'fab four' – Redding's quartet of great singles: 'Mr Pitiful', 'I've Been Loving You Too Long (To Stop Now)', 'Respect' and 'I Can't Turn You Loose'. As Redding's star was in the ascendancy, Bluhdorn was voraciously buying up failing companies in the automobile supplies industry. In one audacious corporate swoop, he borrowed $84 million, then the largest unsecured loan in US history, from Chase Manhattan, and purchased a struggling corporation called New Jersey Zinc. The president woke up one day to find he had a new boss and claimed, 'The more you work for Charlie Bluhdorn, the closer you are to the moon.' It was a prescient description that captured Bluhdorn's soaring ambition and his lunar madness. With each new week he identified more failing or vulnerable companies to snap up and turn around. His biggest success came when he bought a dead-end company in Grand Rapids called Michigan Plating & Stamping, which had consistently failed to turn a profit but had one lucrative long-term contract producing rear bumpers for Studebakers.

Bluhdorn had arrived in America as an Austrian immigrant in the early years of Hitler's rise to power. He allowed people to think he had escaped persecution as a Jew although no one was ever sure if he was actually Jewish. Throughout his life he was fiercely patriotic and forced his children to watch *The Sound of Music* nightly, to witness – again and again – how the Austrian family and the emotional passions of 'Edelweiss' tricked the encroaching Nazis. In 1966 he rocked the movie industry by buying up the failing Hollywood studio Paramount, which had not had a hit since *Psycho* in 1960. At the time of the deal, the film industry, wary of outsiders and sneering in its attitude to the seemingly unsophisticated, had scoffed at Bluhdorn, believing he had only struck the Paramount deal to gain access to a glamour that his other businesses could never deliver. Hollywood was baffled by the transaction and claimed it was 'the biggest purchase for pussy in the history of America'. Bluhdorn may well have been vulnerable to passing beauty, but his motives were always more calculating. Miraculously, he turned the ailing studio into a hit factory with *Love Story* (1970), *The Godfather* (1972) and *Chinatown* (1974), but beyond the box office hits lay a more lucrative undercarriage. Paramount owned thousands of old movies, ripe for re-running in the emergent network television market. Bluhdorn slapped a television licence value of $200 million on its accounts, virtually transforming its commercial credibility. The writer Robert Sam Anson, who meticulously pieced together Bluhdorn's corporate history as it zigzagged across America and into nearly every sector of the economy, summarised his success in one simple phrase. Bluhdorn, the ultimate turnaround king, had once told him: 'I buy things no one else wants.'

Difficult as it was for the leadership of Stax to admit, they fitted the profile. Stax had been edged out of a deal with Atlantic and Warner Brothers and had exhausted a list of other potential suitors. It had become a company 'no one wanted' in a high-risk industry littered with corporate failure. Having lost its back catalogue and many of its most bankable stars to Jerry Wexler at Atlantic, Stax was also perceived to have been naïve, unaware of the depth charges that lay beneath the choppy waters of its relationship with Atlantic. It was an exciting but risky business in a declining neighbourhood of a now notorious city. Bluhdorn had precious little time to devote to Stax, but his hunch was that it had found talent before and could do so again. He also liked something else about the label – it had resonance. Wherever he went in America, and even Europe, people had heard of it. Stax's deal with Gulf & Western was finalised on 29 May 1968 for $4.3 million. The broker, Clarence Avant, received ten per cent of all debentures and Stax's original founders Jim Stewart and Estelle Axton became majority shareholders. Their talented executive Al Bell became a minority stockholder, the first African-American to own a share of a company that was steeped in the deep soul of black music.

In May 1968, *Billboard*, the music industry's business bible, greeted the takeover with cautious optimism. 'Jim Stewart will continue to helm Stax/Volt companies, reporting to Arnold D. Burk, Paramount Pictures vice-president in charge of music operation,' a front-page feature informed, going on to confirm that Stax would continue to be distributed by independents and that Paramount would not take on the cost of building a distribution network.

Although the deal has been retrospectively criticised for under-valuing Stax and not bringing enough cash into the company, it acted as a significant confidence boost, bringing uncertainty to an end and stimulating further growth. Stax had been sold for $4.3 million, the majority of which was paid in Gulf & Western stock, but at least for a time there was cash in the company.

Although there is no evidence, either factual or anecdotal, that Charlie Bluhdorn ever visited the Stax studios, his reputation swept through the corridors, and the company found itself in the challenging situation of having to report on a monthly basis to the corporate headquarters of Gulf & Western in Manhattan via its Paramount entertainment subsidiary in Hollywood. It was overly complex from the outset. Stax had to accept management oversight from a company that barely understood the culture, let alone the cut-throat business of R&B. For a while it was able to operate below the radar of corporate control but that was never likely to last, and slowly but surely the internal culture at East McLemore changed. Using the money that Gulf & Western had invested, Bell embarked on an audacious expansion scheme – 'The Soul Explosion' – that launched thirty singles and twenty-eight albums in under a year. The winds of change blew many certainties away. Stax no longer remained fixated with Memphis; it increasingly recorded in Detroit and opened an office in Los Angeles, and in a move that was to kindle mixed emotions, the company hired the talented Detroit producer Don Davis to bring the gloss of Motor City soul to the south.

Beyond business growth, Bell began to implement some of his own long-held beliefs in building a black business and immediately advocated greater recruitment of black staff. The new era was unsettling for some. Estelle Axton felt that the white employees who had helped build the company deserved rewards, too. With substantial evidence on her side, she cited the fact that producer and songwriter Steve Cropper had contributed as much to the Stax story as Bell had. It was a view driven by more than sentimentality. Although Cropper had worked beside her in the Satellite Records store and was a close personal friend, he had also been a driving force in the studio, where he had worked tirelessly as guitarist with Booker T. and the M.G.'s. He co-wrote some of Stax's most durable songs, among them Eddie Floyd's 'Knock On Wood', Wilson Pickett's 'In The Midnight Hour' and Otis Redding's requiem '(Sittin On) The Dock Of The Bay'. But there was, naturally, a touch of sentimentality. Cropper was a friend and collaborator with Axton's wayward son Packy, whom she felt had been short-changed and then ostracised by Stax and by her own brother. It was a sore that had never healed.

Internal strife at Stax had become like Memphis in miniature. Arguments about race and ethnicity were tied up in a confused ball of divided loyalties. Jim Stewart told the Memphis-based writer Robert Gordon that he felt conflicted and caught between business and family. 'I had a decision to make,' he said, 'a very hard decision to make. It involved family versus the company – a very hard choice. Al and my sister did not get along, and it had gotten to the point where Al was ready to leave. In the end I made the decision that more people's livelihoods were at stake than just mine and asked my sister to step down.' Although the racial tensions within Stax and Al Bell's elevated role brought ill-feeling to the surface, in truth Estelle Axton had felt directionless, undervalued and underused for several years. When the departure came it was with all the bitterness that had been welling up for some time. Local music lawyer Seymour Rosenberg, a teenage friend of Jim Stewart, orchestrated a final legal settlement. He hired a suite at the Holiday Inn Rivermont and locked the warring parties in adjacent rooms, shuttling from one suite to another until the lawyers of Gulf & Western, who had flown in for the day from New York, negotiated a severance package with Axton's local lawyers. The so-called 'redistribution of earn-out agreement' gave Estelle Axton $490,000 for her stake in Stax but left her feeling unfulfilled. She invested in a luxury apartment but no longer had the heart to drive along East McLemore, past the store front that had once played host to Satellite Records, the shop that begat Stax. 'I decided to take the money and run,' she said. But there were strict limitations on where she could run. A do-not-compete clause in her severance deal meant that she was unable to work in the music industry – not even to open another record store – for a period of five years.

Martin Luther King's assassination and Al Bell's eventual

consolidation of power at Stax had many unforeseen consequences. One of the most obvious was a shift in the cultural locus of the company. Stax had emerged out of hillbilly roots, integrated a creative and under-represented local community of black artists, and established itself as the most dynamic force in a city founded on segregation. By 1968 it was moving inexorably towards an era where greater black ownership and assertiveness would become a daily reality. First and foremost, there was social change. The civil rights movement, with its tones of Christian tolerance and passive resistance, had reached a point of crisis with King's death and unlocked more strident voices for Black Power. This was not just theatrical protest or activist posturing, it reached deep into the company's culture. Al Bell had been a passionate and consistent advocate of greater change in the workplace, believing that major companies across the country had to step up to the plate and increase their recruitment of black staff. Now he was in a position to put his beliefs into practice, he made it happen. Black recruitment at Stax increased in numbers across all roles, from security to the secretariat to creative leadership. Bell also forged more direct links with opinion formers within the black community, reassuring the ever cautious Jim Stewart as he went.

Bell's views were most persuasively espoused by Jesse Jackson's Operation Breadbasket movement, the Chicago-based spin-out from the SCLC, which was committed to taking civil rights into the local economy and the workplace. Jackson's career was in the ascendancy, and after disputes with the SCLC he set up an entirely new pressure group PUSH – a grandiose acronym for People United to Save Humanity. PUSH was committed to black self-help and had alliances with the soul DJ network NATRA, which was turning the heat up on record companies, demanding greater royalties for black artists and increased visibility of African-Americans in management and ownership roles.

Change was everywhere and Stax tried to adjust. But it was never a hapless victim of Black Power, not in any crude sense of that term. Like many record companies of the time, Stax felt both the pressure and the desire to react to new times and new markets. In that respect, Al Bell was both an advocate and a beneficiary. He believed passionately in greater power for black people in the workplace and, of course, he personally gained from change.

The new mood of black assertiveness made the everyday working environment less cosy but it also laid the foundations for one of Stax's greatest achievements, the toweringly important Wattstax: a festival, a political rally and an innovative documentary film. Wattstax grew directly from Stax's expansion to the west coast. Like Motown before them, the Memphis company had come to realise that opportunities in and around Hollywood were ripe for exploitation, and that the mountain would never come to Mohammad. If they waited for Hollywood to discover Memphis, it would be a long wait. Now part of the Gulf & Western conglomerate, Stax opened up a small Los Angeles office managed by Forest Hamilton Jr, the son of jazz drummer Chico Hamilton and a man described by some Stax veterans as 'frustratingly pushy'.

Wattstax had its origins in social disruption. In August 1965 gangs of black Angelinos had hurled bricks, bottles and improvised Molotov cocktails at a unit of the hated LAPD after the violent arrest of a suspected drunk driver in the Watts neighbourhood. Rioting swept across the ghetto, leaving 34 dead, 1,032 injured and almost 4,000 individuals arrested. At a time when cool heads were needed, the police chief William Parker infamously compared the rioters to 'monkeys in a zoo'. Yet, out of the rubble a few green shoots grew. The Watts Writers Group, the Compton Communicative Arts Academy and Watts Towers Arts Center created a cultural foundation that produced an annual summer festival, the first of which was held in the gym of Jordan High School on East 103rd Street in 1965. It was a small amateur community affair but with Stax's involvement it grew into the biggest festival of black music ever. Often mistakenly described as the black Woodstock, Wattstax was not aimed at the new counterculture: quite the opposite, it was aimed at a burgeoning black neighbourhood, one of the most deprived in the USA. The entry fee was pegged at one dollar to ensure that even the poorest families could come along. The idea began when two members of the Watts-based Mafundi Institute, a black nationalist arts group, contacted Forest Hamilton Jr about sponsoring a concert in the local Will Rogers Park. What began as a simple request for help and some cash grew into a concept – that Stax would showcase its roster of artists to the west coast. As the event grew in stature, the park could no longer contain Stax's vision and Wattstax eventually relocated to the Los Angeles Coliseum in 1972, attracting an audience of 112,000 and becoming one of the most remarkable concerts in the history of soul music.

Historian and critic Scott Saul, the main chronicler of Wattstax, claims that the subsequent movie was a significant breakthrough for African-American culture, too: 'By cutting dynamically between music on stage and interviews over the course of the film, *Wattstax* establishes a sociological vision of the music: a vision that appreciates its artifice – its power as music and as costume drama – while grounding our understanding in the attitudes of the community from which it springs.' The movie broke the rules and drew on a fund of dramatic community stories and great live music. The concert opened with Dale Warren's 'Wattstax Symphony' and former Motown star Kim Weston's haunting rendition of the national anthem 'The Star-Spangled Banner'. What followed was an explosion of styles and statements. Weston returned to the stage and sang the 'Black National Anthem' – 'Lift Every Voice and Sing':

> Lift every voice and sing, till earth and Heaven ring,
> Ring with the harmonies of liberty;
> Let our rejoicing rise, high as the list'ning skies,
> Let it resound loud as the rolling sea.
> Sing a song full of the faith that the dark past has taught us,
> Sing a song full of the hope that the present has brought us;
> Facing the rising sun of our new day begun,
> Let us march on till victory is won.

The concert featured the very best that Stax could bring to the stage – new signings, talent from their newly forged labels, and the very best of Memphis music: the Staple Singers, Melvin Van Peebles, Jimmy Jones, Deborah Manning, Louise McCord, Eric Mercury, Freddy Robinson, Lee Sain, Ernie Hines, Little Sonny, the Newcomers, the Temprees, Frederick Knight, William Bell, Eddie Floyd, the

Golden Thirteen, Rance Allen, David Porter, the Bar-Kays, Tommy Tate, Carla Thomas, Albert King, Rufus Thomas, the Soul Children, Billy Eckstine and Isaac Hayes.

For the Staple Singers, the theatrics of an open-air concert in California was neither new nor daunting. Since the early days of 1968, before they signed for Stax and throughout the Summer of Love, they had regularly appeared on stage for the coffeehouse hippies of the west coast, and appeared in concert with Jimi Hendrix, Love, Steppenwolf and Janis Joplin. The author Greg Kot, the biographer of Mavis Staples (*I'll Take You There*, 2014), wrote that the family 'found themselves immersed in a full-on psychedelic experience when they debuted on 18–19 April, at the Fillmore. The light show alone suggested a church of an entirely different religion, a collage of dancing liquid light and surreal images that mesmerised the audience.' Later in the summer they were to reconnect with Janis Joplin at the Fillmore East and joined her on stage to sing the gospel standard 'Down By The Riverside'. It was the Staple Singers who encouraged Joplin to record at the Stax studios for what turned out to be a fateful trip to Memphis towards the end of 1968.

Heading the bill was Black Moses himself – Isaac Hayes. Hayes' performance, which parodied James Brown and the history of slavery, was a tour de force of musical self-confidence, the real meaning of Black Power. Scott Saul describes it in all its layered detail: 'Isaac Hayes assumes the stage like a boxer entering the ring, wearing a full-length, swirling pink-and-brown cape that disguises the shape of his body. Then this "Black Moses" throws off his cape – and we see his body both triumphantly revealed and ceremoniously disguised again: topless except for a weave of gold chains, which extend down his chest, thicken into a belt, then descend to his knees; his lower half encased in skin-tight hot pink leggings. He's a self-consciously costumed messiah – so free that he can flaunt the signs of his people's slavery, so manly that he can use hot pink to draw attention to his manhood.'

The speeches were kept to a minimum, respecting the size and potential restiveness of the crowd. But one speech stood out and left the strongest surviving image of Wattstax: Al Bell on stage with Jesse Jackson and next to them a black senior manager of the beer sponsors, the Schlitz Corporation. All three have their fists clenched in the now familiar style of the Olympic Black Power salute. 'This is a day of awareness,' Jackson exhorted. Then he began to recite passages from 'I Am – Somebody', a praise poem written in the fifties by Reverend William Holmes Borders, the one-time pastor at Wheat Street Baptist Church, Atlanta, and an influence on Martin Luther King. It was a poem that was about to enter the vocabulary of soul music and the language of the street. By 1971 a song called 'I Am Somebody' was recorded by Johnnie Taylor at Stax, and then, as the phrase became absorbed in the language of everyday life, it influenced one of the greatest soul records of all time – Glenn Jones' majestic 'I Am Somebody (And The Universe Is Mine)', recorded in 1983, a towering piece of gospel-inspired dance music which smacked of innovations to come in its samples of the voices of Martin Luther King and Jesse Jackson advocating self-awareness and black pride.

Wattstax, and the film that it begat, became one of the most potent statements of black pride that soul music or Stax Records ever gave life to. But in time Al Bell's thermometer, record sales and the success of Wattstax would be forensically analysed by the unforgiving tax inspectors of the IRS.

NOTHING BUT SOUL. Brenda, a young soul girl and resident of
Resurrection City, outside her makeshift home in Washington.

JUANITA MILLER'S LONG WALK TO DC

12 May – 24 June

Juanita Miller was fearless in the face of authority. When she stood up, the tense muscles in her forearms seemed to swell, and when she spoke she seemed to grow a foot in size. Within a few days of Martin Luther King's death, Juanita Miller found an inner strength, as if his death had given her an urgent responsibility. She became passionate to the point of obsession about King's last campaign, the Poor People's March on Washington. She hustled friends and neighbours day and night, standing up to the most vociferous voices in her ghetto community and telling them it was time to stop mouthing off, because it was time to march. She walked into the Invaders' low-rise headquarters at 1310 Florida Street, stuck up notices, and told the guys hanging out there that if they really cared about social change they should get a mule. It became her main focus in life, apart from her children who were disabled and in great need of support.

Prior to his death, King had launched an innovative and

ultimately doomed campaign to take the poor of America to Washington, where the plan was to build a city within a city, an encampment of tents, shacks and wooden walkways. It was to be the biggest civic protest in the history of civil rights and would guarantee coverage in the press and on television. The protestors were to travel to Washington by mule train, harking back to emancipation and to the rural poverty of the Deep South. Scheming away in the shadows, the FBI gave the Poor People's Campaign the secret codename 'POCAM' and tried for months to undermine it by circulating false information, planting negative stories, and arresting local activists across America. Despite the reservations that many had within the civil rights movement and the slow take-up, even among the most politicised communities, King's assassination had ignited a new enthusiasm for change. The protestors came in their thousands, from the dusty towns of the South and the simmering side streets of the urban ghettos. They came to live in a new community, part campsite and part slum, which went by the glorious name of Resurrection City.

As Memphis grieved, Juanita Miller got angry. She was only twenty-three years old, a mother of two children, and at the time she was drawing welfare. Everyone called her Nita and she became the only woman from Memphis to take on a management role within the Poor People's Campaign, leading a team of nearly eighty mules and over forty wagons to Washington. 'We felt like we could run our own lives, build our own community,' she told the Memphis newspaper, the *Tri-State Defender*. 'We might not have had the power, but there was no lack of desire of wanting it.'

Juanita Miller Thornton was born in 1942 and had grown up in devastating poverty, in a slum apartment on Beale Street, before her family were rehoused in North Memphis in an area known as New Chicago. She was a student at Manassas High School, where she shared a classroom with the young restless ghetto kid Isaac Hayes. As Hayes' life gravitated away from poverty towards music, Juanita was drawn to the politics of poor communities and the welfare rights movement. In 1968 another of her school associates at Manassas, the Reverend Harold Middlebrook, had recently graduated from Morehouse College, met Martin Luther King and briefly ran the SCLC's offices in Selma, Alabama. Now back home in Memphis, the Reverend Middlebrook was an assistant pastor at Middle Baptist Church in Whitehaven and had risen to local prominence during the Sanitation Workers Strike when he served on the strike's strategy committee. His job was to organise local young people and recruit teenagers to support the strike, and so Middlebrook became a familiar figure at Satellite Records and at the counters of Poplar Records at 308 Poplar, jive-talking with customers unfazed by his preacher's demeanour and starched white dog-collar. It was Middlebrook who originally recruited Juanita to lead youth demonstrations downtown and picket stores on Main Street in support of the strike, and it was in the intense heat of social unrest that she met and joined the Memphis Invaders. Even at the height of the strike, her interest was not so much in industrial disputes or even Black Power but in welfare and disability rights. She was by now a single mother with a daughter who was deaf and a son who had multiple skin conditions, and they were barely surviving on welfare. One night, dragging her kids along with her, she attended a speech by Willie Pearl Butler, the female president of the Memphis Welfare Rights Organization (MWRO), who at the time was leading a residents' rent strike at Le Moyne Gardens, a decaying public housing project where the gifted blues and soul singer O.V. Wright lived with his mother. That night, a light went on in Juanita Miller's mind. She realised that she, too, had a hidden talent and the capabilities to be a female community leader. So, with no money and two children to support, she volunteered to lead the mule train. It was the beginning of big changes in her life. Within a matter of months she had become the first recipient of welfare to attend Memphis State University. 'They couldn't see that if you were on welfare you could have pride,' Juanita told a visiting academic. 'They are putting men on the moon but felt that paying a woman $97 a month was a lot of money.'

In the harshest ghettos of Memphis poverty was a stubborn presence. The city had long been compared unfavourably with Detroit and Chicago when it came to securing federal aid to combat inner-city deprivation. A major investigation in Memphis's sprawling Southside exposed a systemic failure to secure increased funding from Washington, or from charitable trusts and foundations. Memphis was unintentionally concealing the real depths of its poverty: poor quality housing, rat infestation and, remarkably in the mid twentieth century, six cases of malnutrition among children. Newspapers followed up on the claim and exposed the horrendous lives of the James brothers, who, despite being on supplemental food programmes, were emaciated. Another newspaper reported on the truly horrific life of Mrs Donnie Posey. Confined to bed with cerebral blackouts, her battered refrigerator contained only half a jar of orange juice to feed ten children. She was a widow and had brought her children from a rural shack in the old plantation town of Drew, Mississippi, to Memphis in search of a better life. It was a fruitless journey.

Juanita Miller's first job was to identify people from the Southside of Memphis who would join her on the 'Long Walk to DC'. A few members of the Invaders signed up, but, keen to shift the focus away from youthful Black Power activists, she also encouraged local mothers and their kids to join the mule train and bravely convinced disabled activists to join her. One problem loomed large: where to find a mule? No one in the city owned one and those who had seen a mule talked about them as if they were from the dark days of slavery. But Miller was as good as her word, and with the clock ticking on King's most dramatic idea, she led the Memphis mule train to Resurrection City. It was Miller, more than any of the city's celebrated preachers, or the wild boys of the Black Knights, or the Memphis Invaders, who took an impassioned message to the highest seat of power in America.

It is not entirely clear how Nita's plans converted to music but they did. Still grieving the loss of their spiritual mentor, the Staple Singers had the idea to record a tribute record, a song that could help his cause. After conversations with Ralph Abernathy it became clear that the most productive thing they could do was to bring attention to the Poor People's March. Their first Stax recording, a rousing song called 'Long Walk To DC', was in many respects a throwback to the gospel origins of soul music and the early days of civil rights. With stirring tambourines, gospel hollering and powerful female vocals featuring sisters Mavis and Cleotha Staples, the song was both a commemoration and a call to action. Behind the vocalists and always at their shoulder was their guitarist father, the former preacher Roebuck 'Pops' Staples.

Around the time of the recording, Miller had gone to Stax studios to fundraise and meet up with her old school colleague Isaac Hayes. Word spread through the studios of her audacious plan to take mule trains from Memphis to camp out in Washington. John Gary Williams of the Mad Lads had by now been recruited into the Memphis Invaders, and some of their members had signed up to join the mule train. Homer Banks, a prolific writer within the Stax camp and a man who was always attuned to the city's restless political culture, thought that marching on Washington was now such an established part of the grand narrative of civil rights that it was worthy of a song. Banks claims to have had the idea in his mind many months before, and initially intended the song to be a commemoration of Martin Luther King's epic march on Washington in 1963, but the Memphis mule train brought the idea back to the forefront of his mind, and the song had already been written and recorded in a demo form when the Staple Singers signed for Stax on 25 July 1968.

With the clock ticking, Miller had to source old plantation mule trucks and farm vehicles, which had long since disappeared from the ghetto streets of Memphis. She had made contact with the grieving leadership of the SCLC, who told her that the local base for the march was in the tiny village of Marks, Mississippi, seventy miles due south of Memphis. It was where the southern leg of the march was scheduled to begin, and Miller was advised that it would help to launch publicity if the Memphis mule train could assemble there. The plan was to leave Memphis by mule train and farm carts, ensuring that local press photographers got powerful images of young ghetto radicals being driven to Washington surrounded by bulls, cows and goats. Then, when the press call ended, the protestors would decamp onto a fleet of buses and drive south to the national assembly point in Marks, which was at the time one of the poorest communities in the United States.

It was in a dirt-poor schoolhouse in Marks that Martin Luther

King had first conceived of the idea of the Poor People's March on Washington. King and Abernathy had visited the village a year ago and watched the children, most of whom were from illiterate families with no hope that parents could even understand their rudimentary homework, let alone help. It was the teacher's job not only to teach but to nourish what was a depressed and emaciated class. 'We watched as she brought out the box of crackers and a brown paper bag filled with apples,' Abernathy wrote in his autobiography. 'The children sat quietly as she took out a paring knife and cut each apple into four parts. Then she went round each desk and gave each child a stack of four or five crackers and a quarter of an apple.' It was a scene that touched King deeply and nudged him away from core civil rights issues such as desegregation to the wider and more ingrained problems of poverty. 'I watched with growing awareness of what we were seeing,' Abernathy wrote. 'This was not just a snack. This was all these children would be eating.' When the two men drove away from Marks later that day, King in tears, they vowed they would return to shine a torch on the school and the grim lives of these children who were struggling to learn despite near starvation. Over time, the commitment to return evolved into a national campaign against poverty, and the mules that King's car had to negotiate on the drive back to Atlanta became their symbol. Whenever King or Abernathy was called on to explain the Poor People's Campaign they returned to the story of the 'soul children' in the school in Marks, Mississippi, and used their plight to arouse sympathy.

In January of 1968 King had made a speech to rally support for the campaign. In his sonorous voice, always heavy with dramatic foreboding, he spoke directly to the congregation and outward to the world: 'We are tired of being on the bottom. We are tired of being exploited. We are tired of not being able to get adequate jobs. We are tired of not getting promotions after we get those jobs . . . And as a result of our being tired, we are going to Washington, DC, the seat of our government, to engage in direct action for days and days, weeks and weeks, and months and months if necessary, in order to say to this nation that you must provide us with jobs or income.'

From the outset, the Poor People's Campaign attracted donations from all the major soul singers and independent labels of the time, from Motown in Detroit, from Stax in Memphis, and from Wand Records in New York City. It had touched a nerve in the glamorous bodies of the newly rich. Inevitably, many of the soul singers who had come to prominence in the sixties and early seventies identified with the campaign; some visited Resurrection City and many more helped with funding or appeared at benefit concerts. But by far the biggest connection was poverty itself. Many of soul music's most successful artists had emerged from the deprivation that the campaign was designed to highlight. Bill Withers, whose classic love song 'Lean On Me' was yet to be released, had been born into brutal poverty in the coal-mining town of Slab Rock, West Virginia. Withers had a stutter, struggled at school, and lost his terminally ill father as a teenager. The great southern soul singer Millie Jackson was born in Thompson, a depot town on the Georgia railroad where her father laboured as a sharecropper. Like Withers she grew up in a single-parent family, her mother dying when she was a child. The troubled singers who rehearsed in Roosevelt Jamison's segregated blood bank and then signed to Goldwax Records were inevitably poor and drawn from the scattered townships of Mississippi. James Carr was from Clarksdale, Mississippi, a former slave town where local black families were brutalised and then forced to leave when machinery replaced cotton picking by hand. The town had been home to Sam Cooke, Ike Turner and to blues troubadours John Lee Hooker and Son House. One of Stax's most gifted singers, J. Blackfoot of the Soul Children, took his name from the streets of Memphis. Too poor to be able to afford his own shoes, he wandered the tar-smeared streets of the ghetto and earned the nickname 'Black-Foot'. His real name was John Colbert, and as a teenager he became embroiled in petty crime, stealing cars, breaking into convenience stores, and shoplifting. By his late teens he was imprisoned in the notorious Tennessee State Penitentiary in Nashville, where by sheer chance he ended up in the same prison wing as the incarcerated soul singer Johnny Bragg, who formed soul music's most intimidating harmony group, the Prisonaires. Bragg had been an inmate since 1943, convicted for six charges of rape; Ed Thurman and William Stewart were both doing ninety-nine-year sentences for murder; they were joined by John Drue Jr, who was serving a shorter sentence for larceny, and Marcell Sanders who was convicted of involuntary manslaughter. Although Blackfoot never officially joined the Prisonaires, he sang with them in rehearsal and vowed that on his release he would pursue a music career despite the barriers in his way. He recorded one non-event record called 'Surfside Slide' on an obscure Nashville label called Sur-Speed Records and then headed home to Memphis where he sang in wine alleys and local juke joints on the corner of McLemore and College, where Stax had its base. Blackfoot was eventually discovered by songwriter David Porter and employed on a short-term contract at Stax, where for months after the death of Otis Redding he was a temporary member of the devastated Bar-Kays. Blackfoot's voice, steeped in the cadences of poverty and rural church pews, set him apart, and he was eventually selected by the Stax management team to form part of a 'manufactured' group, the Soul Children. He was joined by Anita Louis, Shelbra Bennett and Norman West in a double male/female duo. Far from being contrived or in any way second rate, the Soul Children grew to become one of the most talented acts on Stax's books and arguably one of the finest soul groups.

Juanita Miller stayed in touch with the SCLC by phone, seeking advice and asking for help to source mules and wagons to carry the Memphis contingent all the way to the White House. Logic would have suggested they travel to Washington by Greyhound bus but that was not the spirit of the march, and so the Memphis contingent managed to secure farm wagons from the South and the rag-tag army became the last to leave the assembly point at Marks, Mississippi. Theirs were the final wagons to lumber into Washington, by which time Resurrection City stretched out like a shanty town across the Mall. Shortly before the demonstrators were to arrive, Abernathy had been granted a temporary permit by the National Park Service for 3,000 people to set up camp in the grassy surrounds to the south of the Reflecting Pool that stretches serenely from the Lincoln Memorial. It was a near perfect location – at the centre of power and at the seat of democracy – rippling with history and rich in meaning. Poor people had come to shame the powerful. An opening ceremony was held at the Benjamin N. Cardozo High School stadium, in an area of inner-city DC that had been most heavily hit by the riots. Coretta Scott King conducted the ceremony and Resurrection City was officially declared open. Back at the Mall, Abernathy took the ceremonial lead and drove an inaugural stake into the ground, announcing the foundations of a poor people's city within walking distance of the White House. Construction begun and the first of 650 plywood huts roofed with plastic sheeting was built. Resurrection City was designed to have three makeshift dining facilities, a medical tent and a nursery. Food, blankets and medical supplies were provided by churches across the beltway and to echo the democracy of a real community a city hall was built. Reverend Jesse Jackson was declared the Mayor of Resurrection City, his first step on the ladder of public office. Street signs were erected – Martin Luther King Avenue and Fannie Lou Hamer Street – and other sections took their name from famous ghettos: Harlem, Watts and Motor City. Unofficial names began to appear as graffiti on the walls of the shacks. 'Rat Patrol Cleveland' read one, 'Soul Sisters' read another, and in the soul argot of the time another wall paid tribute to the dead and the missing in Vietnam – 'Jimmy Mack – When Are You Coming Back?'

Two days earlier Abernathy had been told by journalists that his family had been arrested in Georgia for trespassing on state highways. The Deep South caravan had made its slow progress mostly by back roads, but when the caravan of mules and farm wagons rocked perilously onto the highway the police intervened. Reactions varied: some mule trains were stopped and searched; others were given a police escort to the state line. Among the last to arrive at Resurrection City was Juanita Miller's Memphis contingent. It was a ragged army of Black Power activists, welfare mothers and children. On arrival, they were allocated a row of shacks on the southern periphery, and on seeing the graffiti that had appeared elsewhere they decorated the sodden brown huts with their own painted slogans: 'Invaders Have Landed', 'Memphis Soul' and 'Le Moyne Goes To Washington'.

The journalist Nan Robertson, reporting for *The New York Times*, wrote: 'Shacks were decorated with slogans and graffiti, funny and inspirational by turn, which illustrated the human need to put a personal stamp on even the most primitive and temporary of shelters.' The photographer Jill Freedman, who travelled down from New York to join the campaign, found herself in the midst of one of the greatest photo opportunities of the sixties – a camp populated by the rural poor, restless children, Black Panthers, urban gang members and devout Christians. She wrote in her personal diary: 'Resurrection City was pretty much just another city. Crowded. Hungry. Dirty. Gossipy. Beautiful. It was the world, squeezed between flimsy snow fences and stinking of humanity.'

On 12 May Resurrection City was given its first significant boost when an additional 5,000 protestors flocked to DC for a Mother's Day March, led by Coretta Scott King. But it was in many ways a false dawn. The place was compromised from the outset; the area around the Reflecting Pool was sodden, and the rudimentary plumbing that had been laid fell far short of the camp's needs. Resurrection City quickly became a swamp as the torrential rains of the summer of 1968 defied the seasonal odds. Only fourteen of the forty-two days that Resurrection City survived were dry, and even as the city moved towards completion, health and welfare officials worried about dangers to public health as pools of urine flooded through the tented encampments. Wobbly planks of wood were arranged as pathways, but they only partly negotiated a way through floating sewage. In the early days the poor conditions did nothing to deter the campaign and a series of protests was under way. On 21 May the residents picketed the Capitol and the State Department, but with time the living conditions worsened and spirits flagged. Abernathy's first-hand witness report hints at deteriorating moods. 'Next day the heavens opened,' he wrote. 'Day after day, the gray skies poured water, huge sheets that swept across the mall like the monsoons of India. The first day or two it was an adventure, sitting in the City Hall tent listening to the persistent rapping of raindrops on the canvas. But after a week the green grass that had provided us with a natural carpeting sank under our feet into soft mud. You could emerge from your tent, take a couple of steps, and suddenly find yourself ankle deep in cold, brown slush.'

Each new day brought further setbacks. The weather worsened and rain poured down. It was election time, but none of the presidential candidates showed up to talk to the campers, and the tolerance of the press, who had initially enjoyed the circus of the first few days, began to wane. A mood of sourness took over. A few unsavoury incidents broke out on the periphery of the encampment in which tourists were threatened and their money stolen, and police were insulted for no good reason. The official permit that allowed Resurrection City to exist was due to expire on 24 June and it became clear that there was little or no chance of an extension. Realising that time was running out, the SCLC leadership planned a final protest, a rally in tribute to Martin Luther King to be held in front of the Lincoln Memorial, the site of the very first Long March to DC, and where King had improvised his most famous speech – 'I Have a Dream'.

The final rally was to be called Solidarity Day and, remarkably, after the torrential conditions, the camp woke to a blisteringly hot day. Over 50,000 demonstrators marched to the Lincoln Memorial and surrounded the Reflecting Pool, singing from the civil rights hymn sheet and listening respectfully as Coretta Scott King, shrouded in her now familiar black mourning clothes, addressed the crowd. It was a day of quiet resistance and determined solemnity, redolent of the early gospel days of civil rights, but within a matter of two days the mood had lurched yet again to one of threat and anger when a gang of Resurrection City youths, led by the Chicago gang the Blackstone Rangers, threw fire bombs at passing motorists. With less than twenty-four hours left on the camp's temporary permit, police moved in with clubs and tear gas. It was a sad metaphor for the summer of 1968 as the power of the peaceful resistance and plea for civil rights gave way to the more strident and aggressive politics of Black Power.

Washington's local Public Broadcast Station WETA reported: 'In the early morning hours of June 23, 1968, thick clouds of tear gas rolled through a multitude of shacks on the National Mall. This shantytown was Resurrection City, and its residents were the nation's poor. As many ran from their shelters, they saw Martin Luther King Jr's final dream of economic equality withering in the gas.

They had been citizens of the city for six weeks, all the while campaigning for rights for the poor around DC. Now their work seemed all for naught. After an increase in violence and with an expiring living permit, the police had come to chase them out. Children were crying, adults screaming, and some were even vomiting. But amid the chaos, a song rang out: "We Shall Overcome".'

SCLC leader Andrew Young claimed: 'It was worse than anything I saw in Mississippi or Alabama. You don't shoot tear gas into an entire city because two or three hooligans are throwing rocks.' The gas soon cleared but the authorities had the excuse they needed to bring the protest to an end. Within twenty-four hours a special Civil Disturbance Squad came and officially shut down the camp, and the dismantling of the dream began in earnest. The tired and bedraggled contingent of Memphis protestors, including the Invaders, made their sombre way home to the poverty programmes and decaying projects of South Memphis.

Slick enforcers. Johnnie Baylor (left) and Dino 'Boom Boom' Woodard (right) at a Stax social gathering.

DINO WOODARD'S TRIP TO MIAMI

August

Dino Woodard had fists that hung heavy like swollen fruit and the intimidating habit of cracking his finger bones as if they were being prepared for action. He had literally grown up on the wrong side of the tracks, and lived by the giant salvage yards off South Main Street where railroads met and merged. As a boy he kept fit by turning the scrapyards and discarded sleepers near Booker T. Washington High School into a ghetto gymnasium. David Porter and Maurice White lived locally, too, and, according to urban folklore, Woodard ran in a local gang with Porter's older brothers in an area that the Stax songwriter once described as 'a dead-end street in the last house on Virginia Avenue'.

Woodard was a young man with an unnerving reputation for violence. Even as a youngster he had behavioural problems and teetered on the brink of sociopathy, yet he often regretted his brutality, was nagged by his conscience and deeply held religious beliefs. One Memphis insider, who had no good reason to like

Woodard, once said, 'He would beat you up, steal your money, but feel bad about it the next day, then come and apologise, and beat you up again.' Despite his violent reputation, Woodard had mood swings that belied his hardness. He was a devout brute in many respects, yet one with a preacher's sensibility and a fondness for quoting tracts from the Bible. He pioneered the shaven-head look that became more readily associated with Isaac Hayes and had a heavy sculpted brush moustache that accentuated a brooding menace. By August 1968 he had become a security guard at Stax, a description that significantly underplayed his real role. Initially, however, he had been hired by the company to repel local thugs and to ensure that Stax's interests were protected in an industry that attracted gangsters and drug barons like moths to a light.

Throughout his teenage years Woodard was a champion boxer, regularly winning high-school tournaments and local amateur fights. He borrowed a nickname from a flyweight boxer Lenny 'Boom Boom' Mancini, out of Youngstown, Ohio, and long after he retired from fighting was often known as 'Boom Boom' or simply 'Boom'. Many thought that the name came from the sound of a gunshot, a misunderstanding Woodard never corrected. After exhausting the potential of the local boxing circuit in Memphis and a move north to New York, he fought as a Golden Gloves contender and trained in the same gym as Sugar Ray Robinson. With his low centre of gravity, orthodox style and forearm strength, he was employed as a sparring partner at gyms in Harlem, and by the age of twenty-four was the stand-in to get Robinson ready for crucial fights with Carmen Basilio and Gene Fullmer, whose styles he imitated. In the case of Robinson's rematch with Fullmer, Woodard was instructed to persistently rabbit punch Robinson to allow him to ward off Fullmer's illegal attacking style. For a spell Woodard was a day-rate boxer at Harry Wiley's Gym at Broadway and 136th Street, where he helped Robinson to train the legendary jazz musician Miles Davis. It was at a time in the late fifties when Harlem was experiencing its last great era as the capital of African-American culture. Robinson drove around the neighbourhood in his flamingo-pink Cadillac – provocatively called 'The Hope Diamond of Harlem' – and, as author Wil Haygood described, turned his life into 'a waltz through the times in which he lived'. By the time Robinson retired, Woodard had already diversified into Harlem's other infamous pursuits, working in and around the late-night jazz and soul clubs, the small record stores and independent labels that were dotted around 125th Street.

It was a world of flamboyance and dark violence. Sometime in the early sixties Woodard befriended Johnny Baylor, another formidable hard man, who had moved north to Harlem from Bessemer, Alabama. Baylor was the real deal, a US Ranger trained in military combat at Fort Benning, Georgia, who on his release from the military became an ice-cold gangster. His sharp suits and dark sunglasses screamed of self-confidence and latent criminality. Irrespective of the time of day, Baylor's shades stared out at the world and the two men working in tandem began to cultivate a name for themselves on the fringes of the Harlem crime scene. Both men carried guns with the intent to use them, and together they dreamed of setting up a successful soul label, initially from a base in Harlem. Stax myth has it that the two were in effect guns for hire and were brought to Memphis to repel a group of local thugs who were intimidating the staff at the studio. Long before the riots of 1968, the area around the Stax studios had been on a spiral of decline and staff, especially the women, frequently complained to Jim Stewart that the neighbourhood was no longer safe. There had been a spate of carjackings and armed hold-ups, and a mood of brooding menace prevailed in the car parks and side streets surrounding the studios. The police were called on occasion, but Stax were told that they had chosen a bad area to base their business in and were left with no option but to provide their own security. It proved to be a darkly prophetic suggestion. At first Stax looked into a local security firm, but the petty criminals at the root of the problem needed a harsher solution, and someone among the ranks of the musicians suggested contacting Dino Woodard. That is the official version of events, but it is almost certainly the surface of a much more complex story. Al Bell already knew the pair from their membership of a nascent industry pressure group called the Fair Play Committee (FPC), which agitated for improved rights for African-American artists, producers and employees in the music industry, and he had met them on several occasions over the years when he was a promotions man and the distance between soul music and petty crime could be measured in inches. Since the fifties the R&B industry had built up its own questionable practices, not least of which was payola – the system that encouraged small under-resourced record companies to pay DJs to play their records. New York had built up its own industry, disguising payola by providing DJs with spurious credits on records, which allowed them to be paid via royalties rather than in cold hard cash. By 1968 soul music was rife with the malpractice. For example, DJ Frankie 'Loveman' Crocker was credited with being the artist on a funk instrumental 'Ton Of Dynamite' on the All Platinum Records subsidiary Turbo. It was in fact a track by the All Platinum studio band, to which Crocker made no real contribution other than playing it on his radio shows. The famous Chicago DJ E. Rodney Jones, the prime-time DJ at WVON, was also a recipient of revenue from a pounding instrumental 'R&B Time' in which he raps over the beat in a primitive hip-hop style. Most transparently of all, Philadelphia DJ Jocko Henderson had the drive-time show on Radio Station WLIB New York. Henderson supposedly 'compiled' two albums for the Wand record label featuring records by Chuck Jackson and Maxine Brown. Jocko's sounds led the compilations with records credited to him, and he was rewarded accordingly.

Far from being recruited as glorified doormen, Johnny Baylor and Dino Woodard were hired as promotions managers, who Bell knew were steeped in the ways of payola. They frequently carried wads of cash to pay off friendly DJs across the major urban areas and handed out threats to weaker contacts, including the gullible young students of college radio. Years later, when Stax had over-reached itself, Baylor was arrested at Memphis airport carrying $129,000 in cash and high-value cheques that could only have been intended either as payola or to disguise taxable income. The court determined that the cash and cheques were 'fraudulent conveyances', and Baylor's arrest triggered the final demise of Stax and its eventual bankruptcy.

Independent soul music on its outer fringes was a criminal subculture, and numerous record labels such as Diamond Jim

Riley's labels in Detroit and George Blackwell's Smoke Records in Newark were little more than front organisations for criminal activity including drug peddling, prostitution and numbers racketeering. In an interview with a Memphis magazine to promote his authoritative book *Respect Yourself*, Robert Gordon described Baylor as 'a pretty brutal man. I think representative of a certain period of business. Especially in distribution . . . distribution of all things. Not just records.' Writer Rob Bowman, the author of *Soulsville U.S.A.* concurred: 'Baylor was a bona fide gangster who wasn't afraid to use force if he felt it was necessary.'

One of the most notorious companies in the battlegrounds of R&B was the Duke-Peacock label in Houston, Texas, where the owner Don Robey either directly, or under the guise of his pseudonym Deadric Malone, routinely cheated artists. In his exposé, *Tell the Truth Until They Bleed*, the author Josh Alan Friedman quotes Jerry Leiber of the celebrated songwriting team Leiber and Stoller as saying, 'Robey was a gangster who managed his various entertainment enterprises using violence, the threat of violence, and murder.' It was a world that Baylor and Woodard knew well, and which Al Bell understood and had to tolerate. But they weren't simply gangsters. Baylor in particular harboured a long-standing desire to be a music producer, and by late 1966 he had plans to set up a small independent record label called KoKo Records – the name was supposedly a nod to the boxing term for a knockout, but more accurately was an abbreviation of the contemporary soul brother catchphrase 'Keep on keeping on'. While flexing their muscles in Harlem, Baylor and Woodard met a frustrated and highly gifted singer Luther Ingram, who had recently released 'If It's All The Same To You', an elegant up-tempo dance record fashioned in the style of Motown. The song had been written and produced in Detroit by local producers Richard Wylie and Robert Bateman and released on Hib Records, a micro-indie based in the basement of a family home at 4862 Parker Street. Local DJs in the St Louis area backed the record, and on the strength of regional success it came to the attention of the Atlantic-owned company ATCO, who gave the song a further boost with national distribution. But again the record failed. Luther Ingram tried one more time with a mid sixties novelty record 'I Spy (For The F.B.I.)', again written and produced by Wylie and Bateman out of Detroit, but this time credited to Luther Ingram and the G. Men. It was eventually released by Mercury's subsidiary Smash Records but yet again Ingram felt short-changed. Despite the obvious commercial potential of the record, Wylie, Bateman and Herman Kelly had simultaneously offered it to a Chicago-based singer Jamo Thomas, who recorded the song several months after Ingram but somehow managed to leapfrog him in the rush for attention and had what turned out to be an international hit.

Bruised, beaten and ready to retire, Luther Ingram considered returning home south to Jackson, Tennessee. Now almost thirty, he appeared as a lonely performer in a bar in Harlem where he met Baylor and Woodard, who convinced him to join them in their plans to set up KoKo. It was a transformational meeting. KoKo became Ingram's lifeline and the best move he ever made. Within a matter of months the threesome were heading for Memphis, where Baylor and Woodard took on front-office roles as hired enforcers and secured a deal that would take KoKo under Stax's wing, eventually driving Ingram to unimagined success. Ingram's great southern soul voice, caressing gospel and blues, found new markets, better distribution and slowly began to have an impact on the charts. Then, after several near misses, his epic single '(If Loving You Is Wrong) I Don't Want To Be Right' took him to the very summit of the *Billboard* charts, becoming a number one R&B hit and a pop crossover classic. It was a song that with time has come to define southern soul: emotional vocals, illicit love and moral ambiguity brought together into an epic story of adultery. Paradoxically, Ingram was soon to discover that his one-time nemesis Jamo Thomas had hit a recording dead end and was now a promotional manager at Stax, where he worked the radio stations and soul shops in Chicago and Detroit, always one of the most corrupt areas of soul music distribution.

Baylor and Woodard's arrival on East McLemore coincided with the old certainties of the Stax studio system being torn up by new leadership. The invisible pressure from new and distant owners and the dark aftermath of Martin Luther King's assassination had sketched a very different landscape, and the last remnants of the one-time family firm were gone for good. According to Chicago-based journalist Aaron Cohen, 'Dino Woodard and Johnny Baylor had their own degenerative impact on the company, making plays for power and threatening and assaulting musicians.' During a heated argument over the direction a rehearsal was taking, Baylor threatened to shoot keyboardist Marvell Thomas, the son of Stax's old trooper Rufus Thomas. Neil Spencer, the former editor of the UK music paper *NME*, writing for *The Guardian*, described the era in two action-packed sentences: 'Harassment of musicians by local thugs ensured that Bell's solution was Johnny Baylor, an ex-special ops ranger who fixed problems with gun and fist. The harassment stopped but Baylor became a toxic presence, on one occasion hospitalising a musician for ordering too much room service.' One Stax employee who chose to remain nameless spoke to authorities and claimed that Baylor had boasted about killing people.

Almost without fail, every historian of the Stax story has portrayed Baylor and Woodard in a malign light, focusing on their disruptive influence and their fearless propensity to use guns or their fists. Too many first-hand witnesses independently verify the pair's violence for it not to be true, but maliciousness is clearly only half the story. It is claimed time and time again that they moved to Memphis to sort out two local hustlers who were intimidating Stax staff. However, it is highly unlikely that two men so deeply immersed in Harlem crime and its self-damaging gun culture would move to Memphis to face up to a couple of neighbourhood thugs. It is even less likely that they would divert their business from New York to take up low-paid work as security officers in Memphis. A much more likely explanation is that they were already negotiating with Al Bell to join the company as producers with the view to grow KoKo Records – and Luther Ingram's career – under the Stax umbrella. Within a matter of months both Baylor and Woodard were salaried staff working as promotions executives at Stax, and in time Luther Ingram became an opening act for Isaac Hayes' live shows.

Baylor and Woodard were already well known to Al Bell from the internecine politics of NATRA, the DJs' union and mouthpiece, where they had emerged noisily as leading figures in the aforementioned New York pressure group the Fair Play Committee. To illustrate its grievances, the committee had drawn up a list of internationally successful records written and recorded by black artists but which had largely benefited the careers of white performers. The so-called British Invasion loomed large in their story. Among its list of exploited records were Arthur Alexander's 'You Better Move On' and the Valentinos' 'It's All Over Now' – both of which were covered by the Rolling Stones. Bessie Banks' 'Go Now' was covered by the Moody Blues, and even Dionne Warwick's 'Anyone Who Had A Heart' was covered by the Liverpool singer Cilla Black. The accusation was that the original artists had neither been remunerated nor fully acknowledged. The Fair Play Committee also campaigned against the major distribution networks, claiming they were slow to pay or simply discounted records by black artists so heavily that there was nothing left to pay the artists. Although the Fair Play Committee had noble ambitions and a strong case, it went about its business with a reckless and angry demeanour. Frustratingly, they weakened their argument by being over emotional and, like many pressure groups before and since, they were too accusatory and not good at working quietly behind the scenes. Nor was the era of Black Power particularly conducive to quiet diplomacy.

A year on from Martin Luther King's triumphant appearance at NATRA 1967, the 1968 convention was held in volatile times and ended in ignominious violence, entering the mythology of soul music in ways that business conventions rarely do. The conference was held at the Sheraton Four Ambassadors in Miami after other hotels had refused to host the event. The Marco Polo Hotel asked the organisers for a security bond of $25,000 in advance, which NATRA could not raise in cash. They proposed a compromise set at $10,000 but were rejected and so sued the hotel for discrimination.

Dino Woodard, a keen golfer until his dying days, travelled ahead of the Stax party to the City of Miami Country Club, where the NATRA golf tournament was being held. By Thursday night the convention began in earnest with Barney Ales, Motown's Sicilian-American head of sales, opening a lavish drinks reception to promote a new super album featuring Motown's two greatest assets together: the Supremes and the Temptations. Speakers lined up for the convention included the Georgia senator Julian Bond, who had only a few months earlier had to decline a vice-presidential nomination as he was below the constitutional age of thirty-five; and the Reverend Jesse Jackson, representing Operation Breadbasket, and Coretta Scott King both spoke at a dinner sponsored by Brunswick.

Stax staff travelled in numbers to Miami but were upstaged in their efforts by a southern rival SSS International, a group of labels based in Nashville. Label owner Shelby Singleton, a master promoter, hired a DC3 passenger plane and co-ordinated what he called 'The Soul Lift', an air service that took southern DJs to Miami. The flight took off from Memphis International and picked up DJs at Nashville, Birmingham and then finally Atlanta, before heading to Miami. SSS International's top soul singers were also on board, among them the country-soul singer Johnny Adams, award nominees Peggy Scott and Jo Jo Benson, Mickey Murray, who was enjoying brief success with 'Shout Bamalama' (imitating Otis Redding), and Danny White, the much travelled vocalist whose song 'Natural Soul Brother' was already charting regionally. A wide range of inducements were available on board, including drink, drugs and SSS International giveaways. It was a soft form of payola high in the skies and left DJs feeling either grateful or indebted to Singleton. A year later the Nashville entrepreneur pulled off an even more audacious coup when he bought Sun Records, the legendary Memphis label that had discovered Elvis Presley and pioneered rock 'n' roll.

The third annual NATRA Awards dinner was the highlight of the convention. It was a black-tie affair at the Bayfront Auditorium, presented by comedian and civil rights activist Bill Cosby and honouring some of the stars of soul music that year: James Brown and Jackie Wilson had tied as Best Male Vocalist; Aretha Franklin retained her crown as Best Female Vocalist; Archie Bell & the Drells were Most Promising Male Vocal Group; the Most Promising Male Vocalist was a close fight with Bobby Womack beating the Philadelphia crooner Fantastic Johnny C.; and the Most Promising Female was Chicago's Barbara Acklin. The Best Instrumentalist was saxophonist King Curtis and Top Duo was Sam and Dave. The argumentative pair had travelled down from New York with senior people from Atlantic, including Jerry Wexler. A special memorial award was made to celebrate the achievements of Otis Redding and the industry award went to the Atlantic producer and studio innovator Tom Dowd, who in friendlier days had helped to transform Stax's studio equipment and masterminded the album *Otis Blue*, recording it over a weekend. But lurking nastily beneath the surface were many unspoken rivalries, not least among them the resentment that still existed between Stax and their one-time partners Atlantic Records of New York.

Supporters of the Fair Play Committee were vocal and boisterous in the key sessions, arguing for a new deal for black artists and a more transparent system of rewards from distributors. Their anger spilled out into the corridors and elevators of the hotel. Violence and intimidation festered, and evenings that had been set aside for networking and social events turned alarmingly sour. Ironically, the first signs of actual violence came at a networking breakfast hosted by one of the industry's least delicate companies, Don Robey's Duke/Peacock from Houston, who offered a high-spirited hospitality suite throughout the weekend. Some of those in attendance claim that tables were overturned and guests threatened, and that white owners and producers were targeted by Harlem gangsters supposedly representing the Fair Play Committee. Del Shields, NATRA's black executive officer, who had drafted the running order for NATRA 68, has since rejected the idea that the attacks were wholly racist, and said that he, too, had been a victim. He claimed that in the run-up to the convention he had been attacked outside his New York office by armed men supporting the Fair Play pressure group. Most subsequent reports have, to a greater or lesser extent, blamed Johnny Baylor and Dino Woodard, but Henry Stone, a local Miami entrepreneur and the owner of the TK group of labels, pointed the finger at another infamous character on the Harlem soul scene, indie producer Joe Robinson, the owner of Sugar Hill Records. Stone claims that the first person to be seriously assaulted at the convention was Marshall Sehorn, the New Orleans producer and co-owner of Allan Toussaint's

Sansu Records. According to Stone, 'whatever the reasons are, these black mafia dudes from New York tried to muscle in on the record business, y'know, they got a hold of him, this white guy Marshall, and beat the shit out of him in the elevator. Busted his face open with the butt of a pistol or something.' Whatever the real story, it was clear that a gang of self-appointed black vigilantes had gathered at the convention to intimidate producers who they believed were not being fair to artists. Sehorn had apparently been targeted as he was in dispute with singer Betty Harris, who had recorded ten records with Sehorn's Sansu Records, among them deep soul ballads and storming up-tempo dance records. Although none were major hits, she had yet to receive a penny in payment. Similarly, the New Orleans funk band the Meters felt cheated, too; they were Sansu's house band but went unrewarded, although their complaints did not surface until many years after the NATRA convention.

Phil Walden, Otis Redding's manager, and his brother Alan, claimed that they were also threatened and that they stayed in their rooms locked away rather than walk the convention floor. Alan Walden has since remarked that it was a simple issue of race – black thugs beating up white executives. He also said that he was accused of cheating Redding. That is a highly unlikely scenario, since Redding was seen by the vast majority of people on the soul music scene as an aspirational star cum businessman, who had secured deals in every major market internationally and who generated an unprecedented income from Europe alone. His wealth was visible and admired. He owned a private plane and a luxury ranch in Macon, Georgia, where he bred stud horses. A year earlier, Redding had hosted NATRA 1967's flagship party at his ranch. The idea that Redding was short-changed goes against the grain of why so many people looked up to him at Stax and within the wider world of black music. The more likely grudge was among smaller and significantly less successful artists. The Walden brothers ran an artists' agency which was a gateway to southern venues for many aspiring soul singers. The circuit had barely improved from the notorious days of the Chitlin' Circuit, when venues were decrepit and of poor quality, and artists were routinely shacked up in black-only hotels. Many singers returned to New York having earned a pittance and with hellish tales to tell. It was hardly the fault of the Walden brothers, but they probably had to shoulder some of the blame.

The most high-profile victim of the Fair Play vigilantes was Atlantic's Jerry Wexler. He attended the convention with his award-winning saxophonist King Curtis, who had narrowly beaten Memphis saxophonist Willie Mitchell into second place in the Best Instrumentalist category. Wexler and Curtis were sharing a table at the convention's Saturday night event – a black-tie affair on the Bayfront – with R&B singer Titus Turner when it is claimed that threats against Wexler escalated. There are mixed versions of events. Some say militants dragged an effigy of Wexler through the hall, but whether that happened or not, Wexler in part blames Bill Cosby, who was there to entertain the delegates. He supposedly told several jokes in support of Black Power and at the expense of white executives in the audience. Wexler has since claimed that Cosby was mixing it and that his comedy routine fired up militants in the audience. 'Emcee Bill Cosby was a vociferous advocate, whipping it up,' he wrote in his autobiography. 'Black Power was on the agenda, and I'm all for it – black political power, black economic power, black management, black ownership, black-run labels. But these shakedown artists had no program: it was just old fashioned, take-what-you-can-get blackmail.' Wexler's autobiography lays out the important role he played in pioneering black music on the Atlantic label, and his right to be at the awards ceremony unmolested is self-evident. Yet his remarkable skills as a raconteur hide a lack of self-awareness of the times. His life story contains a photograph of another ceremony in New York, which took place the day before Otis Redding died, in which Wexler is being given an award for Record Executive of the Year (1967). There are thirty-five record executives gathered together to celebrate his achievement, pictured at the awards luncheon, and none of them is black. It was that frustration that the Fair Play Committee were raging against.

Back in Miami, according to Wexler, 'a certain element thought it was gonna be there to actually take possession of the record companies and the radio stations. And the emcee was whipping them up. "It's your time, boys, go and grab it." I'm sitting there to receive a reward for Aretha Franklin and King Curtis got me and said, "You're out of here right now." He said somebody was coming after me, a part of [what Wexler called] the irredentists' movement, they were gonna off me. It was one of those moments when the surge of Black Power infected the whole record business.' Wexler was rescued when King Curtis and Titus Turner, also carrying guns, escorted him safely from the building to his home in Palm Beach.

Since 1968, the story of the NATRA convention has grown arms and legs. Lurid versions claimed that Aretha Franklin was also threatened and abused. Although she was an award nominee, Franklin was in fact performing at the Newport Jazz Festival and was nowhere near Miami. Others claimed that Otis Redding was intimidated although he had died eight months earlier. Wexler has always maintained that the motives behind the disturbances were to do with an irate Black Power group. But there is an alternative interpretation.

Immediately prior to the dinner, Stax/Volt hosted a session of pre-dinner drinks where invites were extended to all delegates, including Wexler, King Curtis and award nominees Sam and Dave. Relationships between the Stax and Atlantic management teams were still frayed and tensions between the parties only grew worse with alcohol. It was in environments like this that Johnny Baylor and Dino Woodard's worst instincts flourished. Although Wexler may have believed that Baylor and Woodard were Harlem gangsters, they had been adopted by Stax and were taking their instructions from Al Bell and, to a lesser extent, Jim Stewart. It is much more likely that their strong-arm behaviour – which was real and undeniable – owed as much to the tribalism between Stax and Atlantic than any grandiose ideas of black self-determination.

NATRA 1968 was unquestionably spoiled by a dark atmosphere and by reckless acts of intimidation, but it would be misleading to claim that the sole factor was the arrival of Black Power militants. The previous year had also seen an emergent black militant presence in the shape of H. Rap Brown, Minister of Justice of the Black Panthers and once a leading figure in the Student Non-Violent Coordinating Committee (SNCC). Brown's fiery rhetoric lit up the convention and led to heightened demands for a fairer deal for black artists. As a consequence, NATRA chief Del Shields proposed a visionary new training academy that would train young African-Americans entering the industry in skills in studio engineering, production, songwriting and management. Shields had agreed a $25,000 levy from all US majors with black artists on their roster, or an R&B subsidiary, but none of the funding was forthcoming. This resulted in the Fair Play Committee, with some merit, accusing the NATRA executive of ineffectualness and the industry majors of ignoring legitimate complaints. By 1968, in the wake of King's murder, many felt that nothing much had changed and the vacuum was filled with venom.

Whatever their initial reasons for leaving Harlem and moving to Memphis, Johnny Baylor and Dino Woodard quickly established themselves at Stax, by both fair means and foul. Their presence was resented by some, and several key figures in the early years of the Stax story, including the sophisticated William Bell and the musical intellectual Booker T. Jones, left the company. Much has been made of their departure, but it was probably more to do with seeking greater creative freedom under their own direction than a reaction to the presence of Stax's in-house enforcers. However, session musician Sandy Kay claimed that a latent racism was visibly at play: 'I also remember Johnny Baylor and Dino Woodard. I had some run-ins with Dino. I believe he deeply resented white people, or maybe it was just me. Actually, I think he hated me – why, I don't have a clue. Since my hair was long, I had a beard, an earring . . . I suppose I was considered a "hippie" by some. Whatever the case may be, Dino took pleasure in regularly ordering me around . . . He was a *very* confrontational person. One day, we had some words, he hit me in the head with a gun, and I bled all over the carpeting in Stax's hallway. He was pretty well known for hitting people with guns – it was a *really* traumatic day, and required a trip to the doctor. Johnny Baylor never gave me a problem, and I remember him being a very nice guy to me. But I suppose we were never in a situation where we might disagree on anything. There was a whole lot of tension in the building whenever those two guys were around.'

Gradually Baylor and Woodard developed their own careers, as promoters and producers. The KoKo label flourished and Luther Ingram's career at last took off. But they had cleverly noticed another emergent opportunity. Isaac Hayes had slowly but surely been cultivating a solo career and coming out from the shadows of song-writing. As Hayes' solo career was in its early ascendancy, Baylor and Woodard took on the de facto role of his personal management team. Baylor set up shows, first in Memphis and then across the southern states, always insisting on cash in hand and sometimes with a menacing expectation. Woodard rose up the ladder of Stax's promotions team, too, and was named Promotions Man of the Year at the more settled and less edgy 1973 NATRA convention.

It was Woodard, feeding on the food of hype and over-enthusiasm, who had the brilliant idea of rebranding Hayes. One night at the Apollo Theater in Harlem, he announced Hayes to the gathered press as 'The Black Moses'. At first Hayes recoiled from what he thought was a presumptuous and sacrilegious new identity, but it was a moniker picked up with relish by prominent African-American magazines including *Jet* and *Ebony*, and it gave Hayes the final push he needed towards his era-defining album, the supremely innovative *Black Moses*. Hayes came to accept the new name, his initial anxieties proved unfounded, and with time he came to see the name as showbiz, rather than an affront to the Bible. Woodard never had any doubts and moved effortlessly from secular soul to religion and back again. Later in life he became one of the most respected black pastors in Harlem and a minister of the Abyssinian Baptist Church, a congregation he had first joined in the mid fifties when he shared a gym with Sugar Ray Robinson. Such was his presence on the streets of Harlem in his later life Woodard was described as 'a church without walls' and on his death he was given a pastor's burial. 'Boom Boom' returned to the Lord from whom he had come.

Invaders incarcerated. John Burl Smith of the Memphis Invaders behind bars but still wearing the ice-cool look of Black Power.

SONNY YANCEY'S NEW JOB

September

Sonny Yancey cursed the day he took a short cut home from work, and every time he told the story it was with anxiety in his voice. Even his own mother was not sure if he was telling her the whole truth. Edward W. 'Sonny' Yancey was only eighteen and, unlike many of his friends, he had not been conscripted. Against all the odds, he had found a good job, too. It wasn't the best-paid job in Memphis but he was now a lowly kitchen porter at the Top of the 100 Club, a fashionable skyline restaurant at 100 North Main, thirty-seven storeys up in the air overlooking the riverfront. It was one of three revolving restaurants in Memphis at the time, but Yancey was sure it was the best. He had seen Elvis eating there, and had walked past the singer on his way back to the kitchens carrying a box of carrots from the service elevator. Isaac Hayes came in regularly and sat at a private table, wearing his sunglasses. The kitchen staff, who were almost all black, were discouraged from looking at guests and were only ever allowed to use the service elevator. They were forbidden to enter the Japanese Gardens, a decorative retreat at the rear of the restaurant where lawyers and their clients met discreetly to discuss business. The rules were strict, but it was a job that came with a hint of glamour, even though his job was to gut chickens, carry waste to the elevator, and peel onions through smarting tears.

The night Yancey took a short cut home was 24 August 1968. He had come off a long Saturday night in the kitchens and he had gone over the story with police detectives in a gruelling eight-hour interrogation. They had not read him his rights, and he had spent most of the time fearful for his job as they pounded him with questions demanding greater detail and more corroboration. For a time they even told him that he was a suspect. There had been a spate of attacks on police vehicles, and a police officer had been shot. Yancey was in the area at the time and was questioned soon after. He had seen the suspects, and it preyed on his mind like a secret he wished he'd never been told. For the first time in his young life he felt pressurised into assisting a police force he had no good reason to respect.

It was approximately 10.30 p.m. when he headed home to his mother's house on Castex Street. En route he noticed four people crouching by high weeds on an embankment on Davant Avenue, where it dips down to the Yazoo railroad tracks. It was an area steeped in the past – the old bluesmen called the rail track the 'Yellow Dog' and paid tribute to it in song and story – but for boys of Yancey's age it was no more than a short cut home, through the scattered single-storey wooden-frame houses, rusting fences and deserted freight yards. Yancey was nearly home when he spotted the four men. He knew one of them as 'Speedy', the nickname for a nineteen-year-old local youth called Womax Stevenson, and he knew that another was the singer John Gary Williams of the soul group the Mad Lads. He had once dated Sonny's sister. He had no idea who the other two were but suspected they were Memphis Invaders. They were Oree McKenzie (18) and Ben Heard Berry (18), both of whom were already known to the police and had been arrested for participating in a riot at the city's Carver High School earlier in the year.

The Invaders' notoriety had grown since the Sanitation Workers Strike. They had tentacles that reached further than a street gang and an organisational depth that dug deep into the poverty programmes and ghetto streets of South Memphis. The Invaders were feared but also respected. Since the assassination of Martin Luther King, they had armed themselves and spoken openly of insurrection, but like the Black Panthers their activities mostly involved poverty outreach and black educational projects. The Memphis police were their sworn enemy and the police were distrusted by almost every black family in the city. A predominantly white force, who had attacked demonstrators during the strike and had acted at best incompetently in the case of the murder of Martin Luther King, the MPD had been slow to recruit young blacks and alienated even the most compliant youths with heavy-handed tactics and discriminatory stop-and-search procedures. In many areas, particularly in the south of the city, they were seen as an occupying army, patrolling neighbourhoods aggressively in their numbered tactical squad cars.

Across America, the police were retreating into themselves and failing to change with society. There was widespread concern within the law-and-order community that armed militants posed a real and present threat to the country's major cities. Huey Newton of the Black Panthers had been accused of killing an Oakland policeman, Officer John Frey, almost a year earlier. In April 1968 teenager Bobby Hutton was killed in a police ambush in Oakland; fellow Black Panther Eldridge Cleaver was wounded in the same ambush before absconding to Cuba. Police anxiety had been heightened by a volatile summer. In July in Glenville, a racially troubled ghetto in Cleveland, Ohio, a shootout between police and a group of Afrocentric militants led by community worker and bookstore owner Fred 'Ahmed' Evans had been provoked by a low-level dispute over an abandoned car. By the end of the night, seven people were dead: three policemen, three Black Power suspects and one civilian. The incident triggered five days of rioting, and when it became clear that the police were neither trained nor equipped to handle the disorder, Mayor Carl Stokes requested the assistance of the National Guard.

* * *

The Memphis police were regular and unwanted visitors at the Invaders' offices at the Neighbourhood Organizing Project on 1310 Florida Street, which sat among wrecked low-rise buildings near the Illinois Central Railroad. Early in the afternoon of 24 August, police came in force to the Invaders' headquarters and arrested a leading figure in the Black Power movement, John Henry Ferguson, a Memphis teenager who had joined the police's Most Wanted list after he had threatened officers at a Sanitation Workers Strike meeting. He was alleged to have waved a wooden toy gun at a passing car. News of Ferguson's arrest spread like wildfire, and the Invaders and their supporters confronted, disrupted and resisted the police wherever they could. A series of sporadic incidents erupted deep in ghetto neighbourhoods, well away from downtown. Teenage gangs took to intersections and jeered at passing police cars, and fire bombs were thrown at commercial buildings deemed to be unsupportive of local black communities. Laundry outlets owned by the family of the despised mayor Henry Loeb were targeted. Those Invaders who had access to guns were told that the time had come to arm themselves and be public about their rights under the Second Amendment of the Constitution. By the morning of 6 September resentment among the Invaders had grown to fever pitch after their offices were suspiciously burned to the ground in an overnight attack by what were likely rogue agents in the pay of the MPD.

It has never been entirely clear what pulled John Gary Williams into this maelstrom, or what brought him to the corner of Davant and Yazoo on 24 August. He says he was there to discourage his younger cousin Oree McKenzie from getting himself deeper into trouble; the police claim he was there as part of an organised Invaders' plot to shoot and kill a police officer. Always a bright and well-read young man, Williams had become fascinated by the growing radicalism of African-American politics, and although emotionally committed to civil rights he began to feel that the movement for peaceful change was too slow. The assassination of Martin Luther King had convinced him that America was not yet ready for change, and that his generation would have to force it. Although he remained deeply loyal to his religious beliefs and the 'journey of the soul' – and in that respect he was a kindred spirit to King – he was also close to John Burl Smith, the most impressive of the Invaders and a man who had also been to Vietnam and was armed with a library of books that advocated revolutionary social change.

The trial of the Memphis Invaders fell short of being a political show trial, but when it came to court it unfolded with all the intrigue and drama of a television special. John Gary Williams' presence in the dock – charged with ambushing a police car – added a dimension that the local press found hard to resist. Stax was by some distance the most famous record label in Memphis and to have one of their recording artists accused of being a member of the city's most notorious Black Power organisation added spice to an already compelling trial. The facts had been coloured by dramatic reporting. No one died in the incident, but shots had been fired and police were targeted, including one patrol car carrying the city's police chief. Patrolman Robert James Waddell was seriously injured after a bullet pierced the side of his car and he was only able to hobble into court with the aid of walking sticks. An FBI ballistics expert confirmed that the rifle used in the incident was a Russian 7.62mm Mosin rifle, similar to the gun found in the group's car. Unexpectedly, for the defendants, one of their tight-knit group had turned state's evidence and plea-bargained for lesser charges. Ben Heard Berry had been at a private meeting with the Shelby County attorney general in the company of his lawyer and struck a deal. So when Berry entered the court, he came as a pariah, having betrayed the Invaders and his friends. When Judge Odell Horton said that 'his testimony was of great help to the State of Tennessee in the prosecution of the case' the courtroom bristled with indignation.

Williams' presence in the dock caused him to become a minor celebrity in the case. On one occasion he frustrated the court by arriving late, having travelled to Washington to promote a new single 'Love Is Here Today And Gone Tomorrow' (written by Bettye Crutcher). Williams' girlfriend, a trendy afro-sporting teenager by the name of Gloria Fay Goodman, corroborated his story that he was only at the scene to try to discourage his young cousin from taking part in the shooting. Only seventeen and looking like an elegant soul singer in her own right, she was brought to the trial as a ward of the juvenile court and was forced to admit that she had made the bogus emergency phone call that had lured the police car into the vicinity.

Sonny Yancey was by far the most conflicted witness. He changed his story, even in the dock, went back on evidence he had given to the police, and at one stage claimed any evidence he did give might be wrong as he was drunk at the time. He looked petrified and often glanced over at his mother for emotional support. At one point, he enraged lawyers so much that the defence came close to securing a mistrial. He was simply a young man who was scared he would lose his job and concerned that he might enrage the neighbourhood who packed out the public gallery. His mother was so worried about his safety she had sent him to stay with relatives in St Louis the weekend before the trial and had threats of violence relayed to her by phone call.

Williams was compromised by the car that the Invaders had used in the attack. It was a green Chevrolet Camaro with the initials 'JGW' emblazoned on the side, the car he had bought with the proceeds of royalties from Stax Records. Despite the evidence stacked against him, Williams cut a credible figure in court, speaking slowly and lowly, offering contrition for the injury to the officer and at times wiping tears from his face. At least one member of the jury considered acquitting him, but the majority found him guilty on reduced terms. Of the Invaders who stood trial, John Gary Williams was given the minimum possible sentence and charges of attempted murder were dropped. He was found guilty of the lesser charge of assault with intent to commit voluntary manslaughter. It was clear that the jury did not wholly believe the story that he had tried to thwart the sniper attack, but it was apparent that he was the most honest and penitent of the three accused. Williams told the court: 'I would like to say that what I said on the witness stand I learned a lesson from it.' His cousin Oree McKenzie was given the longest sentence, charged with assault to murder in the first degree, and was sentenced to prison for not more than ten years. Williams made one request: rather than go to the tough Shelby County Jail, could he see out his sentence in a more useful way at the Shelby Penal Farm? There he could work outdoors tending vegetables and growing food for the prison population. Ben Heard Berry, the Invader who had turned state's evidence, was also granted a reduced sentence, and it was recommended that he should serve time at the Shelby Penal Farm. Now fearing for his safety, he made an appeal to serve his sentence away from Memphis, in a jail in Nashville, claiming that his wife, children and his mother had all been threatened. Whether that was true or not, it was clear that Berry had made enemies and the Penal Farm would be a dangerous place to serve his sentence. The prison was already populated with convicted Invaders and his life was genuinely at risk. In a very public way he had abandoned the cause and was not going to be quickly forgiven.

John Gary Williams' trial attorney was a fascinating character in his own right. A well-liked figure on the Memphis music scene, Seymour 'Sy' Rosenberg had watched Stax grow from its hillbilly infancy to global success. Music writer Rob Bowman described him as 'a cigar chomping, somewhat portly musician/lawyer with a well developed sense of humour'. Rosenberg had watched the Memphis music scene professionalise from close quarters. In the fifties, he had been a competent trumpeter in Sleepy-Eyed John's band with Jim Stewart, and subsequently invested in a rival recording studio, Chips Moman's American Sound Studio. As soul music surfaced, Rosenberg became a father figure to the generation of garage bands who grew up in the wake of Beatlemania and was an entertainment agent for the unconventional Rufus Thomas and, later, for country music star Charlie Rich. He even launched a local label into the burgeoning Memphis independent scene, Youngblood Records, and recorded Isaac Hayes' debut single 'Laura We're On Our Last Go Round' back in the days when Hayes was a young protégé who had been talent-spotted on a local radio show on WDIA. Rosenberg was a man who preferred conciliation to brutal argument and he was a key negotiator in the days when the Stax family split nearly brought the company to its knees. He acted as a lead attorney in Estelle Axton's legal battle with her own brother and managed her eventual departure from the company.

It was probably through Axton that John Gary Williams came to hire Rosenberg in the first place. She had remained friendly with Williams since his return from Vietnam and was more tolerant than her brother of Stax artists embracing politics. Al Bell also shared many of Williams' political views and it is quite possible, although never confirmed, that the Stax management underwrote Williams' defence costs. Ultimately it was Rosenberg who managed to mitigate the threat of a lengthy jail sentence. He was acutely aware that, in the final analysis, all cases have to find a point of compromise, one where the parties will agree – or agree to disagree – and seeing the evidence stack up against Williams, he advised his client to show some penitence and not to unduly alienate the jury.

By 1968 up to twenty members of the Memphis Invaders were being held at the Shelby County Penal Farm – a mixed bunch of hardened political activists, street criminals and ghetto kids. The FBI's COINTELPRO project and undercover Memphis police officers, led by Agent 500, had relentlessly targeted the group, regularly charging them with crimes relating to drugs and prostitution. While there was indeed an Invaders pimp corps working on the corners of Vance and Hernando near Beale Street, it was unusual for the group either to advocate or tolerate sex crimes. Coby Vernon Smith, a former member of the Invaders who was already under FBI surveillance when he first met Williams, has since described the Invaders as a product of their time and the unprecedented radicalism of 1968: 'We were, in effect, mostly young men who had resisted the war. Some were veterans who had been to Vietnam. And for the most part, we were the underprivileged youngsters who were talking simply about being recognized as men ourselves. In fact, we had spent over a year organizing in Memphis, and we hoped that some of our attempts to organize encouraged the sanitation workers to go ahead and take the stand that they took. We welcomed this kind of challenge to start speaking up. We were at that time mostly young Black Power advocates who thought that the numbers and the energy and the synergism of the whole community, the whole South – the whole country, for that matter – dictated that we step up and speak up.

We were traditional organizers, for the most part – young and foolish, perhaps, arrogant and obnoxious, in many respects. We just didn't look the part that they wanted us to look. None of us were ministers. So we didn't fit into the strategic mould that they wanted.'

And so, for a second time, John Gary Williams' career was disrupted. First, his military service in Vietnam, and then a spell working in the sun-baked fields of the Penal Farm. During incarceration, when he continued to write songs and read voraciously, he began to imagine a solo career far beyond the harmony soul of the Mad Lads. He stayed in touch with Stax and in turn they stood by him. On his release he returned to his second home, the studios on East McLemore, where he discovered that the city, the studio and the times had changed dramatically. There was a more intractable political mood.

At the time of his release, Stax were mining a tiny seam of gold, deconstructing pop classics. Isaac Hayes had dismantled and rebuilt 'Walk On By' and 'By The Time I Get To Phoenix', and Williams brought out a haunting version of George Harrison's 'My Sweet Lord' and a strident reworking of the Four Tops' song 'Ask The Lonely'. But it was one self-penned single that stood head and shoulders above those creative cover versions. In 1973 Williams recorded one of Stax's greatest-ever songs, 'The Whole Damn World Is Going Crazy'. Heavily influenced by the concept soul of the late sixties, especially Marvin Gaye's classic social commentary 'What's Going On' and the Temptations' view of a confusing world, 'Ball Of Confusion', 'The Whole Damn World Is Going Crazy' was a song written from the depths of an incarcerated mind, describing a world of discrimination, gun crime and a city engulfed in hate. It was a song that spoke of the dark and confused forces that engulfed Memphis at the time, and it remains one of soul music's unsung classics – a sign-of-the-times message that few have bettered.

The album from which the single was taken makes vivid the change Williams had undergone. On one side he is pictured in a purple stage suit adorned with bow tie, sitting by a dressing-room mirror about to go on stage. It is the kind of image that many great singers such as David Ruffin or Teddy Pendergrass might have posed for. But the image on the reverse side sees him staring into another mirror, in a fully grown afro, bare-chested in a distressed denim jacket sawn off at the shoulders, Memphis Invaders-style. It is a powerful image of the soul singer: first as romantic and then as street revolutionary.

John Gary Williams is back living in Memphis; he reformed the Mad Lads and performs regularly on the southern soul circuit. Fellow Invader Coby Smith completed his doctorate and is still active in Memphis community politics as a councilman for the city's Ward 7. Charles Cabbage died in 2010 after years of diabetic-related illnesses and John Burl Smith, one of the original Invaders, has retired and now lives in Atlanta.

Black Power salute. Tommie Smith and John Carlos at the
Mexico Olympics, October 1968.

BILL HURD'S FASTEST RACE

16 October

Bill Hurd was the fastest young man in Memphis. He proved it time and time again, on the sidewalk outside his home, at school competitions, and eventually as a high-achieving college athlete. In the eventful summer of 1968 Bill Hurd was on the starting block of greatness, a member of the finest generation of American sprinters ever. Hurd first came to public attention in 1965 as a senior at Manassas High School, when he ran a 100-yard race in 9.3 seconds at the old Fairgrounds, destroying the existing record, which had been held for over thirty years by the legendary Jesse Owens. Hurd trained in the worn grass and white-hot cinder of Tully Street in the North Chicago neighbourhood that fed Manassas High, and he came to dominate high-school athletics in Mississippi throughout his teenage years. Like a character from television drama, he ran the streets to and from home, carrying a battered saxophone case and dreaming of greatness. The trophies and medals he brought home with him went on proud display in a glass cabinet at his family home and his saxophone lay next to him by his bed.

For three years as a teenager, Hurd had played out a local rivalry with Melrose High School sprinter Willie Dawson, from Orange Mound. It was a rivalry that bewitched the Memphis press and drove both boys to the fringes of international recognition. Both were offered university scholarships and invited to compete in the US Olympic trials, having dominated competition in the Mid-South. Hurd had his mind set on attending Massachusetts Institute of Technology, but was targeted by coaches in Indiana and eventually accepted a scholarship from Notre Dame, becoming one of the few black students on the prestigious campus. Hurd's best event was the rarely run 300-yard dash, in which he set an American indoor record of 29.8 seconds, but he also ran a 6-seconds dead 60-yard sprint, when the world record was 5.9 seconds. In 1968 he clocked up impressive times across all the sprint categories and was invited to join the Olympic track and field squad for their trials at Echo Summit, in Lake Tahoe, California, where new and profound challenges awaited him. Perhaps mistakenly, Hurd had no clear sprint specialism and elected to run in the most competitive category of all – the unforgiving 100-yard sprint, where the margin between winning and losing was measured by a hair's breadth.

Lake Tahoe was situated on a mountain pass, 7,000 feet above ground level, with a track carved out of the mountainside, and was chosen as the preferred venue because it replicated the high-altitude thin-air conditions expected at the forthcoming Olympic Games in Mexico. The complex had been fitted with a revolutionary 'tartan track', the first generation of synthetic surfaces. It was a surface that suited Hurd, and as a five-time All-American sprinter, who had shattered nearly every record on Notre Dame's athletic roster, he was seen from the outset as a strong contender to make the Olympic team. But the competition was unprecedented and unforgiving. Hurd found himself up against the greatest generation of sprinters the USA has ever produced. The warning signs were obvious on the night of 20 June 1968 at the US National Championships, at a meeting that track historians have since dubbed 'the Night of Speed'. The competition was awe-inspiring. Among their number were: Jim Hines from Oakland, California, the first man to smash the 10-second barrier for the 100 metres; Charles Greene from

Pine Bluff, Arkansas, the reigning American Athletic Union champion; Tommie 'The Jet' Smith aka the Clarksville Kid, who had overcome pneumonia and childhood disability to become the fastest man in the world over 200 metres; and the Harlem-born Cuban-American John Carlos, who unexpectedly beat Smith in the trials, but had his world record nullified for wearing unregistered brush spikes. In the 400-metres category was Lee Evans, a runner Hurd had never faced nor met, but their records were nearly identical: unbeaten at high-school level, high academic achievers, and then in Evans' case the offer of a prestigious athletics scholarship that led to a Fulbright. Records tumbled like decaying trees. Over ten intense days of competition, the trials produced two hand-timed world records: one for John Carlos in the 200 metres and another for Lee Evans in the 400 metres; while the spidery Bob Beamon, soon to smash the world long-jump record in the thin air of Mexico, equalled what was then the standing world record. In one day, four world records were broken in what were only the trials.

Hurd ran a time that would have easily qualified him for almost every other country in the world but he was eventually squeezed out of the time-dominated 1968 Olympic team by 0.1 seconds. He ran 10.2 in the 100 metres, the same recorded time as another rival Mel Pender, who qualified in front of him and eventually went to Mexico where he won gold in the 4x110 metres relay team. Hurd's life was changed in that fraction of a second, and he returned to a successful season in collegiate sports, out of the Olympics in the blink of an eye. It was a bitter disappointment, but over the few days he spent in Lake Tahoe Hurd began to sense that something quite spectacular was afoot. He became aware of the anger that was growing among the elite athletes of the day. The US athletics chiefs had been measuring speed and distance using the most sophisticated mechanisms available to them at the time but they had not measured the political temperature or the deep feelings of resentment that were festering within the camp.

Success and circumstance had conspired to bring a generation of militant athletes to the Olympics, a group of supremely self-confident young black men who were unlikely to concede to any form of discrimination. Throughout the trials at Lake Tahoe, Hurd listened as his rivals discussed civil rights and the vagaries of sport and politics long into the night. He played his saxophone back in the dormitories, offering virtuoso jazz solos to the assembled athletes. Among them were Tommie Smith and John Carlos, founding members of the controversial Black Power organisation the Olympic Project for Human Rights (OPHR). OPHR was an organisation of major athletes committed to combating racism in athletics, segregation in the USA and apartheid in South Africa. For a tense period in 1967, the group had threatened to boycott the Games of the XIX Olympiad, leaving the US Olympics body with the prospect of either withdrawing from competition or having to accept the humiliating prospect of fielding an all-white team. The idea for a boycott had been hatched by former sports star turned professor of sociology Harry Edwards, who, when he taught at San Jose State University, had come to realise that black students were discriminated against in campus housing provision. Some of his best black athletes were allocated rooms at the furthest distance from the campus facilities. One of Professor Edwards's students, the sprinter Tommie Smith, took up the cause. The campaign soon diversified into a sporting movement. Hurd first heard of the campaign from a fellow student at Notre Dame and became a cautious supporter. He was eager to make the Olympic team, but since his school days at Manassas High he had grown up in an area where civil rights campaigns were commonplace.

The OPHR had its first major success when the towering basketball prodigy Lew Alcindor, who later changed his name to Kareem Abdul-Jabbar after converting to Islam, joined the fray. At the time Alcindor was collegiate box office. From his freshman year at UCLA, the seven-foot-two Hoops giant was the likeliest candidate to join the professional NBA as first-choice draft pick. Alcindor was a Catholic who had been the star player in a New York Catholic basketball league, but as he read and witnessed change in the world he converted to Islam and announced his decision to join the Olympic boycott movement at a game in Los Angeles. Alcindor told the crowd: 'I'm the big basketball star, the weekend hero, everybody's All-American. Well, last summer I was almost killed by a racist cop shooting at a black cat in Harlem. He was shooting on the street – where masses of people were standing around or just taking a walk. But he didn't care. After all we were just niggers. I found out last summer that we don't catch hell because we aren't basketball stars or because we don't have money. We catch hell because we are black. Somewhere each of us have got to make a stand against this kind of thing. This is how I take my stand – using what I have. And I take my stand here.' The crowd erupted in approval, the first time the movement had attracted popular support. Alcindor paved the way for others, and in the days prior to his assassination the movement elicited the support of Martin Luther King, who said, 'No one looking at these . . . demands can ignore the truth of them . . . Freedom always demands sacrifice.'

Not everyone agreed, even among prominent black athletes. The conservative-minded heavyweight boxer Floyd Patterson, usurped by Muhammad Ali at the time, refused to support the campaign; and O.J. Simpson, originally an international-class track athlete and running back at the University of Southern California – and poised to be the most expensive athlete in the world in the 1969 draft – said the campaign did not matter much to him and declined to participate.

The OPHR had five central demands: to restore Muhammad Ali's title after his refusal to join the draft and fight in Vietnam; to remove the white supremacist Avery Brundage from his role as head of the United States Olympic Committee; to exclude apartheid regimes in South Africa and Rhodesia from international sporting competition; to increase the number of black coaches hired by colleges and professional teams; and to boycott the selective whites-only New York Athletic Club.

All of the movement's key demands were discussed in the feisty and cloistered environment of the US trials. Hurd shared some of his experiences with his rivals, talking about events back home in Memphis and his own role in organised campus protest at Notre Dame. He was one of only twelve black freshmen back in 1965 when he led a campus-wide protest against a visiting speaker, Senator Storm Thurmond, the notorious segregationist and vociferous opponent of civil rights. In a failed attempt at the presidency, Thurmond had once said: 'I wanna tell you, ladies and gentlemen, that there's not enough troops in the army to force the Southern people to break down segregation and admit the Nigra race into our theaters, into our swimming pools, into our homes, and into our churches.' Paradoxically, as a young man he had impregnated the family's black maid and had a mixed-race daughter who he secretly funded through a black college. Hurd and a small group of supporters from Students for a Democratic Society (SDS) harangued Thurmond throughout his visit to the Notre Dame campus.

When Bill Hurd returned to Notre Dame, his athletic career peaked, and he set no fewer than eight university records and was named Athlete of the Year for 1967–68. Narrowly missing out on what was destined to be the most politically resistant Olympics ever remained a sore defeat among many victories. He then followed the path of many sprinters before him and accepted an invitation to join the Fighting Irish and use his speed as a member of Notre Dame's famous football team. He was back on campus watching television when Smith and Carlos took to the podium in Mexico to receive their gold and bronze medals for the 100 metres. The silver had been won by the liberal Australian Peter Norman, who as a mark of support accompanied the black athletes to the podium wearing the outlawed badge of the OPHR. Smith and Carlos came to the ceremony dressed to protest: wearing black socks and no shoes to symbolise African-American poverty and single black leather gloves to express African-American strength and unity. As the US national anthem played and an international TV audience watched, each man bowed his head and raised a clenched fist. Silence reigned.

In his own inimitable style John Carlos has since described the tension inside the stadium: 'You could have heard a frog piss on cotton. There's something awful about hearing 50,000 people go silent, like being in the eye of a hurricane.' Carlos was so concerned about the silence that greeted their stance he genuinely feared assassination. 'I remember telling Tommie, "Look, man, if someone has a rifle and they're going to shoot us, remember as sprinters we are trained to listen to the gun. So you keep that foremost in your mind."' The demonstration had all the dramatic street imagery of the Black Panthers and the Memphis Invaders, and the two were promptly banned for life, but the image of their medal ceremony resonated around the world and entered the iconography of protest. Although it is now seen as a momentous event in the politics of racial protest, at the time it divided opinion, even within the fractured black community, where some cautioned against any public demonstrations of anger or demands.

According to Douglas Hartmann, the author of *Race, Culture, and the Revolt of the Black Athlete*, 'it was a polarizing moment because it was seen as an example of Black Power radicalism. Mainstream America hated what they did.' Pressure mounted on the US Olympic Committee. A spokesperson for the Olympic movement said it was 'a deliberate and violent breach of the fundamental principles of the Olympic spirit'. The words had been carefully drafted by Avery Brundage, the doggedly unsympathetic president of the committee. In less than twenty-four hours, the US Olympic Committee ordered Smith and Carlos out of the Olympic Village. Smith never raced at international level again. Both men were sent into athletic exile, and in the case of Carlos his subsequent career was ruined. Stalked by the FBI for much of the remainder of his life, his wife committed suicide and his children carried the stigma, struggling to find work. 'I had a moral obligation to step up,' Carlos has since said. 'Morality was a far greater force than the rules and regulations.'

Bill Hurd's remarkable athletic career took him back to his old school regularly, to reminisce about the old days and discuss the athletic records he had broken, many of which were still defiantly in place decades later. But more often than not, his memories drifted back to the other great love of his life: the brilliance of black music. If Booker T. Washington was the training school for soul music and Memphis funk, Hurd's Manassas High School was synonymous with jazz and the marching band tradition. In the sixties, the pupils of Manassas were driven to new levels of musical sophistication by their tutor and band leader, Emerson Able Jr, a strict music disciplinarian and talented jazz saxophonist who once excluded Isaac Hayes from the school band for falling behind with his sheet-music reading lessons. Happily, the punishment never rankled with Hayes, who invited his old teacher to join him as a guest musician on-stage at Wattstax.

Emerson Able's father owned a store in a dank basement near Madison and Front, where he repaired and reconditioned brass instruments, particularly tubas, trombones and saxophones. It was those big meaty horn sounds that came to define the Manassas High School band and infuse the city's musical style. Able famously applied emergency repairs himself, filling worn holes in saxophones with slugs of chewing gum. He pushed his pupils hard, using carrot and stick, and the reputation of Manassas, which was already huge in the Memphis area, achieved a national reach. Professional musicians and local studio heads often called at the school looking for talent. Willie Mitchell, the overseer of Hi Records, was a frequent visitor, and most of the Stax in-house producers drew on the talent academy. Among its most gifted former pupils were hard bop jazz pianists Phineas Newborn Jr and Harold Mabern, and trumpeter Booker Little. Newborn Jr was the musical talisman who tied the threads together and may well have been the greatest Memphis soul musician that never was, turning his back on the repetitive simplicity of funk for the technical complexities of jazz.

Newborn Jr came from a remarkable musical family. His father was the drummer with the Plantation Inn house band, an R&B band which at its height featured Ben Branch and Willie Mitchell. The Plantation Inn was something of an institution for the enlightened and the curious. Situated on Highway 70, across the Mississippi Bridge in West Memphis, Arkansas, the venue dubbed itself 'The South's Finest Nightclub' and with liquor laws more lenient than in Memphis the club became a magnet for the musically inspired and the underage. 'When I was a kid I always heard about the Plantation Inn,' Stax trumpeter Wayne Jackson told local newspaper *The Commercial Appeal*. 'It was one of those places the adults went. They had linen tablecloths, good steaks and good music. Then as time went by, and we became teenagers, we would go and sit around and listen to the bands and the singing. They'd serve us a beer and look the other way. We thought we were big time. But we got to hear what was being played and fall in love with the music.' The veteran producer Jim Dickinson went there as a young teenager. 'There were times where I couldn't get in,' he recalled. 'Like if I didn't have a phony ID or something. So many a night I just went over there and got drunk in the parking lot, stayed in my car listening to the music, because you could hear it from outside.' Dickinson is one of many who see the Plantation Inn as the real root of Memphis music, more important than either Sun Studios or even Stax itself. He has argued that Ben Branch and the Largos, for years the house band there, encapsulated what were the primitive origins of Memphis soul. 'They were the single most significant influence on what became the Memphis sound. All of what became soul music was derivative of what Ben Branch and Largos were doing,' Dickinson claimed. 'But overall, the Plantation Inn itself developed a kind of sound . . . and how the same group of musicians developed a kind of interplay and a style.'

The Plantation Inn house band, which sometimes went by the initials PI, took its name from the slave plantation era, and became something of a crossroads for young Memphis musicians, who would be required to play all forms of music from old dancehall standards through jazz to R&B, rock 'n' roll and soul. Performing as underage musicians, they came under the brutal leadership of strict senior professionals such as Ben Branch, Willie Mitchell or, in the case of Phineas Newborn Jr, his own demanding father. Branch in particular was suspicious of young ambitious musicians. He turned down Isaac Hayes on several occasions and never fully acknowledged his talent, even at Hayes' creative height. Unlike Manassas High School, which remained conservatively wedded to jazz and classical, still insisting that its students could read music, the Plantation Inn was an informal, sometimes reckless, hive of improvisation, a place where jazz became contaminated with the new forms of popular music.

Drummer Howard Grimes, who became a mainstay session drummer at Hi studios, was another prodigy of North Memphis. 'I went to Manassas High School, where I was under the teaching of the great bandleader Emerson Able. I never knew that he was in my corner, but he was,' he told journalist Andria Lisle. 'He'd take me on his own gigs at the Plantation Inn in West Memphis, and let me out of school at two p.m. so I could catch the bus over to

McLemore Avenue. But he'd never tell you how good you were – he'd keep you working as hard as you could to please him.' In his own young days Able had been a disciple of the legendary Jimmie Lunceford, who had preceded him as a Manassas bandleader. Lunceford, the ultimate renaissance man, had joined the high school as an English teacher cum football coach but also organised extracurricular music classes. In the Depression era, he established a Manassas High School student band called the Chickasaw Syncopators, and then eventually left the school, taking many of his best students with him to form the world-famous Jimmie Lunceford Orchestra.

The legacy of the Plantation Inn band and Manassas High School brought the best of North Memphis to prominence. Ben Branch went on to lead one of the great bands of the civil rights era, the Operation Breadbasket Orchestra; Willie Mitchell pioneered two eras of Memphis music, the up-tempo instrumentals of the sixties with Bill Black's Combo, peaking in 1968 with his own 'Soul Serenade', and then driving Hi Records to new levels of success with the emotional soul of Al Green and Ann Peebles in the seventies; and Phineas Newborn Jr became one of the great figures of jazz (the respected jazz musician and writer Leonard Feather saying of him: 'in his prime, he was one of the three greatest jazz pianists of all time'). But, like so many before and since, Newborn Jr struggled with substance abuse and nagging mental health problems that necessitated his incarceration in the Camarillo State Mental Hospital in California. Undervalued and out of the reach of the music scene, Newborn Jr returned to Memphis in 1968 but recoiled from invitations to join legions of his old friends who were earning money as session musicians in the Memphis studios. He struggled to earn money through music despite short residencies at the legendary jazz club Sweet Basil in Greenwich Village. Throughout his early years Phineas Newborn Jr had been the virtuoso most likely to find greatness, but he could never find it in himself to compromise, and he died prematurely, still doubting his own formidable ability and emotionally distancing himself from the story of the band he had once graced.

* * *

Bill Hurd's athletic career faded into history, and he became a successful ophthalmologist, frequently travelling around the world to perform eye surgery on patients in Senegal, Mexico, Ghana and Trinidad and Tobago. Later in life he returned to the faithful friends in his life: the saxophone and the lessons he had learned at Manassas. Now an accomplished bandleader in Memphis, he has recorded four albums, one of which features the city's finest vocalist, J. Blackfoot of the Soul Children. Another features the late Maurice White of Earth, Wind and Fire, and yet another stars his wayward schoolfriend Isaac Hayes. Hurd has reconnected with former pupils of Manassas High School, the irreducible thread that runs through the Memphis jazz scene.

Hurd's experiences of 1968 are inevitably framed by the photograph he never appeared in: the iconic image of Tommie Smith and John Carlos, heads bowed in solemnity, their black gloved fists raised aloft. Of all the many images that 1968 gave to the world, this powerful statement of black resistance, beamed around the world, stood out as *the* defining image of the era.

Gospel franchise. Mahalia Jackson, businesswoman and gospel superstar.

MAHALIA JACKSON'S GLORI-FRIED CHICKEN

November

A stately voluptuous Mahalia Jackson emerged from the kitchen bearing a plate of her famous fried chicken. The cameras sparked into life, and Ernest Withers pushed his way to the front, tangled in straps and with his cumbersome Graflex Crown camera nestled in the palms of his hands. Jackson strode into the heart of her new restaurant and held the steaming plate of chicken aloft, teasing the photographers, as if fast food was cooked with sacred sauces and in the most celestial of kitchens. It was a press launch for Jackson's soul food franchise, a series of restaurants that were briefly popular in 1968 before economic reality and poor distribution brought the venture crumbling to its knees.

Jackson had been adamant that the restaurant chain respect gospel heritage and not exploit the name of the Lord, and so decided that the fascia of the fast food restaurants would be designed to look like a church and carry her name. She rejected several recipes and a host of terrible puns on the draft menu but agreed that the franchise could call its centerpiece dish 'Glori-Fried Chicken'. An image of the gospel star hitting a joyous top note adorned the cardboard buckets of fried chicken. The design was far from original, being boldly derivative of the pseudomilitary gait of Colonel Sanders and his Kentucky fried chicken franchise, by then an institution in the white South. Jackson was a magnificent singer, a soaring contralto who remained fiercely loyal to gospel music throughout her life. A frequent visitor to Memphis, she was known first as a gospel star, then as a celebrity chef who specialised in southern soul food, and then as an astute businesswoman who made the clever decision not to invest in fast food but to license her image rights to others.

There were four restaurants in different parts of Memphis, all of them in African-American communities, but the flagship had been cleverly located at Stax corner, which uniquely attracted musicians and journalists from all over the world. According to the African-American historian Alice Randall, 'Mahalia Jackson sought to use franchise food as a kind of Trojan horse to introduce economic vitality into the belly of black communities. There was a bit of Marxism in her recipe. A bit of black Muslim self-reliance. And a whiff of gasoline.' Jackson had secured a partnership with Gulf Oil, who stated in a press release at the time, 'we are pleased to be associated with Miss Jackson, a respected and renowned personality, and her company. Since Mahalia Jackson's Chicken System is black-owned, managed and staffed and is hiring in the communities in which it operates, Gulf hopes it is helping to provide blacks business and employment opportunities.'

The issue of black-owned businesses had been a key plank in the civil rights movement for decades, but in Memphis the cause was magnified by a city-wide NAACP campaign led by Maxine and Vasco Smith, who co-ordinated picket lines at stores in predominantly black neighbourhoods. The most visibly successful protest was at the Bellevue-McLemore shopping mall, close to both the Stax studios and Jackson's flagship chicken restaurant. The objective was to secure jobs and management posts in stores that had predominantly black clientele. As the NAACP jobs campaign gathered momentum and small but significant successes, by contrast Jackson's venture crashed and burned. After the initial enthusiasm of the launch period, interest dwindled and a high-profile robbery at the drive-in restaurant on South Parkway had a negative effect on trade. By 1971, the managing company had filed for bankruptcy.

Despite the commercial setback, Jackson's reputation was unscathed and she was able to point to the noble ambitions of her Glori-Fried Chicken. The chain had been ambitious in its aims, offering jobs, decent wages, paid vacations, low-cost life insurance and major medical benefits to its employees. It was also in the ambitious process of building a management school for African-American recruits when the roof fell in. Despite her detour into the fried chicken industry, Jackson was at the towering height of her career as the most successful gospel singer black America had ever produced. It was hard earned, deeply deserved and had provided her with substantial wealth. She had received many approaches to convert her from her gospel roots, first to blues and then to sixties soul music, but had always refused. She believed that the church was something more than a place to worship and saw it as the great sanctuary of life and the breeding ground of the civil rights movement. Al Green was even more explicit: he saw the church as a social response to segregation, once telling *Esquire* magazine, 'Church is so important for black people because it's the only place we had to go when we couldn't go no place else. Couldn't go to the bar – wasn't allowed. Couldn't go to the hotel because we weren't able to rent a room. Couldn't go to the restaurant because we weren't allowed to be seated. So we went to church.'

On her long journey to fame, Jackson had sung in churches from the beating heart of the Chicago South Side to the flooding levy banks of Louisiana, and she had performed in Memphis on hundreds of occasions, staying at the Lorraine Motel in a specially sourced double bed. Across her remarkable career she had defied age and seen off a younger generation of female singers, including Aretha Franklin, Dionne Warwick and Gladys Knight, most of whom escaped to pop or soul music. Franklin had briefly threatened to steal Jackson's crown when she signed for Columbia Records on what was euphemistically called a jazz contract, but Jackson knew that was just corporate code for pop and soul, and told people indiscreetly that the worm of fame was eating away at Franklin's soul. It was never a happy relationship; the often dogmatic Jackson felt that Franklin had betrayed her sacred gifts to the music industry, and for the rest of her life she held her in silent contempt. Although they were civil and ambassadorial when they met, the painted smiles hid many bitter jealousies. Franklin, for her part, was equally scathing. She considered Jackson to be a conniving fraud, a woman too busy making money to make great music, and she had never quite forgiven Jackson for withholding payments that she claimed were due to her when they performed at a concert in Chicago at a time when both were established stars of the gospel circuit. Who could ever fathom the many mysteries of the gospel circuit? It was lucrative, bitchy and strewn with a sometimes bogus love for God. It was the Miami soul singer Paul Kelly who dramatically severed his links with the Christian gospel tradition when he released 'Stealing In The Name Of The Lord', a savage critique of religious parasites, false preachers and the furious commercialism of the new church.

Mahalia Jackson was a gospel traditionalist who was suspicious of blues and soul. She once told a journalist, 'I'd never give up gospel for the blues. Blues are the songs of despair, but gospel songs are the songs of hope. When you're through with the blues, you've got nothing to rest on, but when you sing gospel, you have a feeling that there's a cure for what's wrong.' At times her Christianity projected a resoundingly pompous view of other musical forms but it was not without a core truth. Of soul music, she could be even more damning, revealing a seething disrespect for musicians who traded in their brilliance for cheap thrills. 'It seems to attract people who are a flashy mess,' she once said in a diatribe against the drugs, toxic glamour and financial failures that seemed to blight the great soul singers of her time, such as Little Willie John, David Ruffin and Marvin Gaye.

Al Green, then on the cusp of signing to Hi Records and moving his life to Memphis, was more philosophical about the musical culture he worked in. 'The battle between the secular and the sacred,' he wrote in his book, *Take Me to the River*, 'has brought down more great Black musical artists than drugs or loose living or any other hazard of the trade.' He was not simply pointing his finger at others. The magazine *Rolling Stone* said prophetically of Green, 'to a greater extent than even his predecessors Sam Cooke and Otis Redding, Al Green embodies soul music's mix of sacred and profane'.

Gospel had dominated Jackson's life from her birth in a shanty town by the Mississippi, where she was surrounded by jazz and Dixie, to her death in the Little Company of Mary Hospital in Chicago in 1972. She had married and divorced twice, and the one constant in her life was gospel. Her reputation had two consequences. She influenced generations of black musicians to use their voice as an instrument and she brought a level of social acceptability to African-American music that no one before had successfully done. Curiously, her dedication to spiritual music – rather than funk or atonal jazz – made her an unthreatening figure to the powerful. During her remarkable career she sang for three presidents – Eisenhower, Nixon and Kennedy – notably appearing at John F. Kennedy's inauguration and at a Royal Command Performance for the Queen in London, and becoming the first westerner to perform for Emperor Hirohito of Japan. Politicians loved her godly conservatism, and, strange as it may seem, she struck up a friendship with the most unlikely figure, President Richard Nixon, who once sent a US Air Force jet to bring her home after she collapsed on-stage in Munich. It was the preface to a string of health problems that ended with her death from heart seizure. In a line that could have been on her gravestone, she somehow managed to combine her love for food, gospel and the entrepreneurial spirit: 'I've been singing for over forty years, and most of the time I've been singing for my supper as well as the Lord.'

Unlike almost every other singer who visited Memphis in 1968, Jackson was one of the very few who attracted the attention of the notoriously white and conservative daily the *Memphis Press-Scimitar*, who described her as 'a mountain of soulful serenity'. Unlike the sexually explicit soul stars of the funk revues, or the message music that had hardened since civil rights, Jackson was solid and dependable, and she radiated family values. She was eventually entombed in a white granite grave in Providence

Memorial Cemetery, Chicago, and then moved to a resting place designed in the style of Martin Luther King's tomb. Dick Gregory, the comedian, said in her memory, 'The night before the final push a lot of folks would be sitting round and not knowing if we were going to live or die. After you left Mahalia singing about heaven, dying didn't seem too bad.' Jackson's final visit to Memphis was to sing at a benefit concert for the Riverview-Kansas Day Care Center, which at the time was a vacant warehouse at 1424 Florida, near the offices of the Memphis Invaders. The plan was to convert the space into a centre for the poor, providing daycare for working mothers and offering medical and dental services to local infants.

Throughout the sixties she had appeared regularly in the African-American press, dispensing culinary wisdom, sharing recipes and proselytising on behalf of traditional forms of southern soul food. Rural food featured prominently in southern soul music, which used cooking as a metaphor for everything from love to celebration. The name of the old Chitlin' touring circuit was derived from chitterlings, the culinary delight of boiled hogs' intestines that were sold in the venues. It was called soul food, and it was a passion Jackson shared with the Stax studios. Much of the back catalogue of Booker. T and the M.G.'s could have fallen from the menus at her franchise restaurants. In 1962 Booker T. and the M.G.'s' international hit 'Green Onions' brought Stax a global reputation and was immediately followed by a string of culinary instrumentals extolling soul food, among them 'Jelly Bread', 'Burnt Biscuits', 'Mo' Onions', 'Red Beans And Rice' and 'My Sweet Potato'. They shared a repetitive and instantly recognisable formula of funky bass, metronome percussion and a meandering organ sound with flashes of guitar: it was as if a sixties Modernist had been let loose in a post-war cinema chain, so redolent of an era when the organ – once a staple of religion – was being reinvented. By 1965 the Mar-Keys were also in on the act with 'Banana Juice', but probably the best of the lot was Wendy Rene's irrepressible Motown-styled dance record 'Bar-B-Q'. It had a natural energy, as if a youthful and self-confident black girl had decided to dance outrageously at a whites-only garden party in the Memphis suburbs. Rene was the stage name of a local Memphis singer Mary Frierson, a one-time member of the Drapels. They were a local Memphis group led by her better known brother Johnny Frierson and featuring Marianne Brittenum and Wilbur Mondie. Frierson was a regular feature on the Memphis gospel circuit and played guitar for the Sunset Travellers in numerous concerts and on at least one recording, O.V. Wright's 'Another Day Lost'. Frierson and the Drapels recorded for Stax's subsidiary label Volt, and for a time were the favoured backing singers at the Stax studios. Stax were keen to rename Rene as Wendy Storm, but she took advice from Otis Redding and adopted the more subtle stage name Wendy Rene. Already heavily pregnant when 'Bar-B-Q' was released, she left Manassas High School prior to graduation to pursue a professional career as a singer, recording a catalogue of obscure songs for Stax that have since been sampled by Wu Tang Clan and Alicia Keys. This gave her work a new lease on life, long after the originals had been forgotten and deleted. By 1968 Rene's career was all but over, and she made the prophetic decision to turn down what would have been one of her last professional performances, the chance to travel with Otis Redding on his fateful journey to Wisconsin. According to the Stax publicist Deanie Parker, 'She had all the ingredients. She wrote her own songs, had a distinctive style. But she didn't fit into the mould typically associated with the sound of Stax. So it was difficult to launch the kind of career she really did deserve. But she was enormously talented.' Rene's vivacious style may have been more suited to the pop sound of Motown, but that was not to be. She had returned to gospel singing at the Church of God in Christ at Mason Temple. By 1968 her brother Johnny and his friend Marianne had crossed town and were employed as backing singers at Hi Records.

Memphis had become a place where gospel singers could cross over and yet somehow maintain their dignity. Unlike the flashy Cadillacs of Harlem or the sinful ghetto bars of Detroit, something about Memphis still respected the old ways, and even Beale Street, with its late-night saloons and dens of iniquity, held out a pious hand to religion. It was in November 1968, as Mahalia Jackson worked double-time singing by night and promoting fried chicken by day, that the two Margarets arrived in Memphis. Neither would ever be known by that name, and for different reasons they had both tried to leave their Christian names – if not their Christian faith – behind. Margaret Joseph and Margaret Ann Peebles brought with them the deep and pleading soul of the great gospel heritage. Margaret Ann Peebles was from St Louis, Missouri, the daughter of a preacher man and the seventh child of a gifted gospel family. As a young teenager she had risen to be the featured singer in her father's Peebles Family Choir, who toured extensively in the Mid-South opening shows for Mahalia Jackson, Aretha Franklin and Sam Cooke. After a fight with her father, Margaret Ann Peebles walked out on gospel to join a St Louis revue band led by local saxophonist Oliver Sain, a masterful musician who had worked with Howlin' Wolf, Little Milton and Fontella Bass. Her father knew and distrusted Oliver Sain, considering him a serpent-like figure who profited from the devil's music. It was on tour as a featured singer with Oliver Sain's Revue that Peebles arrived in Memphis. There she met trumpeter Gene 'Bowlegs' Miller, who had held various residencies the length of Beale Street at the Flamingo Room, Club Handy and Club Paradise. It was Miller who saw star potential in Peebles. He took the inspired decision to introduce her to Willie Mitchell, the driving force at Hi Records, foregoing a chance to take her to the overstretched and overpopulated Stax studios, where too many good acts had fallen by the wayside. Much more comfortable with her middle name, and preferring to be known as Ann Peebles, the young gospel singer took up a residency in a bar on Beale Street, singing standards, pop ballads and soul classics. Within a few short weeks, Willie Mitchell took her to the infamous NATRA convention in Miami as part of the Hi Records stable of artists and she was heavily promoted as a star of tomorrow. It was her first significant outing as a recording artist and the first tantalising hint that Memphis was about to launch a new generation of talent on the world.

The second Margaret, who insisted from an early age on being called Margie, Margaret Joseph, arrived in Memphis in the autumn of 1968 to promote her new release. She had learned to reconcile body and soul long ago. A gifted singer and actress as a child, she had a self-assured deportment supported by years of training in stagecraft. Her debut album, *Margie Joseph Makes A New Impression* (Volt, 1970), sees her resplendent in a full afro, sitting on a stool dressed in a figure-hugging halter-neck dress. The image screams of soul power, the rise of black assertiveness and the triumph of sexuality.

Born in Pascagoula, Mississippi, she was a singer in her father's choir. She went on to graduate from Dillard University in New Orleans, where she studied Speech and Drama. While at university she befriended a generation of much more streetwise musicians from the Calliope Housing Project, in uptown New Orleans, among them the Neville Brothers and her eventual producer Wilson Turbinton, better known by his preferred name Willie Tee. Joseph was a determined, confidently sexual and talented singer who went on to record at Fame's Muscle Shoals studios in Alabama and sign for the legendary OKeh label in Chicago. The last months of 1968 saw her ready to take another tilt at fame. She briefly signed for Stax, who assigned her to the Volt subsidiary, but she was crowded out by the relentless pace of releases there, lost amongst songs by Jimmy Hughes, the Mad Lads, the Emotions, Darrell Banks and Jeanne and the Darlings. But her torch song 'Never Can You Be', backed by an immense mid-paced crossover song 'One More Chance', has somehow survived and clung on for several decades as an underground classic. Paradoxically, it was 'Never Can You Be' that alerted Atlantic Records to her talents. In the past that would have been a simple exchange of phone calls, and she would have stayed in Memphis to work with the Stax house band and record for Atlantic; but the mood music had changed in the intervening months, and the idea of recording at Stax while signed to Atlantic – the norm until May 1968 – was now as close as it gets to musical betrayal.

Before she left Memphis, her visit too fleeting, Margie Joseph made a contribution to a style of African-American music that was about to become yet another Memphis-inspired trend. Working with Isaac Hayes and the producer Fred Briggs, she covered a version of the Supremes' 'Stop! In The Name Of Love', dismantling the song and then rebuilding it as a ballad, which she prefaced by a long narrative rap. The informal rap introduction and the deconstructed pop classic had become the creative signature of Hayes, used most compellingly on his ground-breaking version of Glen Campbell's 'By The Time I Get To Phoenix'.

By the end of 1968 Mahalia Jackson's southern fried chicken franchise was careering towards bankruptcy and the singer's diseased heart was failing her. Time had moved on, and the classic gospel tradition she represented, with all its demanding constraints, was fading in the rear-view mirror. Soul music was poised for another eventful episode in its hectic rush to modernity.

It is rare for a city to define a moment in music. Detroit had done it with Motown and Liverpool with the Mersey Sound, but Memphis stood ready to achieve it twice. First, with the raucous Stax-inspired songs of the mid sixties – Otis Redding's 'I Can't Turn You Loose', Sam and Dave's 'Hold On I'm Coming', Wilson Pickett's 'Mustang Sally' and Eddie Floyd's 'Knock On Wood' – but this time round it would be tear-drenched sophisticated soul – Al Green's 'So Tired Of Being Alone' and 'Let's Stay Together', the Soul Children's 'Move Over' and 'The Sweeter He Is', Margie Joseph's 'Never Can You Be' and Ann Peebles' unblemished classics, 'I'm Gonna Tear Your Playhouse Down' and 'I Can't Stand The Rain', a song that Peebles composed in a single night with her partner Don Bryant during a Memphis thunderstorm. It was the song that virtually invented a subgenre of soul music, a subtle mid-tempo sound that radio programmers dubbed 'the quiet storm'.

Al Green was the maestro of the quiet storm. His sweetly nurtured gospel style was woven in heaven and delivered to romantics here on earth. It was music that was never intended to be raucous, or even revivalist; the style was devotional but cast in the familiar world of love, romance and relationships. Green is one of soul music's most popular vocalists, selling over twenty million albums in a decade. Wherever he roamed, Albert Green was instinctively a southern singer. He was born into a poor share-cropping family in the so-called 'Jewel of the Delta', Forrest City, Arkansas. His family soon uprooted and tried to find a better life as part of the great migration north to Michigan. They settled for a while in Grand Rapids, where his father took low-paid factory work but never totally overcame heavy drinking. Green joined his school's gospel choir, where he stood out from the chorus and soon became a featured vocalist in church gospel groups across Michigan. At aged sixteen, in a now familiar pattern for aspiring soul singers, he fell out with his father, who in an act of petty hypocrisy refused to allow his son to join an R&B band because they were likely to play in bars and nightclubs. The overbearing and self-righteous father figure has been a recurring figure in soul music, impeding the careers of David Ruffin and Marvin Gaye as well as Al Green. Deciding to ignore his father, Green joined a group called the Creations and walked out of the family home. He entered a new world, unsafe and unprotected, in which he slept on sofas, rehearsed in corridors and travelled to concerts in a crowded car, heaving with instruments and restless friends. He found temporary refuge with a Michigan prostitute and managed to climb up the local ladder of fame by joining the undercard at Junior Walker and the All Stars shows. Green's group hustled enough money to bring out records on what was then a low-key independent label called Hot Line Music Journal, the most visible of which was a 1968 song called 'Back Up Train'. On the strength of the song's regional success Green secured an opening slot at the Apollo in Harlem, but whatever money the group made drained away and Green left to go solo, with neither family nor much direction to guide him. Fleeing from debt back in Grand Rapids and drifting inevitably southwards, Green found himself in Midland, Texas, where by sheer chance he met Willie Mitchell. In an interview with Andria Lisle, Mitchell tells a story of near desperation: 'I knew even then that Al had the talent to really be something. But he didn't have a follow-up to "Back Up Train", and he was down on his luck, really starving. I offered to bring him back to Memphis and work with him, but he wanted to know how long it would take to make him a star. I told him eighteen months, and you know what he said? "I really can't wait that long." He came around, but first he needed some money – he had some bills to pay up in Michigan. I lent him $1,500 without a contract, and he took it and disappeared up north. About six months later, the doorbell rang at six o'clock in the morning. I thought it was a man coming to paint my kitchen, but the guy said, "Don't you remember me? I'm Al Green."'

For reasons buried in history, Mitchell chose to launch Green's Memphis career with a cover version of the Beatles classic 'I Want To Hold Your Hand'. Undistinguished, it fell without trace, but just as the song was fading out Green's voice shrieked as if he had barely begun. He barely had. By the early seventies Green had recorded a string of songs that came to define both his style and his stature, among them tireless beat ballads like 'So Tired Of Being Alone' (1971), 'Let's Stay Together' (1971) and 'Call Me (Come Back Home)' (1972), which would in time join the pantheon of peerless soul music.

Green had a woman in his life, too. Her name was Mary Woodson, and she was dating him casually but not yet closely. In a story that beggars belief, Green found himself caught in a relationship layered with deceit and hurtling towards tragedy. Woodson was twenty-nine and living a double life. A married mother of four (Green only discovered this after her death), she was petite, vivacious and arrestingly attractive, and had what has been described as 'a megawatt smile'. She had a back story that read like a soap opera. Born in North Carolina, she had been a child bride and fell pregnant twice as a teenager. By 1968 she had remarried – to a quiet and unassuming electrician called Raymond – and was now living in New Jersey. She had a history of dating, pursuing and stalking soul singers and was well known at the Continental Ballroom in Newark, a staging post on soul music's sinful northeast coast. Running away from the confinement of motherhood, she had several unfulfilling affairs and began to became reckless and suicidal. On one occasion she was admitted to hospital in Newark after taking an overdose of sleeping pills. She even talked about suicide to her mother in the family home in Madison, New Jersey, telling her she would shoot herself with a gun and that on her burial she had to have an open casket and wear a favourite red dress so her beauty could be acknowledged. She fell in love with Green at first sight, apparently, when she met him at a prison benefit concert in upstate New York. Green was performing and she was an invited member of the audience, the guest of an inmate. Unaware of her home life, Green courted her with red roses and champagne, which her husband simply laughed off. They continued what has been described as 'a torrid affair at long distance', calling each other obsessively and speaking for unbroken hours at a time. Late one night, after Green had been recording at Willie Mitchell's Royal Studios, they returned to his twenty-one-room mansion at 1404 Saint Paul Road in Millington on the northern outskirts of Memphis. Woodson went to the kitchen to cook a pot of boiling hot grits, the staple of southern soul food. She had mentioned wanting to marry Green and raised the subject again. He brushed it off, saying that they would talk about it in the morning. Woodson pursued him into the bathroom, where Green was stripped semi-naked preparing to shave, and threw the scalding pan of grits across his bare back. She then fled to a bedroom where she shot herself in the head with Green's .38-calibre pistol. Inside her purse the police found a suicide note, and a few days after her death Al Green's secretary opened a letter that contained a second suicide note. Green was rushed to the Baptist Hospital in Memphis, where he stayed for several weeks undergoing emergency treatment and skin graft surgery. The incident triggered a huge emotional retreat in Green's life and he returned to the church claiming he had been born again. His days as a secular soul star were now preciously numbered, and although his drunken father was long gone, he returned to his roots in gospel music. In an exchange that would have horrified Mahalia Jackson, his mentor Willie Mitchell tried to talk him round. Green told an interviewer: 'I don't know what happened, except in 1973, I had this religious conversion, and Willie Mitchell . . . goes, "Oh no! You say you found Jesus! How we gonna make money with that?"'

Now a minister in Memphis, where he regularly sings at the Full Gospel Tabernacle Church on Hale Road, Green has reconciled a war that had fought within him since his teenage years: 'I've come to understand one can't live without the other. You've got a body and then there's the spirit, God did the right thing, he put them together and the body needs the soul and the soul needs the body. We have to reconcile our actions and our work only to the man upstairs.'

Merry Christmas. By December 1968 Memphis was a magnet for visiting musicians. Janis Joplin and Sam Andrew (far right) of Big Brother and the Holding Company join Steve Cropper, Dick Dunn, Carla Thomas and Rufus Thomas at Jim Stewart's party.

JIM STEWART'S CHRISTMAS PARTY

December

As 1968 came to its eventful end, Memphis defied expectations. It had been battered by a divisive rage that few cities in the world could survive, yet it not only survived, it thrived and expanded. An area to the far southeast of the city known as the Mitchell Road sub-region was waving goodbye to its ancient status as arable farmland and came within the jurisdiction of the City of Memphis. So, under the beleaguered control of Mayor Henry Loeb, a small civic restructuring increased the population of Memphis by 20,000 people. It was small but not insignificant, and many seized on the city's growth as a signal of hope for the future. Remarkably, for all its global success in music and the notoriety that the year had brought, Memphis was still a comparatively small city; the population once estimated at 563,800 now peaked at 541,900. By comparison with Detroit and its northern rival Motown it was tiny, and by comparison with New York, the home of Atlantic Records, it was infinitesimal. But size became a matter of civic pride. Like a boxer confronting a heavier opponent, Memphis not only punched above its weight, it came to dominate all the heavyweight categories of black-inspired music.

Soul was now insinuating itself into almost every other form of popular music, stretching the creativity of rock, pop and even country and western. The city had earned a global status that was most tangible not in a single song nor even in a performer, but in a network of studios that spread across Memphis and deeper down to the South, into Alabama, and the Fame Studios in Muscle Shoals. Stax continued its much vaunted 'Soul Explosion', working its studios by day and night, cranking out releases on a daily basis, and testing Al Bell's thermometer to boiling point. What began as a response to the break-up with Atlantic had now become a feverish era of production in which talent was put to work in a studio that literally never slept. William Bell, the Staple Singers, Ollie and the Nightingales, Johnnie Taylor, John Lee Hooker, Eddie Floyd, Carla Thomas, and the tireless Booker T. and the M.G.'s packed the studio schedules to overspill, and by the end of 1968 Stax were using resources across the city and as far north as Detroit and Chicago, reluctant to let a day go by. A checklist of the studio bookings in Memphis across the latter months of the year is a jaw-dropping sweep across pop creativity: Elvis Presley and his great resurgence; Dusty Springfield's groundbreaking *Dusty In Memphis*; Isaac Hayes' rule-breaking concept album *Hot Buttered Soul*; escapees from Detroit's overheated soul rivalry, including Darrell Banks, Mable John, J.J. Barnes and the Dramatics, featuring Ron Banks; and artists from Atlantic who had previously thrived recording in New York such as Wilson Pickett and Sam and Dave, sent to other southern studios by the astute Jerry Wexler to drink an elixir that Manhattan could never adequately concoct. Talent surged to Memphis like iron filings to a magnet. For all its battered reputation in the wake of King's assassination, it remained a special place in the minds of musicians – R&B's answer to Nashville, the place where magic could be heard.

Dusty Springfield's arrival in Memphis was characteristic of Stax's global reputation. Springfield was an emotionally complex pop singer whose nervous insecurities were legend in the recording industry.

Like the Beatles – who had planned to record at Stax's East McLemore Studios back in 1965 – she was a knowledgeable and obsessive soul music fan, inspired and intimidated in equal measure by the great black singers of the era. On signing for Atlantic, Springfield was enthusiastic about recording in Memphis, believing it to be the modern capital of R&B and a place she felt curiously unworthy of recording in. According to Wexler's 1993 autobiography, *Rhythm and the Blues: A Life in American Music*, 'Dusty has to be the most insecure singer in the world. I was criticized for taking Dusty down south – everyone said the south was for R&B, not pop – but I had a hunch. You won't hear black influence in her voice, yet she's deeply soulful, her intonation pure. As with Aretha I had never heard her sing a bad note.' Springfield's love of southern soul was a generational thing. She had grown up in the Mod-fixated world of British teenage life, seeing black American music not as a passing fad but as a world of distant gods with strange but wonderful names – Sonny Boy Williamson, Howlin' Wolf, Big Maybelle and Little Stevie Wonder. When Dusty arrived in Memphis she was not taken to Stax, her first expectation – her dispute with Wexler ruled that out – but to another legendary Memphis studio, Chips Moman's American Sound Studio at 827 Thomas Street. By all accounts, the process of recording Dusty was painful and elaborate. Her confidence had been battered by the company she was about to keep, and undermined by erroneous comparisons with Aretha Franklin. Some singers would have risen with the tide of flattering encouragement, but Springfield retreated into herself, feeling threatened by a studio environment that had once played host to Aretha, Joe Tex and Bobby Womack. Wexler claims that 'Dusty was all raw nerve ends and neurosis', adding with his trademark acidic style that she was nicknamed 'The Ice Queen'. She refused to sing to a practice track and retreated from any help to sing out loud. Eventually, with the undercarriage of an album recorded as instrumentals, Dusty was whisked back to New York, where she eventually added the vocal tracks to a now iconic album, which included one of her most enduring releases, 'Son Of A Preacher Man'. Even then, the process was marred by anxiety and lack of confidence; at one point Springfield threw an ashtray at the methodical but well-meaning studio engineer Tom Dowd and vowed never to work for Wexler again.

Stax's own celebratory double album *Soul Explosion*, released in Europe in October 1968, was not simply a compilation of much loved singles but a testament to the extraordinary energy that flared up in the troubled aftermath of the company's break with Atlantic. It was a showcase of artists that were stretching soul music both backwards and forwards, from rural gospel to urban street funk, and from subtle harmony to rousing unfettered emotions. But it had another motivation, too, a refusal to be done down, driven by a passionate assertion that the small southern studio would not be bullied by New York.

On 3 December, another great resurgence visited Memphis. Television sets across the city were tuned to the ABC network when the now famous *Elvis: '68 Comeback Special* was aired. The show reached forty-two per cent of the viewing audience and was the network's top show that season. For Elvis Presley, it was a powerful statement that the King was back, and that his saccharine days as a matinee movie star were in the past. It was now nearly twenty years since Presley's career took off at Sam Phillips' Sun Studios at 706 Union Avenue, the place that ignited the epic history of rock music. It was Elvis's nefarious manager Colonel Tom Parker who came late to the conclusion that the movies – or more accurately a string of homely and over-sentimental Hollywood romances – had negatively affected Presley's career. After long periods of regression and declining record sales, Parker was eventually talked into reconnecting Presley with his Memphis roots. Back in January, NBC announced plans to produce a TV special for the 1968 Christmas season. It would be Elvis's first television appearance in more than eight years. The big innovation was to break with the now familiar and schmaltzy log-fire Christmas spectacular, long associated in the minds of Americans with the crooner generation – Frank Sinatra, Dean Martin and Bobby Darin. The original idea was to tell a story, and working against the grain of Colonel Tom Parker's innate conservatism, the programme-makers and newly installed sponsors, the Singer Corporation, favoured a more dynamic approach. A young and in-demand director called Steve Binder was brought on board. He had previously directed the TV series *Hullabaloo* but had also directed the 1965 *T.A.M.I. Show* – Teenage Awards Music International Show – a charitable foundation that pioneered what was in effect the first generation of pop music videos. Rehearsals began in June 1968, and although there was talk of moving the entire project to Memphis, the studios won the day and Elvis moved into his new home – a star dressing room on the NBC lot in Burbank, California. In initial conversations with Presley, the directors were taken by his genuine concern about the spate of assassinations, and the low opinion that many people now had of Memphis. After a conversation specifically about the assassination of Robert Kennedy, Binder commissioned songwriter Earl Brown to write an inspirational song for the finale, which became the triumphant 'If I Can Dream', a song redolent of the imagery of Martin Luther King's powerful sermons.

One night in late June, Binder passed Elvis's dressing room and overheard him laughing and jamming with the so-called Memphis Mafia – a loyal gang of friends who had known Elvis over the years. According to most reports of the *Elvis: '68 Comeback Special*, it was then that Binder had the idea to add a jam session to the television event, in which his original side men Scotty Moore, D.J. Fontana and Charlie Hodge would eventually join him on stage. Rather than return to the rich vein of gospel singers back home in Memphis, where Stax had the Emotions, Jeanne and the Darlings, and the Soul Children on their books, and Hi Records had recently contracted the still unknown Ann Peebles, director Binder dug into his own recent past. He had directed an episode of *T.A.M.I.* featuring Marvin Gaye, who had been backed on the day of filming by the Blossoms, an LA-based gospel soul group featuring Darlene Love, Fanita James and Jean King. And so it transpired that it was Jean King who would sing the gospel refrain from the Negro spiritual 'Sometimes I Feel Like A Motherless Child', in a powerfully emotional section of what was to become Presley's triumphant comeback. Clad in black fifties-style leather biker gear, and in fighting-fit condition, Presley invoked the first threatening years of Memphis rock 'n' roll with 'Hound Dog', 'All Shook Up' and 'Jailhouse Rock'. The 1968 television special has rightly been seen as the greatest comeback ever, rescuing Presley's reputation from a tired and has-been singer to a colossus who stormed back to the summit of the pop charts.

The resurgence of Presley brought with it a wave of sentiment to the city of Memphis. Although it had been stigmatised as the city that tolerated segregation and killed Martin Luther King, its citizens liked to tell different stories, wrapped up in nostalgia, in decency and, most of all, in affectionate sentimentality, that it was a city given to charity.

Walter Forrest Jones and his young wife were destined not to celebrate Christmas 1968. Their desperately sad lives brought the most combustible year in the history of modern Memphis to a regretful end. On Christmas Eve, Walter (24) and Glenda (19) left their low-income apartment home at 639 Looney Street and walked towards Thomas Street, to do some last-minute Christmas shopping at a drive-in mall. They left their baby boy, still only a few months old, in the care of his aunt, Glenda's twin sister Lynda. Presents had been laid out beneath the tree, and festive treats for the family's first Christmas dinner together were stored in their tiny kitchen. They had makeshift furniture and no table, so the newlyweds planned to eat chicken and roast vegetables on plates perched on their knees, feed their baby when he cried, and then toast the season with a few beers and tangerines.

While walking in the direction of Thomas Street, the couple were approached by two youths demanding money. They had nothing much to give them, except for a few dollars that Jones had rolled up in his coat pocket. Guns were pulled and the young couple were shot. When police and emergency services arrived, they were both lying face down on the sidewalk, shot in the back. Jones was dead and his teenage wife, desperately gasping for breath, was taken to St Joseph's Hospital on Overton Avenue with a bullet lodged near her spine. She underwent surgery in the same emergency treatment room where, months earlier, the dying Martin Luther King had been taken.

Police launched a city-wide search for the criminals, who they briefly believed were a street gang engaged in a feud with Jones –

eventually they conceded that they were no more than opportunistic thieves, who had come across the couple by coincidence. It was a killing with the most desperate of motives – a few crumpled dollars, to which Jones clung desperately in his clenched hand. He died much as he had lived, staring the brutal cruelty of poverty directly in the face. The Memphis Police Department, blamed for so much in the year gone by, were powerless. They searched the sewers and ditches in the surrounding area in vain but never found the gun that had killed Jones and wounded his wife. It disappeared into the dark netherworld of Memphis street crime, probably to be used again in another pathetic hold-up. Conscious that their reputation had been battered by the events of the year, Frank Holloman, the city's Fire and Police Director, and most senior police officer, instructed every available officer to be put on the case. Holloman, who had served twenty-five years as a Special Agent with the FBI, much of it in the Washington office close to J. Edgar Hoover, was uniquely conscious that the Memphis Police Department were by now implicated in the assassination of King, and more broadly stood accused of undervaluing the lives of its city's most deprived citizens. Holloman himself brought attention to the crime, urging the local press and his own officers that they had a moral duty to solve it, if only for the surviving widow and infant. The police pushed their resources to the limit and offered a $5,000 reward for anyone furnishing information or descriptions that would lead to the arrest of the criminals. It was the highest sum they were legally allowed to offer. Always the consummate politician, Holloman also used the crime to demand greater police powers, including more permission to 'stop and frisk', to search suspects and known criminals, and to apprehend illegal or unregistered weapons before they could be used in a crime. He also advocated a more demanding punishment structure that raised the fines for carrying a concealed illegal weapon from $50 to $1,000.

The Jones killing and the poignant fate of his infant son, who grew up fatherless and with a disabled mother, launched a season of sentimentality across Memphis public life. It was as if the city had a collective need to dwell on bad luck and appraise itself. The daily newspapers were fascinated by the unfortunate infant, and also by the remarkable life of the 'Muscular Dystrophy Mother', a black woman from the projects who had been left penniless when her husband abandoned her with five children, all of whom had inherited muscular dystrophy. Fearful that her children might be taken into care, the woman refused to give her real identity to journalists and so became known only by the moniker 'Muscular Dystrophy Mother'. Holiday Inn, a company that had been founded in Memphis in 1952, and was now a thriving nationwide motel chain, took the opportunity to attract Yuletide publicity and offered the mother and her disabled children 'a room at the Inn', an opportunistic play on the Nativity. The gesture brought the motel chain priceless publicity across America, but, for all its cloying sentimentality, the theme of disadvantaged children played out across the holiday season in nearly every walk of life. The *Memphis Press-Scimitar* launched its annual Goodfellas Campaign, a predominantly white and suburban campaign to donate toys and clothing to the poor. Many of the stories came from the city's sprawling Southside and areas such as Orange Mound, one of the oldest and most impoverished African-American communities in Memphis. In 1968 Orange Mound was known as the American neighbourhood with the second most concentrated population of African-Americans, behind only Harlem in New York City.

Life in the ghetto was compared unfavourably to a celebrity baby that was already gripping the attention of the press even before birth. Actress and international starlet Sophia Loren was eight months pregnant. After a series of miscarriages, her new unborn child was being tagged 'the richest baby in the world'. Loren's husband, film producer Carlo Ponti, had recently overseen the most popular and financially successful films of all time: David Lean's *Doctor Zhivago* and Michelangelo Antonioni's *Blow-Up*, the quintessential Swinging Sixties film. Famous, and fabulously wealthy, Ponti put in place a remarkable prenatal plan to protect Loren from further miscarriage. At the time, the couple were romantically on the run. Ponti had divorced his first wife at a time when divorce was still technically illegal in Catholic Italy and so lived across the border in Switzerland as a bigamist-in-exile. Sophia Loren for her part was living in 'concubinage' – her relationship unrecognised under Italian law.

To provide a safe haven for his pregnant partner, Ponti had hired three adjacent villa-apartments in Geneva, at an estimated cost of $1.4 million, and had kitted out the villas with $960,000 of medical equipment. Ponti had hand-picked the villas for their proximity to Geneva's Cantonal Hospital, where the world-renowned gynaecologist Professor Hubert de Watteville practised. De Watteville was the president of the International Federation of Gynaecology and Obstetrics, and a world expert on difficult births. A son, Carlo Ponti Jr, now a renowned classical composer and concert conductor, was born on 29 December 1968. It was the same day that an infant boy from South Memphis was swaddled in blankets and taken by car to a funeral parlour, where he lay on the lap of his disabled mother, crying unknowingly for a dead father.

On 30 December, as the year ended, one of the last court cases of 1968 featured a group of Memphis Invaders charged with assault. Horace Hall, who was brought to the court from Shelby County Jail where he had been incarcerated on previous charges, was accused of pulling a pistol and threatening the night manager of the Jump & Grab Drive-In Grocery, 591 E.H. Crump, just before midnight on 29 November. It was a case that hinged on the meaning of a short but highly combustible word – 'boy'. Hall had overheard the night manager using the word 'boy' to a fourteen-year-old black assistant and resented what he considered a racist slur. An argument ensured. The Invaders were all found guilty of brandishing weapons and causing a disturbance, but, significantly, the most infamous among them, Lance 'Sweet Willie Wine' Watson, not only denied the charges but refused to acknowledge the use of the term 'Invaders'. He claimed to be a leader of an entirely new militant group – the Black United Front. Watson was a character who fascinated local journalists; one described him as 'wearing a blue, green and brown poncho, draped over his shoulders, of the kind worn by the Manish tribe in Africa'. Watson and another co-accused, Robert 'Cornbread' Wilson, both spoke of their new-found African origins, an early sign that the Invaders were transforming: the group's original leaders were incarcerated and new recruits were exchanging their community radicalism for Afrocentrism. On the last day of the year, all of the Memphis militants failed to make bond and were taken to the Shelby County Penal Farm, where many other members of the Invaders were already imprisoned. By the end of 1968 the Memphis Invaders, who for nearly two years now had scared the authorities and provoked genuine fear of insurrection, were in decline and faced near annihilation. With many of the founders in jail and others scared off by persistent police harassment, new members who came to the group in 1968 had joined an organisation that was short of resources, had been infiltrated by the FBI, and was hounded daily by the police. Ultimately they were compromised by their own mistakes and snagged by the most basic of shortcomings – they had next to no money and were floored as much by cash flow as overzealous policing.

Cash flow was also proving a problem for Stax. In late December they had hosted a poorly attended Christmas concert at the Mid-South Coliseum. The event was ill conceived, having tried to reach out to the local counter-culture by hiring Janis Joplin and her newly assembled band, the Kozmic Blues Band, to headline. Joplin had recently left Big Brother and the Holding Company, and was flourishing on the new festival circuit and among the alternative clubs on the west coast. She had become obsessed with the Stax sound and, according to those close to her, would play Carla Thomas records forty times in a row, scratching the disc and destroying styluses as she tried to identify sequences that most impressed her.

Bill King, briefly the Kozmic Blues Band's pianist and musical director, recorded a diary of their trip to appear at the Memphis show. 'A rehearsal was set for mid afternoon, 20 December, at Soulsville U.S.A. Studios. First sight of the shattered movie marquee made me question if we'd been driven to the wrong location. I would eventually learn the broken panes of glass were fronting an immensely successful, sophisticated operation. As the doors spring open a cacophony of sounds unleash while several bands put the final touches to performance material. We wait until Booker T. and the M.G.'s complete a run through of prepared concert material then take positions behind our respective instruments. It was truly one of the most awkward situations I'd ever been in. First, the studio floor was on a slope due to its previous incarnation as a public cinema. Secondly, the number of certified super stars walking about not only excited but also added a level of intimidation. I mean these were my big heroes.'

King's diary provides some clues as to why the Coliseum show failed in such a calamitous way. 'After a complete run through we drove on to the Coliseum for set up. The sound check was a disaster. With an event [of this] magnitude you would have assumed the promoters would have spent decent coin to rent adequate amplification. Instead, they propped up a couple column speakers found mostly in rural churches at the time. Enough wattage for a sermon but not reliable enough to carry the power of a raucous singer. Janis was flabbergasted. To compound matters, she spotted a poster of the event with her image and name posted larger than the other participants. The thought of headlining amongst such prestigious talent sent her into an apologetic rant.'

The concert was a disaster. Al Bell had called it wrong. All the major Stax acts were on the bill, but many of them, including the Bar-Kays who were the featured group at the Tiki on Bellevue, had local residencies, and so were already familiar to core fans. Joplin was all but irrelevant to black audiences, and the audience she normally attracted did not exist in sufficient numbers and stayed away. Stax lost out. Paying the musicians' bloated bill and funding the loss to the Coliseum proved tricky but it was nothing compared to the cash shortfalls to come. Bell had borrowed the idea of an annual Stax homecoming show from Motown, who staged an annual week of spectaculars at the Fox Theater in Detroit. But another idea – again borrowed from Motown – proved to be more successful. Bell was an admirer of Motown's annual sales convention, a major opportunity for the company to showcase its artists and new releases in one spectacular event. Using the ballrooms of the Rivermont Hotel, he earmarked 16–18 May 1969 as the dates when twenty-eight albums would be unveiled, all with accompanying singles. Work began in November 1968, and for a relentless six months Stax never slept. It was at the May 1969 convention that Isaac Hayes' virtuoso performance of 'By The Time I Get To Phoenix' thrilled the visiting buyers and brought his album *Hot Buttered Soul* to the top of the pile. What began as a flicker of interest ignited into a flame, and by the end of 1969, in an unforeseen surge of success, the album featured on four charts simultaneously: jazz, easy listening, R&B and pop. Somehow, magically and improbably, it had appeal to them all.

In the run-up to Christmas, Stax boss Jim Stewart and his wife moved into a new suburban mansion on the outskirts of Memphis. The couple threw a house-warming party that must rank as one of the truly bizarre events in the history of soul music. Secluded in an exclusively white neighbourhood, and recently decorated with snow-white carpets and the latest fashionable furniture, it was a home that oozed wealth. The couple did the decent thing and invited their new neighbours and work colleagues. The party was not only a clash of cultures but a theatre of the bizarre: Rufus Thomas in a gangster-pin tie; members of the Bar-Kays in polyester leggings and fur coats; Isaac Hayes in an ocelot suit; and the Stax security force in razor-sharp suits, dark shades and stone-cold killer shoes. The neighbours – bless them – were politely dressed in sober standard-management suits and understated cocktail dresses. Then, stumbling into an already high-octane environment, came one of rock music's most troubled souls – the singer and heroin addict Janis Joplin. With her unkempt hair, her satin blouse stained with drink, hippie beads hanging down to her waist and ostrich feathers decorating her wrists, Joplin, in the withering words of the magazine *Rolling Stone*, looked like 'a Babylonian whore'. According to Peggy Caserta, Joplin's friend and occasional lover, by late 1968 Joplin was shooting at least $200 worth of heroin daily and downing Southern Comfort as if it were soda water. Between the summer of 1968 and late 1969, Joplin reportedly overdosed six times, and, according to her friend, the virtuoso blues guitarist Michael Bloomfield, she was snared by full-blown addiction. 'A junkie's life is totally fucked,' he said, speaking of Joplin. 'Shooting junk made everything else seem unimportant.'

Sometime after midnight, as the party edged further into discomfort, Joplin began stubbing out her cigarettes on the brand-new carpet, and she was eventually asked to leave by Jim Stewart's furious wife. Joplin left Memphis soon after, never to return. One of rock music's most tragic characters, in September 1970, only twenty-seven, Joplin died of an accidental overdose in the Landmark Hotel, Hollywood, clutching some change from the cigarette machine. Her obituary in the *New York Times* described the white woman who saw Stax as the pinnacle of all that was brilliant in modern music. 'She would stand before her audience, microphone in hand, long red hair flailing, her raspy voice shrieking in rock mutations of black country blues. Pellets of sweat flew from her contorted face and glittered in the beam of footlights. Janis Joplin sang with more than her voice. Her involvement was total.'

Jim Stewart, resplendent in a brilliant white suit, reluctantly called his guests together. By way of a toast to his new home, he reflected on a year that had been among the most tumultuous in recent history. Never a great public speaker, he did what many have done before and since – focused on the good news, the company's achievements and the hit records. He thanked those who had contributed to the Stax sound and what was once again a renewed and growing business. But what was left unsaid still bruised him. The divorce from Atlantic had been bitter and costly, and the loss of the precious back catalogue bore heavily on him. The death of Otis Redding, exactly a year before, still left an aching gap at Stax, and although Johnnie Taylor and, latterly, Isaac Hayes would emerge from the studio to seize international fame, that was yet to come. The death of Martin Luther King still weighed heavy on Memphis, too, and the stigma would linger for decades. Stewart lived and breathed Stax, and as he wandered from room to room he quietly, almost shyly, paid tribute to those living and dead who had played such a vital part in the Stax success story. He often came close to calling it an empire, but there was a modest side to his personality that could not quite use the word; maybe because he thought it was too arrogant or, more likely, that he was intelligent enough to know that empires rise and then just as dramatically fall.

By the close of 1968 the Stax empire was discovering an emperor in its midst. The year had begun with the pathetic sight of Ben Cauley trying to fight off tears as journalists probed him for details of the tragic plane crash that killed Otis Redding. Rather than retreat, Cauley and his friend, bassist James Alexander, agreed that giving up was not an option, and so they slowly but surely began to rebuild the Bar-Kays. The brother of dead drummer Carl Cunningham was drafted in and so, too, were other close friends, and quietly the group was reimagined as pioneers of street funk. The Bar-Kays had always been an ultra-reliable backing band, but by the end of 1968 they resurfaced as a formidable act in their own right, eventually hiring their first dedicated lead vocalist, Larry Dodson, from rival Memphis group the Temprees, and putting in place a new vision of a group that went on to record the hard-edged disco classic 'Shake Your Rump To The Funk'. By December the Bar-Kays were back recording at the Stax studios and at weekends holding down a profitable residency at the Tiki Club, an African-American nightclub on Bellevue, which at the time was owned by a local music operator, Gene Mason, a helpful mentor in the band's re-emergence.

It was at the Tiki Club that soul history was made. Isaac Hayes had been flirting with recording an album for months and was considering a new wave of songs. For reasons now long buried in time, he began to favour great songs he knew and liked rather than record songs he had written with his long-time songwriting partner David Porter. Two of his favourite songs of the time were Burt Bacharach's 'Walk On By', which had been a hit for Dionne Warwick in 1964, and Jimmy Webb's 'By The Time I Get To Phoenix', which, by 1968, was a country classic most readily associated with the singer Glen Campbell. Neither song shouted soul. Nor were they ones that audiences associated with the Stax sound. Nonetheless, Hayes rightly championed them as great songwriting and, in the anything-goes era at Stax as the soul explosion smashed apart categories and expectations, he was given late-night studio time to record them. The songs were probably conceived as traditional cover versions and, in the minds of Al Bell and Jim Stewart, would be no more than filler tracks for an Isaac Hayes album. But something unpredictable and magical happened. Hayes asked the Bar-Kays if he could join them at the Tiki Club to try out new material. He took to the stage in front of a noisy and inattentive crowd. Rather than launch straight into his first number –'By The Time I Get To Phoenix' – Hayes paused and asked the new Bar-Kays to strike up a long repetitive loop of percussive funk, and then he began to tell a story in a spoken rap style now so familiar to black music you might forget it had to be invented. Hayes started to imagine the story of the man travelling to Phoenix. What has driven him there? How did he get there? And what was he escaping from? Rather than honour the original song and make the driver white, Hayes cast him as a young black man escaping from LA and making an intense, frenetic journey to Phoenix, Arizona. Frank Sinatra called it 'the greatest torch song ever', and, along with Gladys Knight's 'Midnight Train To Georgia' and Millie Jackson's 'If You're Not Back In Love By Monday', it remains one of *the* most complex love songs – a mesmerising piece of soul alchemy that took classic Nashville and reimagined it as Memphis soul.

The audience at the Tiki Club took a while to settle, but gradually they quietened, and, finally, as silence reigned amongst the once rowdy tables, Hayes launched into the song proper. The rapped intro became a trademark device for decades to come, but more importantly Hayes returned to the studio with the Bar-Kays and fashioned *Hot Buttered Soul,* a formidable act of musical deconstruction that fast-tracked his career and gave birth to the concept album and new ways of seeing black American music. The album contained only four lengthy tracks: a reinterpretation of 'Walk On By'; a song called 'One Woman'; an epic rendition of 'By The Time I Get To Phoenix' that stretched to nearly nineteen minutes in length; and the surreally named 'Hyperbolicsyllabic-sesquedalymistic', which, at a modest ten minutes, ended the first side and was later sampled by Public Enemy, Ice Cube and many others. As Hayes expressed in *Rolling Stone* in 1972: 'I felt like what I wanted to say, I couldn't say it in no two minutes and thirty seconds, because I wanted to speak through the arrangement, I wanted to speak through singing . . . I cut that record with all the freedom in the world and it was a beautiful release for me.' With the obvious exception of jazz, most forms of popular black music had been constrained by the needs of commercialism and the demands of radio stations. Motown had perfected telling stories of teenage love in under three minutes and not until Hayes broke the mould had any soul artist ever dared to extend songs or disrupt the rules of the marketplace.

Hot Buttered Soul had its origins in the fertile months of 1968, as Hayes tried to shake himself out of what was in many respects a breakdown, triggered in part by the circumstances of Martin Luther King's death and his proximity to the events. But it was equally a product of his own unfettered self-confidence. Born into abject poverty, he now had a modicum of wealth; unsure whether he was a songwriter or a performer, he had a chance to take centre stage. Raised and then rejected by a high school that favoured jazz over R&B, he realised that it was a false choice he was no longer obliged to make. *Hot Buttered Soul* is in some respects a jazz album forged in the furnace of soul. Composed mostly of free-form cover versions, it is bravely disruptive and broke all the cardinal rules of the radio stations of the day. The tracks are too long to satisfy playlists, and the vocal hooklines are tangled in looping and adventurous backing tracks. But what is rarely said about the album is that it is visionary in the true sense of the word: it anticipates the future of black music. The long rapped intros point not only to jazz-funk and rap itself, but to the soliloquies of bedroom soul pioneered by the great women artists of the seventies, including Millie Jackson, Denise LaSalle, Doris Duke and Shirley Brown. Something about its laconic and almost druggy tone looks forward to trip-hop and the ambient soul that found a flourishing electronic heart in the UK's 'Bristol sound', with artists like Portishead and Massive Attack. And, most clearly of all, *Hot Buttered Soul* was the flag-bearer for concept albums in the black music market and the LP that gave permission to Marvin Gaye and *What's Going On*, Curtis Mayfield's *Superfly*, Funkadelic's *Maggot Brain* and Swamp Dogg's *Cuffed, Collared & Tagged*. It broke decisively with the racist presumption that soul and R&B artists were best suited to the singles market and that only white rock musicians could cope with the demands of the album. The basic tracks were recorded at Memphis's Ardent Studios – Stax was already straining with the weight of bookings – and then Hayes worked with the producer Dale Warren, a classically trained violinist who had joined Stax from the Motown empire. Warren convinced Hayes that they should head to the Motor City, where they hired East European émigrés working for the Detroit Symphony Orchestra to add elegance, depth and unexpected subtlety to the score. This was Stax like never before – a gut-bucket southern soul sound reimagined. But it was also soul like never before – creative, disruptive and unconcerned with the limitations that the marketplace had traditionally heaped on black music. Hayes had in many respects coincided with the growth of Memphis soul, having emerged from the ranks of local high-school talent contests and basic studio work to become one of Stax's most reliable writers. It might have ended there, with a comfortable career as a studio producer, but Hayes had one last transformation to come: the frenzy of fame.

Hayes was determined to go the full distance and create a persona that stood astride music as a colossus. His style was daringly political, with the torso of a slave decked in symbolic gold chains and his head shaven to the bone. Over the next decade he would rise to be one of the superstars of a newly emancipated black music, the emperor of a generation who would no longer confined to the ghetto – or what had once been called 'race music'. He would strike out in a new direction, disrupting the classics, barnstorming the movies, his name emblazoned in lights. Isaac Hayes became Black Moses.

EPILOGUE

The Final Pay Cheque

William Brown had seen it all. His life had almost exactly corresponded with the birth and death of Stax Records, and, more importantly, he knew where the bodies were buried. Brown had the archetypal Stax background. He had attended Booker T. Washington High School and had been a member of a gang of precocious teenagers who hung around the doorway of Satellite Records. He worked in the store and became friends with Estelle Axton. By 1964 he had joined the Mad Lads, singing in local talent contests and then touring on the under-card of some of the biggest shows at the towering height of sixties soul, supporting James Brown, the Temptations, Marvin Gaye and the Four Tops. He shared a stage with Otis Redding when they were both hopeful artists on Stax's subsidiary label, Volt Records. Then, in 1966, when the Mad Lads were beginning to establish a reputation as recording artists, he was swept up in the wave of conscription that focused on the inner cities of the USA. He was drafted to fight in the war in Vietnam, and along with his schoolfriend and singing partner, John Gary Williams, he had to abandon a musical career for military service.

Axton regularly sent him surprise boxes to Vietnam: chocolate, hair gel, newspaper clippings and good wishes from the Stax team back home. On his return from Vietnam, the second generation of Mad Lads had no great desire to see Brown return to the group, and had become a settled new unit enjoying their own success. But out of respect for a returning veteran, the Stax management team was adamant that they could not abandon him. So Jim Stewart created a new role and encouraged Brown to build an alternative career and pursue his interest in studio engineering. As his friend Williams drifted towards the political insurgency of the Memphis Invaders, eventually spending time in jail, Brown became obsessed with the voodoo sounds that came from the knobs and dials of Stax's burgeoning studio. In time he became the first African-American to hold down a job in studio production, working off-microphone at Stax as an engineer, and then later as an engineer at Ardent Studios and at Hi Records with Willie Mitchell. In 1971 he was one of the engineers on Isaac Hayes' Oscar-winning smash 'Theme From *Shaft*' and two years later worked on Elvis Presley's sessions at Stax.

William Brown succumbed to a stroke in July 2015, but before he passed away at a rehabilitation centre in East Memphis he confided in those close to him that the saddest day of his life was the one when his last pay cheque from Stax bounced. IRS officers had locked and bolted the doors of the studios and, with no guaranteed income, Brown struggled to meet mortgage payments. Sadly, his home was repossessed.

The decline of Stax Records began in earnest on 30 November 1973, when producer and 'security executive' Johnny Baylor was apprehended at Memphis airport by FBI agents. Security had checked his hand luggage and found a case carrying $129,000 and a cheque to the value of $500,000. Baylor told the FBI that he was suspicious of banks and so was taking the money to Birmingham, Alabama, to lodge with his mother, whom he trusted more than a savings account. A more likely explanation was that Baylor was travelling to Birmingham to meet up with local DJs and dispense payola – cash gifts to induce them to promote current releases by

Stax and his own label, KoKo Records. KoKo's success with the Luther Ingram classic '(If Loving You Is Wrong) I Don't Want to Be Right' had taken it from the fringes to the forefront of soul music, and the latest releases 'Always' and 'Love Ain't Gonna Run Me Away' were in urgent need of greater promotion. Others have since claimed that he was taking the money on Stax's behalf out of sight of the tax authorities.

According to the *Guardian*, 'behind Stax's hip, happening façade lay a bloated organisation of 200 employees, where excess flourished and rumours of gangsterism and payola flew'. Baylor's arrest seems to have been the fuse that ignited a tangled set of circumstances, to the extent that many consider him as the principal cause of Stax's demise. That would be to simplify a much more complex situation. The singer William Bell said in his defence, 'Johnny was an outside entity, but I don't think he was the cause of the collapse of Stax. There were some choices made that were not right for Stax. One was leaving Atlantic, because they knew our music, they knew the artists. Then, for the sake of trying to get into the movie industry and all that, they changed from Atlantic to Paramount, which was a big mistake, because them being out of California, they knew nothing about what we were doing at Stax. So even though the financiers were at Paramount, the support was not.' But Bell's clarity obscures the degree of difficulty Stax had found itself in. Like many empires before and since, Stax Records collapsed for reasons that were in the main of its own making.

First, and in common with almost every dying empire, it had expanded too far from the centre, with offices in Los Angeles, investments in the movie business, and, following Isaac Hayes' lead, diversifying into real estate. Even within the record business, Stax had pushed it too far. What had once been two strong labels servicing the soul market (Stax and Volt) became an array of labels: Enterprise became a branded vehicle for Isaac Hayes; We Three became the label of songwriters Bettye Crutcher, Raymond Jackson and Homer Banks; Truth was the down-home soul label that showcased Shirley Brown; and Gospel Truth was the home of Jo Armstead and the Rance Allen Group. This only scraped the surface of a bewildering catalogue of labels, deals, co-productions and distribution arrangements that baffled the staff, confused the market, and stretched the loyalty of even the most ardent followers. Stax had also bought pressing plants and was on the lookout for a radio station.

Then, Stax was battered by a perfect storm. Relations with new distributor CBS were at an all-time low, and its record division Columbia warehoused Stax product rather than release it to shops. According to journalist Ericka Blount Danois, writing for *Wax Poetics*, 'CBS deliberately put the squeeze on Stax. And Bell claims that he and Stax employees were told in no uncertain terms that they were aiming for Stax's jugular and intending to take down the "biggest nigger" from the company.'

Meanwhile, the US Attorney's office and the IRS began an investigation into Stax's finances. Management changes at its local bank in Memphis led to a separate investigation into bad loans. This investigation claimed that Bell, representing Stax, was in conspiracy with a rogue bank employee, Joseph Harwell, who in turn was accused of falsifying the signature of Jim Stewart and creating bogus accounts in the name of real and fictitious Stax employees. Then the roof really caved in. Once the most successful company on the books of Union Planters Bank, it now transpired that Stax owed the bank $10 million. The new regime petitioned for bankruptcy. Stax could no longer meet its payroll and was forced to ask employees if they would take a fifty per cent cut in salary. Unable to stomach the fears and anxieties around him, songwriter David Porter, who was cash-rich from publishing royalties, settled some wages from his own pocket and paid the bills of desperate friends. Stewart put up his luxury home as security to allow the company to limp on, but it was too little, too late. Stewart lost the house as years of over-expenditure caught up with Stax.

Bell and Stewart made a final desperate bid to keep the doors open. Bell's father funded a trip to Europe to find investors, and Stax came close to pulling off a masterstroke; first with Egypt's Anwar Sadat and then with Saudi Arabia's King Faisal, both of whom talked about making a significant investment in the label – enough to pay off the now despised CBS and clear outstanding debts. But, in an unscripted twist of fate, on 25 March 1975, as Bell was planning to travel to Riyadh, King Faisal was assassinated by his own nephew – Faisal bin Musaid – who was eventually beheaded in the public square in Riyadh under the blistering Saudi heat. Stax's pursuit of oil money drained away with the blood.

Over-indulgence had in part brought Stax to its knees, and conspicuous consumption played a role in the downward spiral of the label's most successful artist, Isaac Hayes. In 1976 the IRS filed a tax lien against the singer for $463,969.73 and took ownership of his property and assets. Hayes' financial problems have always been blamed on 'bad management', a euphemism for much more complex problems, not least a parasitic inner circle who openly leeched off Hayes. In the case of the now-notorious Johnny Baylor and Dino Woodard, they functioned as a well-heeled Praetorian Guard who protected Hayes from everything, including the truth. Another drain on Hayes' fortune was the cost of his increasingly bloated concept albums, which since the success of *Hot Buttered Soul* in 1968–9 became costlier by the day, depending on orchestras, new electronic instrumentation and expensive talent. Hayes spent without restraint, and in an industry accustomed to lavishness he was a hopeless spendthrift. Nor was he good at controlling his loins. He had a string of lovers and had lost significant sums of money on alimony and expensive child support settlements. He had married his teenage wife Emily in 1966, and when they divorced, she took ownership of his home at 3628 Old Dominion and took out an injunction to prevent him moving assets from Shelby County. The assets cited in the suit were five vintage luxury vehicles, including two Cadillacs and two Jaguars, furs valued at $40,000, and a hidden bank account in the name of Hot Buttered Soul Ltd, which Hayes had been building up, away from the marital assets. By 1977, despite the phenomenal success of his albums and movie career, Hayes was broke. He owed whopping sums of back tax, and in 1977 his estate was put up for auction by the Delta Auction Company. One of the many assets up for grabs was the Oscar he had won for the soundtrack to *Shaft*. Moments before the auction began, a last-minute appeal allowed Hayes a meagre $2,500 exemption, and his attorney stepped forward and took down five platinum album awards, for sales in excess of $2 million. The auction itself was a circus, with people climbing on chairs and chests of drawers to attract the eyes of the auctioneer; many turned up simply to gaze at the haul. Much of Hayes' characteristically flamboyant clothing was up for sale, including a floor-length tiger-skin coat, which the auctioneer said could never be made again as tigers were now an endangered species. Fans flocked to buy little pieces of the life of the man they called Black Moses; one fan bought a bathroom mirror for $7; another bought his TV set; and one lucky bidder went home with a little box of toothpicks.

As the Stax empire and Isaac Hayes tried to ward off insolvency, another brutal and inexplicable episode scarred the final days of the company. On the evening of 30 September 1975, Al Jackson Jr, the drummer of the legendary Booker T. and the M.G.'s, drove to Memphis airport to catch a flight to Chicago. He was scheduled to produce a session with soul singer Major Lance, who at the time was signed to a Memphis indie called Osiris Records. As he headed towards the airport, a radio advert alerted him to one of the major sporting events of the era – the Thrilla in Manila – Muhammad Ali's final fight in his blood feud with Joe Frazier. Jackson made an impulsive decision to return home and secure tickets for the fight, which was being aired live at the Mid-South Coliseum. He called Major Lance and they agreed to bump the recording session to a day later in the week. Ali won in the fifteenth round on a technical knockout and Jackson returned home unexpectedly, later that night. What happened when he returned home is one of soul music's great mysteries and remains an open case on the desks of the homicide squad at the Memphis Police Department. Writer Andria Lisle described the event: 'Jackson was found lying face down, shot in the back five times. As the police later told the press, "Whoever killed him really wanted him dead." The robber, never apprehended, made off with jewellery as well as the contents of Jackson's pockets. He was described as a tall black man, twenty-five to thirty years old, with an afro haircut and a moustache, wearing dark clothing at the time of the murder. Despite the Memphis Police Department's pledge to Stax Records and the black community to catch Al Jackson's killer, the case remains unsolved.'

Jackson's death inevitably became caught up in the collapse of

Stax, but there was no evidence to connect the two. In fact, a more likely explanation was much closer to home. A police officer who was passing the Jackson household on Central Avenue found Jackson's wife Barbara screaming, with her hands tied behind her back. When he entered the house, he found Jackson lying on the floor and noticed that he had been shot several times. Mrs Jackson, who had been accused of wounding her husband a few months previously, claimed that she had arrived home from a beauty parlour at 11 p.m. and was ambushed by a young black man brandishing a gun. The intruder demanded money and, after she told him there was no money in the house, tied her to a chair and ransacked the house.

The rumour mill went into overdrive. Then, on 1 May 1976, the *Tri-State Defender* reported that a source inside the Attorney General's office had named widow Barbara Jackson and southern soul singer Denise LaSalle as two of the suspects about to be indicted. The other suspects were not named, but speculation grew that the killer was probably an escaped armed robber from Springfield, Ohio, whom LaSalle had been accused of harbouring. His name was Nathaniel Doyle Jr, a young gangster who used the pseudonym Nate or Nat Johnson. He was soon to join the FBI's Ten Most Wanted list as fugitive number 341. LaSalle co-operated with the FBI and, under her real name Ora Denise Allen, was acquitted of assisting Doyle back into Ohio. He had escaped arrest and was still on the run. It raises the as-yet unresolved question of whether Doyle had moved to Memphis to hide out with LaSalle, who was signed to Detroit's Westbound Records but recording locally in Memphis. The homicide squad's investigation faced a massive barrier in July 1976, when Doyle was killed in a gun battle with police officers in Seattle, Washington. The truth almost certainly died with him and his one-time girlfriend LaSalle lived to record another day. Her bestselling album *The Bitch Is Bad!* showed her posing by a Memphis swimming pool, resplendent in a shimmering black satin dress split to the thigh, and with her white stilettos firmly planted on a dead tiger. It is an album cover that screams of bitchy self-confidence and violent power.

Al Jackson Jr's murder had another consequence. It ended the Memphis Group for ever, the famous M.G.'s who had given Stax such powerful symmetry in the early days of the label as segregation still presided in Memphis. Two black men – Booker T. Jones and Al Jackson Jr – and two white men – Donald 'Duck' Dunn and Steve Cropper – came together to defy the worst prejudices of a divided city, and through their cultural backgrounds created a truly unique sound. That was now gone and would only survive in memory.

For all the intrigue and murderous side stories, the end of Stax Records was banal and ignominious. In December 1975 the Union Planters Bank foreclosed, forcing the company into involuntary bankruptcy. The bank had secretly worked with three minor creditors to force bankruptcy on a debt of only $1,900. One creditor had supplied Stax with photography services, another with small electronic parts, and, most galling of all, the third creditor was the company that supplied the studio's toilet rolls.

Stax employees were given fifteen minutes to gather their personal possessions and leave the premises. Security guards surrounded the building and chained the doorways. It was a moment that had desperate memories for the singer Eddie Floyd, whose 'Knock On Wood' remains one of Stax's evergreen releases. His two-year-old daughter had been playing at the family home with Floyd's gun and accidentally shot herself. Desperate to fund her emergency care, he called Stax to discuss his medical insurance policy, and was told it was too late, that marshals were already closing the doors. Then, in a final humiliating transaction, the building that had once housed the most vibrant studio in the history of southern soul music was sold to the Southside Church of God in Christ for ten dollars. It would be forty years before a degree of dignity returned to the old cinema at 926 East McLemore Avenue, when it was reborn as a museum and music academy. By day tourists stream through the renovated building, surveying the exhibits of an era rich in social history and musical memories. Next door the newly discovered musical talent of Memphis, some still living in the decaying streets nearby, are tutored in performance skills and the curious ways of the music business. It is a building that can never be reborn but at least a flame still flickers.

Black Moses. The mercurial singer, actor and superstar Isaac Hayes abandons his robes for a gold watch and a gun in the film *Tough Guys*.

BIBLIOGRAPHY

Primary Sources

The Commercial Appeal and *Memphis Press-Scimitar* newspapers, 1967–1969, McWherter Library, University of Memphis, Memphis, TN.

The *Tri-State Defender* collection, LeMoyne-Owen College, Memphis, TN.

Blues and Soul magazine, 1968–1975, author's own collection.

Michigan Chronicle, 1962–1972, Detroit Public Library, Detroit, MI.

Pittsburgh Courier, 1960–1968, University Library, University of Michigan, Ann Arbor, MI.

Cuttings on segregation, Memphis life, Beale Street, Stax Records, the Memphis Invaders, Isaac Hayes and other related subjects, courtesy of the Preservation and Special Collection Department, McWherter Library, University of Memphis, Memphis, TN.

The COINTELPRO Papers, The FBI Education Center, Pennsylvania Avenue, Washington, DC.

Home Select Committee on Assassination (HSCA) 1976–1979, Library of Congress, Washington, DC.

NAACP Collection, cataloguing the activities of the National

Association for the Advancement of Colored People and its related activities, 1909–1979, University Library, University of Michigan, Ann Arbor, MI.

The Papers and Correspondence of the Reverend Martin Luther King Jr, The Martin Luther King, Jr. Center for Nonviolent Social Change, Atlanta, GA.

FBI and Memphis Police Department documents released under the Freedom of Information Act and made available via www.vault.fbi.gov and other specialist sites.

Secondary Sources

Abernathy, Ralph David, *And the Walls Came Tumbling Down,* Chicago: Lawrence Hill Books, 2010.

Beiffus, Joan Turner, *At the River I Stand,* Memphis: St Luke's Press, 1990.

Blackstock, Nelson, *COINTELPRO: The FBI's Secret War on Political Freedom,* New York: Pathfinder Press, 1976.

Bowman, Rob, *Soulsville U.S.A.: The Story of Stax Records,* New York: G. Schirmer Inc., 2003.

Branch, Taylor, *At Canaan's Edge: America in the King Years 1965–1968,* New York: Simon & Schuster, 2006.

Carpenter, Bill, *Uncloudy Days: The Gospel Encyclopaedia,* San Francisco: Backbeat Books, 2005.

Donner, Frank J., *The Age of Surveillance,* New York: Alfred A. Knopf, 1980.

DiEugenio, James & Lisa Pease (eds), *The Assassinations: Probe Magazine on JFK, MLK, RFK, and Malcolm X,* Port Townsend: Feral Press, 2003.

Dyson, Michael Eric, *I May Not Get There with You: The True Martin Luther King, Jr.,* New York: Free Press, 2000.

Freeman, Scott, *Otis!: The Otis Redding Story,* New York: St Martin's Press, 2001.

Gentry, Curt, *J. Edgar Hoover: The Man and the Secrets,* New York: W.W. Norton & Co., 1991.

George, Nelson, *The Death of Rhythm and Blues,* New York: Random House, 1988.

Gordon, Robert, *Respect Yourself: Stax Records and the Soul Explosion*, New York: Bloomsbury, 2014.

Gordon, Robert, *It Came from Memphis*, Pocket Books: New York, 1995.

Guralnick, Peter, *Last Train to Memphis: The Rise of Elvis Presley*, London: Little Brown, 1994.

Guralnick, Peter, *Sweet Soul Music: Rhythm and Blues and the Southern Dream of Freedom*, New York: Harper & Row, 1986.

Hamilton, Marybeth, *In Search of the Blues*, London: Jonathan Cape, 2007.

Howard, Josiah, *Blaxploitation Cinema*, Surrey: Fab Press, 2008.

Hauser, Thomas, *Muhammad Ali: His Life and Times*, London: Robson Books, 1991.

Hughes, Charles L., *Country Soul: Making Music and Making Race in the American South*, Chapel Hill, NC: University of North Carolina Press, 2015.

Pepper, William F., *An Act of State: The Execution of Martin Luther King*, New York: Verso, 2003.

Jones, Roben, *Memphis Boys: The Story of American Studios*, Jackson, MI: University of Mississippi Press, 2010.

Kamin, Ben, *Room 306: The National Story of the Lorraine Motel*, East Lansing, MI: Michigan State University Press, 2012.

Kot, Greg, *I'll Take You There: Mavis Staples, the Staple Singers and the March Up Freedom's Highway*, New York: Scribner, 2014.

Kotz, Mick, *Judgment Days: Lyndon Baines Johnson, Martin Luther King, Jr., and the Laws That Changed America*, Boston: Mariner Books, 2006.

O'Reilly, Kenneth, *Racial Matters: The FBI's Secret File on Black America, 1960–1972*, New York: Free Press, 1991.

Powers, Georgia Davis, *I Shared the Dream: The Pride, Passion, and Politics of the First Black Woman Senator from Kentucky*, Far Hills, NJ: New Horizon Press, 1995.

Ribowsky, Mark, *Dreams to Remember: Otis Redding, Stax Records and the Transformation of Southern Soul*, New York: Liveright, 2015.

Ritz, David, *Divided Soul: The Life of Marvin Gaye*, New York: McGraw-Hill, 1985.

Sides, Hampton, *Hellhound on His Trail*, London: Allen Lane, 2010.

Salvatore, Nick, *Singing in a Strange Land: C.L. Franklin, The Black Church, and the Transformation of America*, New York: Little Brown & Co., 2005.

Ward, Brian, *Just My Soul Responding: Rhythm and Blues, Black Consciousness, and Race Relations*, London: UCL Press, 1998.

Warner, Jay, *Just Walkin' in the Rain: The True Story of the Prisonaires: The Convict Pioneers of R&B and Rock & Roll*, Los Angeles: Renaissance Books, 2001.

Wexler, Jerry & David Ritz, *Rhythm and the Blues: A Life in American Music*, London: Jonathan Cape, 1993.

Whiteis, David, *Southern Soul-Blues*, Chicago: University of Illinois Press, 2013.

INDEX

53, 66, 68, 71, 77, 79, 90–3,
102, 122, 124, 125, 127, 263
Beale Street Players 83
Beamon, Bob 245
Beatles, The 12, 135, 266, 271
Beifuss, Joan Turner 90
Belafonte, Harry 89, 144
Bell, Al (Alvertis Isbell) 25, 73,
151, 152, 158, 169, 181–90,
198, 199, 221, 278, 290
and Baylor/Woodard 218,
219, 227
and civil rights 183, 184, 238
and *Hot Buttered Soul* 176,
282
and Willie Mitchell 100
driving force at Stax 186
office thermometer 181, 182,
199, 270
race relations at Stax 31, 161,
162, 193–5
trying to save masters 51
Bell, Archie and the Drells 223
Bell, Reverend Ezekiel 46
Bell, William 26, 28, 31, 51,
122, 173, 187, 197, 270
and Martin Luther King 152
and Vietnam 79, 85–7, 110
as top Stax songwriter 73
founding Peachtree 163
leaving Stax 228, 289
Bennett, Shelbra 208
Benson, JoJo 223
Benton, Brook 124
Bergard, Fr Coleman 107
Berger, Bettye 153, 154, 162
Bergman, Ingrid 134
Berry, Ben Heard 232, 237

Bevel, James 116
Beverley Glen Records 135
Bial, Daniel 141
Big Brother and the Holding
Company 278
Billboard (magazine) 31, 58,
132, 173, 192, 220
Binder, Steve 272, 273
Binford, Lloyd 134
Black, Bill 252
Black, Cilla 222
Black Monday campaign 84
Black Moses *see* Hayes, Isaac
Black National Anthem 197
Black Organising Project
(BOP) 83, 84
Black Panthers 83, 88, 159, 168,
175, 210, 227, 233, 249
Black Power movement 40,
118, 159, 195, 222, 227, 238
and Juanita Miller 203, 204
and Vietnam 82–5, 87
at Olympic Games 246–9
at Resurrection City 209–11
infiltrated by FBI 111, 113,
126
music of 78, 79, 198, 199
politics of 168, 172, 226
protest marches and riots 92,
93, 233, 234
Black United Front 277
Blackfoot, J. (John Colbert)
207, 208, 253
Blackstone Rangers 159, 211
Blackwell, George 219
Bland, Bobby 2, 3, 44, 125, 135
Blossoms, The 273
Blue Seal Pals 9

blood transfusion,
     controversies over 5, 6, 13
Bloomfield, Michael 280
Bluhdorn, 'Hurricane Charlie'
     190–4
  buying Paramount 191
  controlling Stax 193
Bond, Julian 223
Bongalis 114
Booker T. and the M.G.'s (see
     also Jones, Booker T.) 2, 51,
     100, 167, 173, 193, 278
  as Stax house band 24, 187,
     270
  death of Al Jackson 292
  success with 'Green Onions'
     31, 80, 260
  working on film music 169
Booker T. Washington High
     School 22, 29, 30, 80, 81,
     91, 94, 166, 215, 249, 287
Borders, Reverend William
     Holmes 199
Bowman, Rob 26, 28, 54, 132,
     219, 237
Box Tops 45, 57
Bragg, Johnny 208
Branch, Ben 68, 97–107, 145,
     250–2
  and the Downhomers 97
Branch, Taylor 47, 90, 91
Brandon, Bill 59
Briggs, Fred 263
Brittenum, Marianne 261
Brooks, Verdell 115
Brown, Bill 79, 80, 82, 287, 288
Brown, Earl 273
Brown, H. Rap 87, 190, 227

Brown, James 10, 18, 22, 24, 33,
     34, 78, 79, 125, 160, 198,
     223, 287
  and the Famous Flames 10,
     33, 160
Brown, Maxine 59, 187, 218
Brown, Ruth 125
Brown, Shirley 135, 136, 284,
     289
Brundage, Avery 247, 249
Bryant, Don 264
Buddha Records 135
Burk, Arnold D. 192
Burke, Solomon 33, 60
bus boycotts 99, 123
Butler, Jerry 25
Butler, Willie Pearl 203
Butterball, D.J. 186
Butterfield, Paul 74
Byles, Earlie 162
Byrds, The 86

C., Fantastic Johnny 223
Cabbage, Charles 85, 87, 88, 93,
     104, 118, 240
Cake, Pat T. 24
Caldwell, Ronnie 22
Campbell, Glen 264, 282
Canes, The 148
Canipe, Guy 147–51, 163
Cannon, Gus 71
Capitol Movie Theater 28
Carlos, John 245, 246, 248, 249,
     253
Carmichael, Stokely 78, 87, 117
Carnegie Hall, New York 6
Carousel Ballroom 74
Carr, James 1, 8–12, 207

Rainey, Ma 2
Randall, Alice 256
Rare Breed (band) 160
Rawls, Lou 133
Ray, James Earl 119, 149, 150, 159, 160
Ray, John Larry 159
RCA Records 189
Redding, Otis 3, 10, 12, 15, 28, 50, 51, 56, 160, 190, 225–7, 261, 264
    career 21, 24
    death of 16–20, 22, 32, 125, 132, 161, 208, 281
    'fab four' singles 191
    funeral 23, 24, 33–5
    in Paris 170
    intensity of 25, 26, 186
    memorial award 224
    posthumous albums 59
    tributes to 86, 194, 224
Redding, Zelma 20, 23, 33, 34
Redditt, Ed 105, 140
Redemption Harmonizers 10
Reed, Jimmy 44, 72
Regal Theater 2
Reid, James R. 82
Rene, Wendy see Mary Frierson
Resurrection City 202, 204, 208–12
Rice, 'Sir' Mack 55
Rich, Charlie 237
Richard, Little 20, 24, 53, 54
Richbourg, John 143
Riley, Diamond Jim 218, 219
Rinzler, Alan 175
riots 83, 84, 92–5, 124, 144, 151–8, 169–72, 190, 196, 232, 233
Robertson, Nan 209
Robey, Don 10, 219, 224
Robinson, Freddy 197
Robinson, Joe 224
Robinson, Smokey and the Miracles 80, 114
Robinson, Sugar Ray 216, 217, 229
Rockett, Gerlean 133
Rogers, Taylor 40
Rolling Stone (magazine) 153, 259, 280, 283
Rolling Stones 10, 24, 54, 74, 222
Ronettes, The 148
Ronstadt, Linda 11
Rosemart Records 54
Rosenberg, Seymour 194, 237, 238
Ross, Eddie Jr 41
Rossellini, Roberto 134
Rowland, Linda see Lyndell
Royal Spades, The 30
Royal Studios 13, 100, 267
Royal Theater 7
Ruffin, David 239, 258, 265

Sadat, Anwar 290
Safice Records 185
Sain, Oliver 262
St Jacques, Raymond 172
St Joseph's Hospital 107, 274
Salt-N-Pepa rap group 161
Sam and Dave (*see also* Sam Moore and Dave Prater) 50, 52, 53, 59–62, 132, 160, 186, 224, 227, 264, 270

STUART COSGROVE'S CRITICALLY ACCLAIMED SIXTIES SOUL TRILOGY

Detroit 67

Memphis 68

Harlem 69

Published October 2016

'Such is the depth and breadth of his research, and the skill of his pen, at times you actually feel like you are in Berry Gordy's office watching events unfurl like an unstoppable James Jamerson bass line'
Paolo Hewitt

'Written with precision, empathy, and a great, deep love for the city of Detroit . . . there is much to learn here'
Detroit Metro Times

'Big daddy of soul books'
TeamRock

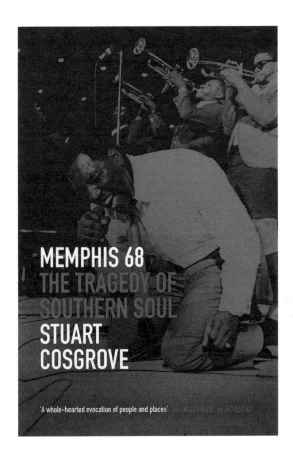

Published October 2017

And coming in
October 2018 . . .

HARLEM 69:
THE FUTURE OF SOUL